THE GRA
FROM CELTIC M\
CHRISTIAN SYMBOL

THE GRAIL

FROM CELTIC MYTH TO CHRISTIAN SYMBOL

BY

ROGER SHERMAN LOOMIS

PRINCETON UNIVERSITY PRESS
PRINCETON, NEW JERSEY

Published by Princeton University Press, 41 William Street,
Princeton, New Jersey 08540
Copyright © renewed 1991 by Princeton University Press
All Rights Reserved

Library of Congress Cataloging-in-Publication Data
Loomis, Roger Sherman, 1887–1966.
The Grail : from Celtic myth to Christian symbol /
Roger Sherman Loomis.
p. cm.—(Mythos)
Includes index.
ISBN 0-691-02075-2 (alk. paper)
1. Grail—Romances—History and criticism. 2. Christian art and
symbolism—Medieval, 500–1500. 3. Arthurian romances—
History and criticism. 4. Mythology, Celtic. 5. Grail—Legends.
I. Title. II. Series: Mythos (Princeton, N.J.)
PN686.G7L6   1991
398'.353—dc20   91–18021   CIP

This book was originally © 1963 by Roger Sherman Loomis,
and published by the University of Wales Press
(in the United States by Columbia University Press).
The Princeton Mythos edition is reprinted
by agreement with the Loomis Estate
and by arrangement with the University of Wales Press.

First Princeton Paperback printing in the Mythos series, 1991

10 9 8 7 6 5

Princeton University Press books are printed on acid-free paper,
and meet the guidelines for permanence and durability of the
Committee on Production Guidelines for Book Longevity of the
Council on Library Resources

Printed in the United States of America

TO

GERTRUDE SCHOEPPERLE LOOMIS

AND

LAURA HIBBARD LOOMIS

IN

GRATEFUL AND LOVING

REMEMBRANCE

WHETHER in the Teutonic countries, which in one of their corners preserved a record of old mythology, or in the Celtic, which allowed mythology, though never forgotten, to fall into a kind of neglect and to lose its original meaning, the value of mythology is equally recognizable, and it is equally clear that mythology is nothing more than Romance. Everything in the poets that is most enthralling through the mere charm of wonder, from the land of the Golden Fleece to that of the Holy Grail, is more or less nearly related to mythology.

w. p. KER, *The Dark Ages*, p. 47

LA GRANDE originalité de notre romancier, c'est d'avoir ressenti à la fois le charme, en vérité très prenant, des contes celtiques et l'incomplète satisfaction qu'ils apportent à l'esprit.... L'imagination est ravie, mais l'intelligence déconcertée: elle aspire à ordonner ce chaos charmant. L'auteur de la *Queste* était loin de se douter que tout cela n'avait pas toujours été une vaine fantasmagorie, et que ces contes étranges n'étaient pour la plupart que l'expression déformée d'antiques croyances païennes. Mais il eut la clairvoyance rare de comprendre qu'en l'état où les Français de son temps le trouvaient, le merveilleux celtique, malgré son charme incomparable, n'était plus qu'une forme vide. Ce qu'il y introduisit, ce fut tout naturellement sa conception chrétienne de l'univers et de l'homme.

ALBERT PAUPHILET, *Études sur la 'Queste del Saint Graal'*, pp. 192 f.

FELIX, qui potuit rerum cognoscere causas.

VERGIL, *Georgics*, iv. 490

PREFACE

In 1927 I first ventured to publish my speculations about the Grail legend in a book entitled *Celtic Myth and Arthurian Romance*. Though I still hold to many of the opinions there set forth, I came to realize within a few years that other opinions were mistaken, and a retraction of certain chapters was inserted in the copies which remained. I retracted in particular my adherence to Dr. Jessie Weston's ingenious hypothesis concerning the Grail and Lance, for lack of valid and clearly pertinent evidence. In 1949, after twenty-two years of reconsideration and research, I published *Arthurian Tradition and Chrétien de Troyes*, and I have not found it necessary to withdraw from the ground there taken. Brief studies bearing on the Grail have since appeared in *Wales and the Arthurian Legend* (1956) and *Arthurian Literature in the Middle Ages* (1959). In this book I have tried to bring together the soundest results of scholarship, such as the publications of Alfred Nutt, Albert Pauphilet, and Joseph Armitage Robinson, and to fit them into a comprehensive theory which would explain not one or two or three of the many forms of the Grail legend but the whole complex fabric. Obviously, that theory must take account of the multifarious influences which shaped the variegated forms of the legend, but it may be simply stated in the words: from Celtic myth to Christian symbol.

It is a theory favoured by antecedent probability. For what is more likely than that an important branch of Arthurian literature should have first arisen in what has been called the Celtic Fringe in the Dark Ages as a medley of semi-pagan traditions, and that it should have gradually been rationalized and Christianized in conformity with the tastes and beliefs of French and Anglo-Norman society. That is what one would expect to happen to a Celtic vessel of plenty: at first, a thing of mere magic, it would become in time possessed of miraculous and sacred powers, and emerge at last a Christian symbol.

But it may well be asked, why, if the solution of the Grail mystery is so obvious, is there no general agreement among scholars as to the answer? Why is there, on the contrary, heated controversy? I believe there are four principal reasons.

1. The proponents of Celtic origin, particularly Sir John Rhŷs and A. C. L. Brown, made such a weak case that they roused scepticism, and my own first book on the subject was marred by rash claims, with the same effect.

2. The evidence on some of the most important issues is scanty owing to the complete disappearance of early literature in the Breton language and the paucity of early Welsh material. And such evidence as exists has been overlooked because it sometimes lies in out-of-the-way, though by no means inaccessible, texts, such as the *Phantom's Frenzy*, the list of the Thirteen Treasures of the Isle of Britain, and *Sone de Nansai*. But facts are not to be disregarded just because they are not found exactly where one would expect them.

3. There is a lingering belief among some literary historians that the dates of manuscripts in which texts first appear are roughly the dates not only of composition but also of the origin of the material. Ergo, it is argued that no evidence from manuscripts after 1200 has any validity for the early stages of Arthurian romance. But not only are Irish sagas, preserved in manuscripts of the twelfth century, dated by the authorities back as far as the eighth century, but their contents bear unmistakable signs of pre-Christian origin. The same may be said of much of the fragmentary Welsh material. The antiquity of a tradition cannot be judged by the date of its earliest record, and even a fifteenth-century manuscript may supply the missing piece in the jigsaw puzzle.

4. There is a popular school of criticism which attempts to explain the eccentricities of Arthurian romance not by its origins and early history but as an intentional mystification, whereby occult meanings are conveyed through fantastic narratives. One scholar has declared that 'in these wonderful adventures nothing whatever is without its meaning; everything is symbol or delicate allegory'. The fact is, however,

that when a medieval author intended to convey a hidden significance he took it out of hiding and expounded it at length, as witness the *Queste del Saint Graal* and Wolfram von Eschenbach's *Parzival*, not to mention the *Roman de la Rose* and the *Ovide Moralisé*.

The task attempted in this book, the task of illuminating the obscurities and interpreting the peculiarities of the Grail romances, involves a variety of problems. Some may be solved readily by reference to common preoccupations of the Middle Ages, such as the miracle of the mass and the cult of relics. Other puzzles may be answered by a study of an author's environment, his personal idiosyncrasies, and his reading, as in the case of Wolfram von Eschenbach's acquaintance with the *Iter Alexandri Magni ad Paradisum*. Then there is the curious and crucial difficulty presented by the word *graal*, which demands a semantic and liturgical study. To these various types of problem I have given, I trust, due attention, but the conclusions I have come to are, for the most part, those already reached by other scholars, and for which I can claim no credit.

I would, however, make bold to assert that in two obscure fields I have brought new light. There is the type of confusion and distortion which occurs through mistranslation and misinterpretation, and, unless I am completely mistaken, such confusions had an enormous influence on the development of the legend in sacramental and evangelistic directions. Then there are certain bewildering peculiarities of the legend, even the emergence of the tradition itself, which demand explanation and which can be explained only by a patient and detailed examination of its remote sources in Irish and Welsh literature and its transmission to the French and Anglo-Normans. Though others have pioneered in this field, and though the analogy between the Grail and the *Dysgl* of Rhydderch was noted as far back as 1819, yet it is here that I may claim to have made my most important contribution to the understanding of the mysteries of the Grail.

ROGER SHERMAN LOOMIS

TABLE OF CONTENTS

LIST OF ILLUSTRATIONS

See description on p. 280.

I

The Chief Romances of the Grail
A Preview

No legend of the Middle Ages, except those endorsed by the Church, has had so strong an evocative and provocative power as the strange fictions which grew up about the Grail. Thanks to Tennyson and Wagner, Galahad and Parsifal have become types of chastity, and the quest of the mysterious vessel has come to mean, on the one hand, a vain following after 'wandering fires', or, on the other, the arduous search for supreme mystical experience. The stories of the Grail—for there are many of them—have exercised a potent fascination on eminent literary men of our time, with surprisingly varied results—on T. S. Eliot, Arthur Machen, John Cowper Powys, T. H. White, and Julien Gracq.[1] They inspired Charles Williams to the writing of a modern 'thriller' about the struggle between the forces of evil and those of good for the possession of the vessel, as well as to the composition of a spiritual epic, ranging from Wales to Byzantium, and from the edge of Hell to the region of the summer stars.[2]

It is not strange that the medieval legends should have engendered in our century so diverse an offspring, for they form a bewildering assortment of battle and banquet, earthy magic and sacramental miracle, blood-feuds and mysterious rites. Bewilderment begets curiosity and seeks a solution, and over the last hundred years, scholars and would-be scholars have tried to discover the secrets of the Grail, with such contrasting results that the reading public, eager for enlightenment, may well feel more puzzled than ever.

[1] For an excellent discussion of modern British and American treatments of the Grail theme see Nathan Starr, *King Arthur Today: The Arthurian Legend in English and American Literature, 1901–1953* (Gainesville, Florida, 1954).

[2] *War in Heaven* (1949). *The Region of the Summer Stars* (1950).

The quest of the Grail has led to the Punjab in India, to the palace of Atreus at Mycenae and the temple of Zeus at Dodona, to the monastery of Montserrat in Spain, to the palace of Chosroes in Persia, and the Christian shrines of Constantinople. Pick up a book on the subject, and you may be told, with a great show of erudition, that the object itself was derived from the cauldron of the Irish god Dagda, from the eye of the Egyptian god Thoth, from a symbol of the female organ of generation, from a pearl of the Zoroastrian cult named Gohar, from a talisman of the heretical Albigensians, once adored in a cavern of the Pyrenees, or from a 'Great Sapphire', formerly preserved in the sacristy of Glastonbury Abbey. On the other hand, there are those scholars who are content to believe that the Grail was *ab origine* conceived as a peculiarly holy eucharistic vessel.

Not all these speculations are as fatuous and incredible as they seem, and some find their excuse, if not their justification, in the diversity and the contradictions of the medieval texts themselves, for in them too there is a strange disagreement. The Grail may be described as the dish from which Christ ate the Passover lamb at the Last Supper; or as the chalice of the first sacrament, in which later the Saviour's blood was caught as it flowed from His wounded body; or as a stone with miraculous feeding and youth-preserving virtues; or as a salver containing a man's head, swimming in blood. It may be borne through a castle hall by a beautiful damsel; or it may float through the air in Arthur's palace, veiled in white samite; or it may be placed on a table in the East, together with a freshly caught fish, and serve as a talisman to distinguish the chaste from the unchaste. Its custodian may be called Bron or Anfortas or Pelles or Joseph of Arimathea or simply 'the Fisher King'. He may be sound of wind and limb or pierced through the thighs or wounded in the genitals. The hero who achieves the quest may be the notoriously amorous Gawain or the virgin Galahad.

Whence came this fantastic development of the Arthurian legend—a development of which the first record is found in a French poem dated about 1180, and which in the next fifty years produced so many wildly variegated forms? How did it come to be linked with relics of the Passion? What did it all mean?

Let us first take a sweeping glance at the body of literature most of which we shall later examine in detail in the endeavour to solve its problems.[1] The principal texts concerned with the Grail fall into two classes: (1) Those which relate the adventures of knights of King Arthur's time who visit by chance or by design the castle in Britain where the vessel is kept; (2) those which relate the history of the vessel from the time of Christ to the time of Merlin and which account for its removal from the Holy Land to Britain. There are eight important texts in the first group, and two in the second.

The romances of the first group are:

1. The *Conte del Graal* or *Perceval*, composed by Chrétien de Troyes, a poet of Champagne, for Philip Count of Flanders.

2. Four long continuations of the same, two anonymous, one by Manessier and one by Gerbert de Montreuil.

3. The *Parzival* of Wolfram von Eschenbach, a Bavarian knight, which was the main inspiration of Wagner's *Parsifal*.

4. The Welsh prose romance, *Peredur*, included in Lady Guest's collection called the *Mabinogion*.

5. The *Didot Perceval*, a French prose romance, so called from the name of a former owner of a manuscript.

6. *Perlesvaus*, a prose romance from northern France or Belgium, translated by Sebastian Evans as the *High History of the Holy Grail*.

7. The Prose *Lancelot*, which forms the third member of a vast compilation, known as the Vulgate cycle.

8. The *Queste del Saint Graal*, the fourth member of the same cycle. Malory has made us familiar with most of the Grail material in the *Lancelot* and with the *Queste* by his abridged version in Books XI to XVII of the *Book of King Arthur*.

[1] For bibliography of scholarly treatments of the Grail legend and of the major texts see Appendix I.

The two romances dealing with the early history of the Grail are:

9. *Joseph d'Arimathie*, by the Burgundian poet, Robert de Boron.

10. The *Estoire del Saint Graal*, the first member of the Vulgate cycle, but probably composed after the *Lancelot* and the *Queste*.

This classification is by no means absolute, since the continuations of the *Conte del Graal*, Wolfram's *Parzival*, the *Didot Perceval*, and the *Queste* introduce variants of the early history of the holy vessel. A later and much neglected poem, *Sone de Nansai*, describes a visit to the Grail castle, located strangely on an island off the coast of Norway, and contains a brief early history of the vessel, derived in part from the *Estoire del Saint Graal*. Besides the romances listed, there are numerous medieval translations of French texts into other languages—Norse, Irish, Welsh, English, Spanish, Portuguese, Italian, German, and Dutch. The total bulk of the Grail romances produced before the Renaissance was prodigious and attests the wide and enduring fascination which the mysterious vessel exerted on the medieval imagination.

It is noteworthy, however, that all the basic texts listed above were composed within a period of about fifty years. The earliest, Chrétien's poem, was written about 1180, the first two continuations of the same may be placed before 1200, Manessier's between 1214 and 1227, and Gerbert's about 1230. Wolfram's *Parzival* is fixed between 1200 and 1210. The dates of the other versions cited are still uncertain but probably precede 1230. *Sone de Nansai* alone of the romances to be discussed belongs to the second half of the thirteenth century.

If these dates convey little to the imagination, it may be helpful to recall some of the more memorable historical figures and events of the period in question. Between 1180 and 1200 there stand out the ageing but vigorous Henry II, ruler of dominions which included England, Ireland, and western France; Eleanor of Aquitaine, his queen, patroness of poets and mother of Richard Coeur-de-Lion; Richard himself, who nearly succeeded in winning back the Holy Sepulchre from Saladin; his rival and enemy, the young king of France, Philip Augustus. To the thirty years after 1200 belongs an even longer list of notable figures and events. King John lost most of his continental possessions to Philip, was worsted in his struggle with the great pope, Innocent III, and was compelled by his barons to sign the Magna Charta. St. Francis and St. Dominic revitalized the Church by founding the mendicant orders. There were three Crusades: one against the Albigensian heretics in southern France, which had the effect of crushing the gay world of the troubadours; one which was diverted to Constantinople and resulted in increased hostility between Western and Eastern Christendom and in flooding the West with relics; a third expedition by the wily, free-thinking emperor, Frederick II, which secured by negotiation for a brief time the city of Jerusalem.

None of these personages or events except the Crusades influenced perceptibly the Grail romances, but what surely, though subtly, affected them was the artistic and intellectual ferment of the time. For this half-century saw the building of Notre-Dame at Paris, the cathedrals of Rheims and Wells, and the choir of Lincoln; it also witnessed the growth of the universities of Paris, Bologna, and Oxford. At no period in the history of Western Europe have the arts and the zest for knowledge attained a higher level. The greatest literary masterpieces were yet to come, but the men of our period listened to the lyrics of the goliards and Walther von der Vogelweide, the rugged *Brut* of Layamon, and the tragic *Tristan* of Gottfried von Strassburg. The Grail romances belong to a great experimental and creative epoch.

The ten listed above, it is worth noting, were all composed on the continent of Europe, except for *Peredur*, and it is generally agreed that this romance consists for the most part of confused reminiscences of French or Anglo-Norman texts. No Anglo-Norman treatment of the Grail is extant, and all the Middle English versions, including Malory's, are renderings from the French. This is strange, considering that the geography of the French Quest romances, so far as it relates to reality, is British, and that the possession of so sacrosanct a relic redounded to the glory of Britain!

How is this seemingly unnatural situation to be accounted for? Before seeking a direct answer to this and many other problems through an examination of the texts in modern English renderings, it would be sensible, it is indeed imperative, to look into the circumstances, literary and historical, which have a special bearing on the origin and growth of the fantastic legends. Only after an examination of this material, too often ignored by interpreters of the subject, can we with assurance proceed to a detailed analysis of the principal medieval treatments of the Grail. Of these, the Quest romances and *Sone de Nansai* will be discussed in Chapters IV to XIII; the early history of the vessel in Chapter XIV. The Glastonbury developments will form the subject of Chapter XV, to be followed finally by an attempt to summarize the results of our investigation.

II

The Origins and Growth of Arthurian Romance

Too many investigators, professional scholars as well as amateurs, in their search for answers to the riddle of the Grail have looked in the most unlikely places, and resemble an absent-minded gentleman who hunts for his pince-nez in the refrigerator, the waste-basket, the medicine cabinet, the pockets of his riding-breeches, and the grandfather clock, while the object of his search is resting on his nose. Would it not be sensible to seek the clues to the mystery of the Grail, not in Mohammedan, or Albigensian, or late Hellenic cults, but in the history of Arthurian romance?

As everyone knows, the stories of the holy quest form a part of that larger body of fiction of which Arthur is the central figure. It was at his palace of Camelot that the Grail appeared, covered with white samite, and it was from Camelot that the knights of the Round Table set forth in the hope of seeing the mystic vessel more openly. There can be no doubt that the French men of letters who told of these astonishing adventures regarded them as inseparably connected in time and place with Arthur's reign and Arthur's realm. Accordingly, if we wish to gain insight into the origin and meaning of the legends of the quest, the most sensible procedure is to find out what we can about the Arthurian tradition as a whole and to determine the forces which produced it. The researches of the last hundred years have gradually enabled us to understand whence it came into the possession of the French romancers, and how it developed into the favourite secular reading matter of Western Europe for four hundred years.

It is almost certain that Chrétien de Troyes, the first of the Arthurian romancers whose work has survived, relied mainly on written texts for the plots of his four traditional poems,[1] and in fact he referred to the book which Count Philip of Flanders gave him as the basis for his *Conte del Graal*.[2] But it is also clear that he had heard similar tales from professional reciters. He refers scornfully to those who earn their livelihood by telling stories and who spoil and mutilate the tale of Erec in the presence of kings and counts.[3] Again, he declares that he has never *heard* more about the Knight of the Lion than what he has related in *Ivain*.[4] The second continuator of the *Conte del Graal* describes certain strolling minstrels who go from court to court and in return for a night's lodging tell lying tales without rime.[5] Geoffrey of Monmouth attributes to Merlin the prophecy that the deeds of Arthur will provide food, i.e. a livelihood, for story-tellers.[6] The Norman Wace in a well-known passage speaks of the *conteurs* who have told over so often the adventures which befell in the reign of Arthur and have so embellished them that they seem to be fictitious.[7] There can be no doubt, then, that in the twelfth and in the early thirteenth centuries there was a class of professional story-tellers who entertained kings, counts, and lesser nobles with a repertory of romantic tales about Arthur and his knights.[8] And we have testimony that by 1180 Arthur's fame had spread to the Crusader states of Antioch and Palestine.[9]

It is also evident that this oral tradition furnished material to the French men of letters who have left us the romances in

---

[1] Loomis, *Arthurian Tradition and Chrétien de Troyes* (New York, 1949), pp. 7–11.

[2] Ibid., p. 9. *Erec*, vss. 19–22.   [3] Loomis, op. cit., p. 10.

[4] *Yvain*, ed. W. Foerster (Halle, 1926), vss. 6814–18.

[5] Loomis, op. cit., p. 22, n. 50. J. L. Weston, *Legend of Sir Perceval*, i (London, 1906), p. 265.

[6] *Arthurian Literature in the Middle Ages* (Oxford, 1959), ed. Loomis, p. 58, n. 4. Faral, *Légende Arthurienne* (Paris, 1929), iii. 191.

[7] E. K. Chambers, *Arthur of Britain* (London, 1927), p. 103. Wace, *Brut*, ed. I. Arnold (S.A.T.F.), ii, vss. 9795–8.

[8] *Arthurian Literature in the Middle Ages*, ed. Loomis, pp. 53–63.

[9] Ibid., p. 62. T. Stephens, *Literature of the Kymry*, 2nd ed. (London, 1876), p. 405, n. 1.

verse and prose which we possess, including certain early versions of the Grail quest. The mixed and the short forms of the First Continuation of the *Conte del Graal* retain, as Jessie Weston pointed out[1] and as we shall see in Chapter VI, many characteristics of oral delivery. Again and again the poet addresses his audience as 'Seigneurs'. Again and again he refers to an adventure which they have just *heard*, or to one which they are about to *hear*. Twice he pauses to ask them to recite a paternoster for the dead, and the second time he adds a request for a drink of wine before he resumes. In most of the manuscripts, however, these vestiges of oral recitation have been removed, but the original form calls up a vivid picture of the social setting in which stories of the Grail were told in the twelfth century before they were set down on parchment for readers instead of listeners. A translation of the visit of Gawain to the Grail castle as given in this early text will be found in Chapter VI, and a critical examination of it in Chapter VII.

Let us turn back the clock to the twelfth century and imagine ourselves as guests in the great hall of a castle such as that of Philip of Flanders, Chrétien's patron, at Ghent, or that of the Counts of Poitou at Poitiers, or that of the Kings of England in the White Tower at London—halls still open to the visitor today. It is a winter's evening and many torches set in sockets along the walls enable us to make out the mural paintings illustrating the fall of Troy or the wars of Charlemagne with the Saracens. Candelabra illuminate the high table, covered with white napery. A baron, who holds the office of butler, and his minions stand ready with their pitchers to refill the gilded and silver goblets with spiced wine from Gascony. In spite of the logs blazing in the great fireplace, the atmosphere is chilly and most of the household wear woollen robes lined or bordered with fur. The bearded lord of the castle, his lady with long braids of yellow hair, two tonsured

---

[1] Weston, op. cit. i. 239, 241–3, 246–9, 252. *Continuations of the Old French 'Perceval'*, ed. W. Roach (Philadelphia, 1950, 1952), ii. 453, 503, 512–20, 530; iii. 338, 434, 452, 460, 462, 490.

ecclesiastics, and certain honoured guests are engaged in chatting and laughing at the high table.

There comes a pause. The lord gives a signal to the marshal, the marshal calls for silence, and beckons to a black-haired man in his prime, seated at one of the lower tables. Thus summoned, the man approaches the dais, bows to the lord and lady, and asks what tale they would like to hear. After a brief consultation, the lord calls for the adventures of Gawain at the castle of the Fisher King. This is an old favourite, but the tale is never too stale, for every *conteur* has his own version, an amalgam of those he has heard, with original touches of his own. The audience listens hushed, while, after a pious invocation, he launches into his story. His language is French with a Breton accent. His mobile features simulate the changing moods of the characters, his voice shifts from masculine bass to feminine treble and back, his arms and hands are seldom idle, and he suits the action to the word, the word to the action, in the style Hamlet prescribed for the troupe at Elsinore. At one point he asks for a cup of wine, and swallows it slowly before resuming. The recital lasts for more than an hour and ends with a description of the departure of Gawain.

Before the *conteur* retires, several questions are put to him as to the meaning of this or that, and he replies that he will have the answers next evening if he is permitted to continue the story. One of the clerics challenges him as to the location and the furnishings of the castle, which are quite different from those described by another *conteur* whom he had heard several months before. The minstrel replies, tactfully, that in King Arthur's time God had ordained a periodic change in the sites and customs of the castles visited by knights of the Round Table, so that they would not find their lives too monotonous.[1] This answer satisfies everyone present, and the lord calls a page and bids him fit the minstrel with a pair of stout shoes and give him a warm mantle. Shortly after, the company breaks up, while the menials put out the torches and stretch themselves out on the benches to sleep.

[1] This explanation is actually given by the author of *Perlesvaus*. See below, p. 101.

The derivation of the early Arthurian romances, more or less directly, from the repertory of the wandering *conteurs* explains two of the most striking characteristics of the genre— their episodic structure and their lack of consistency. Jessie Weston, commenting on the incoherence of the stories about Gawain in the First Continuation of the *Conte del Graal*, wrote :[1] 'There is no logical, much less inevitable, sequence in the tales. If the relative position of the stories were altered, e.g. if Gawain visited the Grail Castle before he won the Chastel Orguellous, or after he achieved the adventure of the shield, the story would be no whit less interesting, or more effective.' Even in that part of the *Conte del Graal* which Chrétien de Troyes wrote himself, the adventures of Gawain are loosely held together and bear no relation to the preceding adventures of Perceval.[2] This episodic structure is a natural consequence of the origin of the romances in separate and more or less independent *contes*, each contrived to hold the interest of the courtly listeners for a single sitting of an hour or two. Poets of the more naïve sort were content to string these episodes together without any regard to unity of plot, and the only satisfactory excuse for Chrétien's own occasional lapses in continuity is the hypothesis that he was following the outline provided by a predecessor indifferent to the claims of coherence. Though some Arthurian poems are marvels of architectonic skill, such as Chrétien's *Ivain* and the English *Gawain and the Green Knight*, the charge of loose organization is one which can justly be brought against many typical romances of the Round Table.

The other inevitable consequence of the derivation of these

[1] Weston, op. cit. i. 250 f.

[2] Some critics think that they find an intentional contrast between the experiences of Perceval at the Grail castle, with their religious and moral implications, and the merely sensational and romantic adventures of Gawain. There is nothing to prove that Chrétien intended any such contrast. According to his own statement at the beginning of the poem, he was putting into rime the narrative which Count Philip had given him, and considering the many flaws and inconsistencies in the poem, it seems unrealistic to credit the author of Count Philip's book with striving for an effect of contrast. In fact, some scholars find the Gawain adventures so irrelevant that they refuse to believe that Chrétien was responsible for them. See *Arthurian Literature*, ed. Loomis, pp. 188 f.

romances from itinerant *conteurs*, ranging over France, England, southern Scotland, and wherever French was understood, each with his own repertory, is inconsistency. It accounts, at least in some measure, for the gross discrepancies between the versions of the Grail quest, which we have already noted. It accounts in part for the fact that characters are differently conceived, and the hero of one author receives shabby treatment from another. Morgan le Fay may be the most beautiful of nine sister enchantresses and the nurse of her brother Arthur in Avalon, or she may be an ugly crone who plots his death. The adventure of the Beheading Test, familiar to readers of *Gawain and the Green Knight*, may be credited to Caradoc or Lancelot in other versions.[1] When a compiler brought together into a continuous narrative a number of tales which he had heard from various sources he was bound to involve himself in strange inconsistencies, and it was the aim of the more intelligent authors to remedy this defect. We find Thomas, the Anglo-Norman court poet, declaring that among those who were wont to tell the story of Tristan there was great diversity. 'Lords,' he exclaims, 'this *conte* is right variously related, and therefore I have harmonized it in my verses.'[2]

No episode in the whole vast body of Arthurian romance is handled in more diverse ways than the visit to the Grail castle. Even when the details are similar, the animating conception may be totally different. Over seventy years ago Alfred Nutt wisely declared:[3]

The many forms of the incident found in the Grail romances are not variants of one, and that an orderly and logical original; they testify to the fact that in the body of popular tradition which forms the basis of these romances the incident of the visit to the magic castle was a common one, that it entered into the thread of stories, somewhat similar in outline and frequently centred in the same hero, but differing essentially in conception, and that the forms in the romances which are most likely to

[1] G. L. Kittredge, *Study of 'Gawain and the Green Knight'* (Cambridge, Mass., 1916).
[2] Loomis, *Arthurian Tradition*, pp. 43–45. Thomas, *Tristan*, ed. J. Bédier (S.A.T.F.), i, vss. 2107 f.
[3] A. Nutt, *Studies on the Legend of the Holy Grail* (London, 1888), p. 181.

keep close to the traditional model are those secondary ones with which the innovating spirit, whether due to the genius of the individual artist, or to intruding Christian symbolism, has least concerned itself. These phenomena, so characteristic of the Arthurian romances, are by no means unique. In the development of the Homeric poems, the rhapsodes, the professional entertainers of ancient Greece, are the counterparts of the *conteurs*. Gilbert Murray, referring to the *Iliad* and the *Odyssey*, wrote :[1] 'Our poems are full of the traces of the rhapsode; they are developments from the recited saga, and where they fail in unity or consistency the recited saga is mostly to blame.'

Nothing better explains, then, some of the typical features of Arthurian romance in its early stages—its episodic, loose structure, its glaring inconsistencies—than the fact that it was based on the numberless short *contes* which formed the stock-in-trade of wandering *conteurs*.

But there are other remarkable features of this body of fiction which provoke questions and demand an explanation. Why were these French-speaking *conteurs* so devoted to the glorification of a British chief and his warriors who had lived in the remote past and who had left little or no record of themselves in the pages of history? Why this passionate concern with the love of Tristan, nephew of a Cornish king, for Isolt, an Irish princess? Why this interest in the Welsh youth Perceval, his naïve blunders, and his mysterious experiences at the castle of the Fisher King?

The answer is highly significant and leads to the solution of many problems. Evidence, both external and internal, combines to show that the *conteurs* of the twelfth and early thirteenth century were in the main Bretons, descendants of those Britons who in the fifth and sixth century, as a result of the Anglo-Saxon invasion, had emigrated to Armorica, which we now know as Brittany.[2] Through intercourse with their

[1] G. Murray, *History of Ancient Greek Literature* (London, New York, 1912), p. 20.

[2] Loomis, op. cit., pp. 15–23, 27–32. J. D. Bruce, *Evolution of Arthurian Romance* (Baltimore, 1923), i. 59–70. P. Hinneberg, *Kultur der Gegenwart*, Teil I, Abt. XI, i (Berlin, Leipzig, 1909), pp. 11–15, 60–65. K. Voretzsch, *Introduction to the Study of Old French Literature*, trans. F. M. Dumont (New York, 1931), pp. 309–19.

continental neighbours they had become largely bilingual, and had added French to their native speech, which was akin to Welsh; today their descendants in western Brittany remain largely bilingual. The Norman poet Wace in 1155 said that the Bretons of his time told many tales of the Round Table.[1] Giraldus Cambrensis, descended on his mother's side from the kings of South Wales, attributed, not to his own country-men, the *Wallenses*, but to the 'fabulosi Britones et eorum cantores', 'the story-telling Bretons and their singers', the legend of an imaginary goddess Morganis, who conveyed Arthur to Avalon for healing.[2] Many names embedded in Arthurian literature are of Breton origin. Bédier detected the following in the Tristan romances: Perinis, Rivalen, Hoel, Denoalen; and there are others.[3] In Chrétien's work one finds Brien, Gandeluz, Guigamor, Rindurans.[4] Two of his heroes, Erec and Ivain, bear Breton names, and the name Lancelot has been recognized by the best authorities as influenced by the name Lancelin, recorded in Brittany as early as 1034. Thus, in spite of possible exceptions, it appears that the *con-teurs* who first spread 'the Matter of Britain' throughout the French-speaking world were Bretons.

Unfortunately no literature in the Breton tongue has survived from this period, and the only Latin works which record the deeds of Arthur and which may be attributed to Breton authorship are saints' lives and do not belong to the category of romantic fiction cultivated by the *conteurs*.[5] It has also been urged against the theory of Breton provenance that the culture of Brittany was too crude and sterile to pro-duce so vital, prolific, and enthralling a mass of fiction as the stories of the Round Table, the romance of Tristan, and the mysteries of the Grail. To this objection it may be replied that

---

[1] Chambers, op. cit., p. 102. Foulon in *Arthurian Literature*, pp. 98–100. On the Round Table see Loomis, *Arthurian Tradition*, pp. 61–68.

[2] Chambers, op. cit., p. 272. Brugger in *ZFSL*, xx¹ (1898), pp. 97–100.

[3] Thomas, *Tristan*, ed. Bédier, ii. 122 f. *Romania*, liii (1927), pp. 96 f.

[4] For origin of names in Chrétien, see Loomis, op. cit., appendix, pp. 478–92.

[5] J. S. P. Tatlock, *Legendary History of Britain* (Berkeley, Calif., 1950), pp. 192–4. *Speculum*, xiv (1939), pp. 358–65.

two of the greatest geniuses of the period, Abelard and Adam of St. Victor, were Bretons; and in the opinion of the latest authorities Geoffrey of Monmouth, the learned and clever fabricator of a pseudo-history which raised Arthur to the rank of a Charlemagne or a Caesar, was, though born in Wales, of Breton descent.[1]

Of course, the talents of the *conteurs* were not in the same category as those of Abelard or Geoffrey of Monmouth, and the fascination which they exercised over their listeners must have been due more to the startling novelty of their matter and the histrionic arts of gesture and intonation with which they mimicked the action and speech of the characters than to the logical planning of their narratives. Though their talents must have varied greatly from individual to individual, they were far from contemptible, and according to Peter of Blois, himself of Breton parentage, their sad tales of Arthur, Gawain, and Tristan moved their audiences to tears.[2]

Now it goes almost without saying that this preoccupation with Arthur, and with events long since past in Arthur's Britain, was due to the fact that the early *conteurs* were descended from those Britons, Arthur's countrymen, who had emigrated centuries before to Armorica. Even after the lapse of six hundred years, the Bretons still cherished the hope that he was alive and would return, as a Messiah, to win back their ancestral home: in Brittany anyone who disputed this belief was in danger of stoning.[3] But, though the Breton expectation of Arthur's return was the object of condescending smiles and derision throughout the non-Celtic West and Italy, the *conteurs* succeeded, with the aid of Geoffrey of Monmouth's pseudo-history, in establishing throughout the same territory the concept of Arthur as a model of chivalry and the belief in Arthur's reign as a golden age.

---

[1] *Arthurian Literature*, p. 57. On Geoffrey's Breton descent see Tatlock, op. cit., pp. 396–402, 440, 443; Bruce, op. cit. i. 19; Chambers, op. cit., pp. 23 f.

[2] Chambers, op. cit., p. 267.

[3] *Arthurian Literature*, pp. 54, 64 f. R. H. Fletcher, *Arthurian Material in the Chronicles* (Boston, 1906; reprinted Burt Franklin, New York, 1958), index, p. 289.

If it be asked how the Bretons, whose ancestors had left Britain six hundred years before, came to possess such a rich fund of fantastic stories about the legendary king and the knights and ladies of his court, the answer is not difficult. They took them over from the story-tellers of Cornwall and Wales, their remote cousins who spoke almost the same language as the Bretons and were, like them, passionately devoted to the memory of Arthur.

Unfortunately, the early vernacular literature of Cornwall, like that of Brittany, has perished. In the famous collection of medieval Welsh tales entitled the *Mabinogion* only two of the five concerned with Arthur and his knights, *Kulhwch* and the *Dream of Rhonabwy*, are of native inspiration; only these two and some very obscure poems remain to us of the purely insular traditions attached to the British hero.[1] A cursory perusal of these remains, dating from the tenth to the thirteenth century, is likely to leave the impression that there is little in common between the Welsh tradition and the French romances of the Arthurian cycle. And some reputable scholars have denied any significant Celtic contribution to the great body of European fiction of the Round Table.

As a matter of fact, however, it requires no microscopic examination of *Kulhwch and Olwen*, written down about the year 1100, to discover some clear resemblances to Chrétien's poems, composed sixty years or more later.[2] Kulhwch sets out for Arthur's court; Kai, on hearing of his arrival, counsels against his admission, but is promptly rebuked by Arthur. Kulhwch then rides on horseback into Arthur's hall, where the king and his warriors are at meat, and asks a boon, which Arthur grants.[3] Likewise, Chrétien's juvenile hero, Perceval, sets out for Arthur's court, and rides on horseback into the hall, where the king and his knights are seated at table. When Perceval asks to be made a knight, Arthur consents. Kay, however, mocks the youth and is promptly rebuked by

[1] *Arthurian Literature*, chs. i, ii, iv.
[2] Ibid., p. 39.
[3] C. Guest, *Mabinogion*, Everyman's Lib., pp. 98–100.

Arthur.[1] Another striking parallel is afforded by Kulhwch's meeting with a herdsman, clad in skins and surrounded by a great flock of sheep. When Kulhwch reveals his errand, the herdsman warns him to proceed no farther.[2] Compare this with the scene in Chrétien's *Ivain*. Calogrenant meets a herdsman, clad in hides and surrounded by bulls. When he reveals his purpose, the herdsman warns him of a perilous adventure.[3] Here, then, are two obvious correspondences between a Welsh romance and the poems of Chrétien—correspondences which can be accounted for only by the hypothesis of transmission of Welsh themes to France. That the transmitters were Bretons is suggested, at least, by the fact that the meeting of Calogrenant with the herdsman is localized in the forest of Broceliande in Brittany.[4] Add to these resemblances the fact that other figures mentioned in *Kulhwch*—Bedwyr, Llenlleawc, Edern, and Gwenhwyvar—reappear in Chrétien's work as Beduiier, Lancelot, Ider, and Guenievre. There can be no reasonable doubt of the French poet's indirect debt to Welsh fiction.

If we extend our search to texts other than *Kulhwch*, we find that two Welsh poems of the tenth or eleventh century furnish us with the names Uthir Pendragon and Mabon, which are familiar in French romance; with the monster Cath Paluc, which turns up as the monster Chapalu in several French texts;[5] and, as will be shown in Chapter IX, with a description of the island castle of the ageless elders which anticipates that in *Perlesvaus*. The first four tales in Lady Guest's *Mabinogion*, which were composed about 1060, though they do not introduce Arthur or immediately recognizable counterparts of persons associated with him, provide, nevertheless, on closer study the originals of certain outstanding characters in Arthurian literature and particularly, as we shall discover, in the romances of the Grail.

---

[1] Chrétien de Troyes, *Roman de Perceval*, ed. Roach, 2nd ed. (Geneva, Paris, 1959), vss. 900–1032.

[2] Guest, *Mabinogion*, pp. 108 f.   [3] *Yvain*, ed. Foerster, vss. 278–407.

[4] On the forest of Broceliande see Loomis, *Arthurian Tradition*, p. 292.

[5] *Arthurian Literature*, pp. 14 f.

It is of great significance for the investigation of the origins of this 'Matter of Britain' to realize that, just as the Breton tales drew largely on Welsh tradition, so the Welsh tales in turn drew largely on material preserved to us in the Irish sagas. Let me quote Sir Ifor Williams :[1] 'Contacts between the two nations [Ireland and Wales] in the early centuries of our era down to the twelfth century were many and close. Irish tales were borrowed and retold in Welsh with minor modifications.' The theme of the Beheading Test, which occurs in the English masterpiece, *Gawain and the Green Knight*, and was used independently by four French romancers, was proved by Kittredge and Alice Buchanan to have its source in Irish traditions preserved in the eighth-century saga of the *Feast of Bricriu*, and though no intermediate Welsh form has survived, there are in the poem clear vestiges of Welsh transmission.[2] Furthermore, Arthur's sword, called in English Excalibur, in French Calibourc, goes back to a Welsh Caledvwlch, which in turn derives from Irish Caladbolg.

There are many more clues to the origin of the French Arthurian romances than those mentioned in the preceding pages, and they should leave little doubt that the early romances derived much, if not most, of their material, through the Breton *conteurs*, from Wales, and that some of it went back even to Ireland. No wonder that Kittredge declared :[3]

Something produced a great change in the literature of France in the twelfth century,—that is to say, in the literature of the western world, for at no assignable time could French literature have been charged with more momentous consequences to the course of European literary history. That *something* professes to be the emptying into French literature of a large body of Celtic material,—not a little leaven, but a huge mass, operating with extraordinary rapidity and with an effect still traceable not only in subtle ways but even in such obvious phenomena as the externals of plot and dramatis personae. . . The specific results of our study are to emphasize once more the importance of Irish material (and even of 'modern Irish' folk-lore) in settling these questions. They

[1] I. Williams, *Lectures on Early Welsh Poetry* (Dublin, 1944), p. 24.
[2] Kittredge, op. cit. *PMLA*, xlvii (1932), pp. 316–29. *Arthurian Literature*, pp. 535 f.
[3] *Studies and Notes in Philology and Literature*, viii (1903), pp. 265 f.

fall in with what is coming to be more and more recognized as the correct view,—the opinion that a considerable amount of the Celtic material that made its way into France actually came from Ireland, and further, that the function of Wales as an intermediary must not be overlooked simply because early Welsh traditions are sparingly preserved.

If this impressive dictum by one of the most learned of writers on medieval literature holds good for Arthurian romance as a whole, the presumption is that it holds good for the stories of the Grail quest, which form a branch of the Arthurian cycle.

III

Celtic Myths: their Mutations and Combinations

IT is apparent that, since the stories of the Grail belong to the Arthurian cycle, the most likely regions in which to look for their origin and their pristine meaning are Wales and Ireland. It is in the early literature of these Celtic lands, so long and so closely linked by cultural bonds, that we may most profitably pursue our search. Though Welsh literature of the period, as was noted above, is scanty, Irish sagas composed in the twelfth century or earlier are fairly numerous, and even those of later date tend to preserve the outlines of the old tradition. Patient study of this narrative material, Welsh and Irish, enables us to recognize nearly all the basic story patterns employed in the French Grail romances, and the originals of most of the chief characters.

The secular part of this literature is shot through and through with mythology. One group of Irish sagas is generally called the Mythological Cycle.[1] T. F. O'Rahilly has recently maintained that the Ulster Cycle, to which the tale of the Beheading Test, mentioned above, and the long prose epic of the *Cattle-Raid of Cooley* belong, was also mythical in origin.[2] Even in those stories concerned with historic kings of Ireland, the main theme is often a visit to a country or a mansion where, as Professor Dillon has put it,[3] 'there is neither sickness nor age nor death; where happiness lasts for ever and there is no satiety; where food and drink do not diminish when consumed; where

[1] M. Dillon, *Early Irish Literature* (Chicago, 1948), pp. 51–72; P. Hinneberg, *Kultur der Gegenwart*, Teil I, Abt. XI, i. 83; H. M. and N. K. Chadwick, *Growth of Literature*, i (Cambridge, 1932), pp. 255–63.

[2] *Early Irish History and Mythology* (Dublin, 1946), p. 271.

[3] Dillon, op. cit., p. 101. On the Celtic Elysium see E. Hull in *Folklore*, xviii (1907), pp. 121–65.

to wish for something is to possess it; where a hundred years are as one day'. In other words, it is the pagan Elysium, the abode of the immortals. Among the immortals who presided over such blissful mansions one recognizes the sun-god Lug and the sea-god Manannan Mac Lir. The sagas which describe the lavish hospitality extended to privileged mortals in these divine abodes form a group which goes under the name of *echtra*, 'adventure'.[1] This group is of the greatest importance for our study since it furnishes some of the basic patterns for the visit to the Grail castle.

As for the older Welsh narratives contained in the *Mabinogion*, Matthew Arnold came to the same conclusion as to their mythical nature in his lectures delivered a hundred years ago, *On the Study of Celtic Literature*.[2]

> What is Gwyn the son of Nudd, king of faerie, the ruler of the Tylwyth Teg, or family of beauty, who till the day of doom fights on every first day of May,—the great feast of the sun among the Celtic peoples,—with Gwythyr for the fair Cordelia, the daughter of Lyr?. . . Who is the mystic Arawn, the king of Annwn, who changed semblance for a year with Pwyll, prince of Dyved, and reigned in his place? These are no mediaeval personages; they belong to an older, pagan, mythological world.

A pious legend tells how St. Collen visited the castle of Gwyn son of Nudd and found his host seated on a golden throne, surrounded by minstrels making music and by the comeliest men and maidens in the bloom of youth.[3] On the table were the most luxurious delicacies that the mind could desire. Another Welsh description of a divine abode, to be discussed in Chapter IX, tells of a royal hall where the visitors were supplied without stint, forgot every sorrow, and though they remained for eighty years, appeared no older than when they came.[4] Note the recurrent features: unfading youth and an abundance of delicious viands. These blissful dwellings were not

---

[1] Dillon, op. cit., pp. 101–23.   [2] (London, 1867), p. 61.
[3] Guest, *Mabinogion*, Everyman's Lib., p. 311; R. S. Loomis, *Wales and the Arthurian Legend* (Cardiff, 1956), p. 139.
[4] Loth, *Mabinogion*, i. 148; P. Mac Cana, *Branwen Daughter of Llyr* (Cardiff, 1958), p. 102.

conceived as utterly remote and inaccessible. Gwyn's castle was situated on the hill called Glastonbury Tor in Somerset, and the royal hall on the island of Grassholm off the Welsh coast.[1]

And the gods mingled with heroes, much as in the *Iliad*. One of the early Welsh poems mentioned in the last chapter lists among the companions of Arthur Manawydan son of Llŷr and Mabon son of Modron.[2] Manawydan is the counterpart of the Irish Neptune Manannan;[3] Mabon was worshipped by the pagan Britons as Apollo Maponos, and his mother was the Celtic mother-goddess Matrona, who gave her name to the River Marne and whose sculptured images are to be seen in the archaeological museums of France and the Rhineland.[4]

One may safely conclude, then, that the marvellous element which so distinguishes Arthurian romance from other medieval French fiction is a heritage from the mythology of the Irish and the Welsh, which was preserved by bards and story-tellers long after the introduction of Christianity. It is this well-recognized survival of paganism among the Celts which accounts for the fact that we find both in Celtic literature and Arthurian romance an atmosphere of wonder and supernatural paraphernalia such as are characteristic of mythology—revolving castles, sword-like bridges, springs haunted by fays, isles inhabited only by women, enchantresses who take the form of birds, hags changed by a kiss into damsels of peerless beauty, vessels of inexhaustible plenty, vessels moved by no visible agency, banqueters who preserve a youthful appearance in spite of their many years. That eminent scholar, W. P. Ker, was guilty of no rash dictum when he wrote:[5]

Whether in the Teutonic countries, which in one of their corners preserved a record of old mythology, or in the Celtic, which allowed

1 Loomis, *Wales and the Arthurian Legend*, p. 150.
2 Malory, *Morte d'Arthur*, ed. J. Rhŷs, Everyman's Lib., I. xviii.
3 P. Mac Cana, op. cit., pp. 123–9.
4 J. A. MacCulloch, *Religion of the Ancient Celts* (Edinburgh, 1911), p. 123. Hastings, *Encyclopaedia of Religion and Ethics*, iv. 406–11.
5 *The Dark Ages* (New York, 1904), p. 47.

mythology, though never forgotten, to fall into a kind of neglect and to lose its original meaning, the value of mythology is equally recognizable, and it is equally clear that mythology is nothing more nor less than Romance. Everything in the poets that is most enthralling through the mere charm of wonder, from the land of the Golden Fleece to that of the Holy Grail, is more or less nearly related to mythology.

How far Ker was right in thus claiming a background in Celtic myth for the Grail legends the reader may judge from the detailed analysis to be found in later chapters of this book. In the meantime, for a clearer understanding of the transmutation of the Celtic stories into Arthurian romances it is desirable to define and exemplify some of the processes which effected and affected the change. These are: (1) The blending of elements from different stories to form a new story. (2) The adaptation of a story to a new cultural milieu. (3) Misinterpretation.

1. The first of these phenomena is well illustrated by the *Mabinogion*. For instance, *Math* was proved by the brilliant researches of W. J. Gruffydd to be 'a vast conglomeration of themes, most of them, if not all, appearing in a truncated and sometimes hardly distinguishable form'.[1] Similarly, the Tristan romance, as Gertrude Schoepperle demonstrated,[2] is a composite on a large scale of episodes and motifs derived partly from Celtic sagas, partly from Oriental tales, and partly from common stereotypes of European fiction. Nutt deserves to be quoted:[3]

If we rid our minds of the idea that there is *a Grail legend*, a definite fixed sequence of incidents, we need not be discouraged if we fail to find a prototype for it in Celtic tradition or elsewhere. We shall be prepared to examine every incident of which the Grail is a feature upon its own merits, and satisfied if we can find analogies to this or that one. And by so doing we are more likely to discover the how and the why of the development of the legends as we find them in the romances.

One can best understand the Grail romances, therefore, if one realizes their composite nature, if one perceives from the start

---

[1] W. J. Gruffydd, *Math Vab Mathonwy* (Cardiff, 1928), p. 47.
[2] *Tristan and Isolt* (Frankfurt, London, 1913; reprinted New York, 1959).
[3] *Studies on the Legend of the Holy Grail*, p. 181.

that seldom is a complete episode traceable to a single Irish or Welsh source, but that each is a more or less skilful patching together of materials from the large stock of Celtic myths and hero-tales.

2. The adaptation of stories to a new cultural milieu is, of course, one of the inevitable changes which would take place in their passage from the Irish and Welsh to the French and other non-Celtic peoples, and it would take many forms. Already in the Irish stage the sun-god Lug had lost something of his divinity, was referred to as a 'phantom' (*scal*),[1] and was listed among the early kings, while the goddess of Ireland, Ériu, became an allegorical figure personifying the Sovranty or Kingship of the country.[2] The tendency to interpret myths as history, which prevailed throughout Europe in the transition from paganism to Christianity and which we call euhemerism, had a powerful effect on the romances of the Round Table. The Apollo Maponos of the heathen Britons turns up not only in early Welsh poetry as Mabon, a companion of Arthur's, but also in Chrétien's *Erec* as Mabonagrain,[3] a tall knight in red arms. Most significant is the fact that, though Morgan le Fay has precisely the family relationships of the Welsh Modron and is therefore, like her, descended from the Celtic goddess Matrona and is in fact called a goddess in four medieval texts, she is generally presented in Arthurian romance as a benevolent or malevolent enchantress.[4] The old heathen magic could be made credible as the white magic of a Merlin, or as the miraculous power of a saintly character, or merely as a natural endowment such as exceptional medical skill or physical prowess. Whatever his prepossessions may be as to the origin of the Grail stories, the student can hardly escape noticing that in the First Continuation of Chrétien's *Conte del Graal* the vessel is merely a magic

[1] Dillon, op. cit., pp. 107–9. On Lug's divinity see R. S. Loomis, *Celtic Myth and Arthurian Romance* (New York, 1927), pp. 46 f.

[2] S. Eisner, *A Tale of Wonder* (Burt Franklin, New York, 1957), pp. 17–44. *Ériu*, xiv (1943), pp. 11–14.

[3] Loomis, *Arthurian Tradition*, pp. 169, 177.

[4] On Morgan le Fay see *Speculum*, xx (1945), pp. 183–203; reprinted in Loomis, *Wales and the Arthurian Legend*, pp. 105–30.

talisman of plenty, whereas only in an interpolated passage and in later romances does it become a relic of the Last Supper and the Passion. Such are the natural transformations and adaptations imposed by a different or a changing milieu.

3. Most of the phenomena under review have been pointed out again and again by students of Arthurian romance, but there is another equally natural, inescapable tendency which has not been taken sufficiently into account, and that is misinterpretation. To be sure, a few instances have been recognized. Zimmer called attention to a King Caradoc, whose seat was at Vannes in Brittany, and who was nicknamed Brech Bras, *brech* in Breton meaning 'arm', and *bras* meaning 'strong'.[1] In the First Continuation of Chrétien's poem we meet a youth named Caradoc, who became king of Vannes and was nicknamed Briesbras, interpreted as meaning in French 'short arm'. As a result of this misunderstanding a tale was concocted to explain the deformity.[2] Readers of Malory may well have been puzzled by the fact that, though he sometimes refers to the sacred vessel as 'the Holy Grayle', a correct translation of the French words 'le saint graal', he also refers to it as 'the Sankgreal' and takes it to signify 'the blyssed bloode of our Lorde Jhesu Cryste', evidently because of a confused notion that 'Sankgreal' contained the element *sang*, 'blood'.[3]

Not only in Arthurian fiction but also in the lives of saints misinterpretation is a factor which has to be taken into account, as Père Delehaye has amply demonstrated in his *Légendes Hagiographiques*. And if anyone finds it hard to believe that a blundering interpretation of a text could have prodigious consequences for literature and art, let him ponder the establishment of St. Cecilia as the patroness of music. All authorities agree that it resulted from an error. I quote from the article of Rushforth in *Notes and Queries*, 30 Nov. 1935:

The words of the old 'Acts' of St. Cecilia were taken over by the

---

[1] Chrétien de Troyes, *Karrenritter*, ed. W. Foerster (Halle, 1899), pp. cxiii f., cxxiv.

[2] W. Roach, *Continuations of the Old French 'Perceval'*, iii (Philadelphia, 1952), pp. 164–80.   [3] Malory, *Works*, ed. Vinaver, ii (1947), pp. 794, 845 f.

'Golden Legend' and ... we read how the holy virgin, a secret Christian from her early years, was to be married to Valerian, a pagan whom she soon converted; and when the day of the wedding was come, and the festivities were in progress, 'She, hearing the organs making melody, sang in her heart only to God.' The meaning is clear. The organ, which to us is primarily the instrument of Church music, began to appear in Rome under the Empire, where its powerful tones were valued for public entertainments, and it was associated with the names of Nero and Heliogabalus. The saint shuts her ears to the blatant instrument with its hateful pagan associations, and in her heart, that is to say silently, chants her prayer for the preservation of the purity she has vowed. Yet the mention of the organs is the germ from which Cecilia's patronage of music has been developed.

It seems to have come about in this way. In the Breviary services for her day (Nov. 22) this passage is used as one of the antiphons only, ... with the omission of the words 'in her heart', so that the much mutilated text: *Cantantibus organis Caecilia Domino decantabat* was interpreted by someone who knew the Breviary but not the Acts to mean that she sang to the accompaniment of the organ.

Rushforth went on to quote J. N. Pacquot, who as far back as 1771 remarked that, if artists must represent Cecilia in connexion with musical instruments, she ought to be trampling them under her feet.

Mistranslation and misunderstanding, therefore, are to be expected in the transmission of legends, secular as well as sacred, and may, as in this case, completely alter the nature of a tradition. Particularly when one comes across passages in the romances of the Grail which seem freakish or incompatible with good sense should one consider the possibility that the author has inherited, or has himself made, an error. Surely no branch of medieval literature offered more opportunities for misinterpretation than this, when one takes into account its many retellings in the course of its development from Celtic myth to Arthurian romance.

To sum up, then, no true insight into the origin and development of Chrétien's poems and those of his successors is possible without a realization that they inherited through the Bretons a somewhat confused body of largely mythical stories derived from Wales and Ireland; that from the beginning the traditions tended to ramify, to split up into their elements, and to reassemble in new combinations; that the supernatural elements were gradually adapted to the preconceptions of a more sober-minded and more thoroughly Christianized society; and that not only were minor slips of translation inevitable, but major changes in the meaning and character of the tradition may be expected as a result of errors of interpretation. To grasp these facts is to grasp the clues to the proper understanding of the Arthurian cycle as it developed on the European continent in the twelfth and thirteenth centuries. The following chapters will reveal, I believe, that these are also the clues which enable us to find our way through the mazes of the Grail legends and to penetrate their secrets.

IV

The First Grail Story: the *Conte del Graal* of Chrétien de Troyes

LET us begin our detailed study of the Quest of the Grail with a consideration of the relevant parts of the earliest extant version, the *Conte del Graal* of Chrétien de Troyes. It was the last of his five Arthurian romances, was composed probably between 1175 and 1190, and was left unfinished.[1] The poet says that he turned into rime the best tale ever told in a royal court, which Count Philip of Flanders had given him in the form of a book. He thus implies that the source was a prose narrative of more or less similar content, and this is rendered the more likely by the testimony of a contemporary, the Anglo-Norman lady, Marie de France, that she had rimed and turned into poetry tales which she had heard.[2]

Before proceeding with a translation of the passages concerned with the Grail, it seems desirable to define what Chrétien meant by the word *graal*. It is certain that it was not universally understood even in France, for some French miniaturists depicted it as a chalice. Others, misled by the poet's statement that the vessel contained the sacramental wafer, the Host, represented it as a ciborium, a covered goblet surmounted by a cross, the normal receptacle of the Corpus Christi.[3] Foreigners usually avoided the difficulty by taking over the word instead of translating it. Wolfram von Eschenbach, author of *Parzival*, declared flatly that the Grail was a stone, much to the bewilderment of scholars.[4] Today, everybody, except those who have investigated the subject, visualizes it

---

[1] The *terminus ad quem* is fixed by the departure of Count Philip for the Holy Land in 1190.   [2] Loomis, *Arthurian Tradition*, pp. 10 f.
[3] R. S. and L. H. Loomis, *Arthurian Legends in Medieval Art* (New York, 1938), figs. 264, 287.   [4] See below, pp. 209, 213.

as a chalice, thanks to the misinformation popularized by Tennyson and Wagner.

But it is certain that Chrétien conceived it otherwise. Helinand, abbot of Froidmont, whose life overlapped the poet's, writing about 1215, defined the word as 'scutella lata et aliquantulum profunda, in qua preciosae dapes divitibus solent apponi . . .', that is, 'a wide and slightly deep dish, in which costly viands are customarily placed for rich people'.[1] The first continuator of Chrétien's poem mentioned a hundred boars' heads on grails[2]—an impossibility if the grails were chalices. The authors of the *Estoire* and the *Queste del Saint Graal* equated the sacred vessel with the dish of the Last Supper, containing the Paschal lamb.[3] A dish of considerable size was clearly implied by Chrétien himself when he asserted that the Grail did not provide a pike, a lamprey, or a salmon—a silly remark if he or his readers thought of the vessel as a chalice or a ciborium. On this point then, the contemporary testimony is plain and consistent, and one should envisage the Grail Bearer, not with a chalice between her hands, but with a somewhat deep platter, big enough to hold a salmon yet holding merely a single wafer—a picture odd enough to suggest that there has been a misunderstanding. Let me now give a brief summary of the events preceding the arrival of Perceval at the Grail castle.

The boy Perceval, after the fatal wounding of his father in battle, was brought up by his mother in a forest near Snowdon. Fascinated by the sight of a few of Arthur's knights in full panoply, he left her fainting with grief at his departure, and set out to seek 'the king who made knights'. After various exhibitions of his *naïveté* at Arthur's court and elsewhere, he

[1] *Mod. Phil.*, xiii (1916), pp. 681–4. Frappier, *Chrétien de Troyes, l'Homme et l'Oeuvre* (Paris, 1957), pp. 187–9. J. Marx, *Légende Arthurienne et le Graal* (Paris, 1952), pp. 241–3.

[2] H. Newstead, *Bran the Blessed in Arthurian Romance* (New York, 1939), pp. 70–85. Roach, *Continuations of the Old French 'Perceval'*, i, vss. 9649 f.

[3] Sommer, *Vulgate Version*, i. 13, ll. 24, 27; vi. 190, ll. 32 f. *Queste del Saint Graal*, ed. A. Pauphilet (Paris, 1949), p. 270. 'Ce est . . . l'escuele ou Jhesucriz menja l'aignel le jor de Pasques o ses deciples.' Since for Chrétien and his readers the word *graal* was a common noun and did not denote the unique relic of the Last Supper, the initial is not capitalized in the following translation.

was given a brief training in the management of horse and arms by a friendly lord and was knighted by him. This lord, Gornemant (who bequeathed his name to Wagner's Gurnemanz), strictly forbade his ingenuous pupil to talk too much, and declared: 'Qui trop parole, pechié fait.'[1] After an amorous interlude with a chatelaine named Blancheflor, Perceval started for his home, anxious to learn whether his mother was alive or dead, and one day found himself riding along the bank of a river. I now translate.[2]

He rode along the bank till he came to a cliff washed by the stream, so that he could not pass. Then he caught sight of a boat floating downstream, and two men in it. He waited, expecting them to come up to him. But they stopped in the middle of the river and dropped anchor. The man in the bow had a line and was baiting his hook with a fish somewhat larger than a minnow. The knight, not knowing where to find passage, greeted them and asked: 'Sirs, tell me if there is a ford or a bridge on this river.'

The fisherman answered: 'No, brother, on my faith there is not for twenty leagues, up or down, a boat larger than this, which would not carry five men, and one cannot cross on horseback, for there is no ferry, bridge, or ford.'

'Then tell me, in God's name, where I may find shelter.'

The fisherman replied: 'Indeed you will have need of that and more. I will myself give you lodging tonight. Ride up by the cleft in this rock, and when you have reached the top, you will see before you in a valley a house where I dwell, near the river and near the wood.'

Without further pause the knight ascended, and at the top of the hill he gazed long ahead without seeing anything but sky and earth. He exclaimed: 'What has brought me here? Stupidity and trickery. God bring shame on him today who sent me here! Truly he put me on the right path when he said that at the top I would spy a house! Fisherman, you foully deceived me if you spoke out of malice!'

[1] *Percevalroman*, ed. Hilka (Halle, 1932), vs. 1654. The verse numbering is the same in W. Roach's edition (Paris, 1959).

[2] Ibid., vss. 2994–3687. This translation is reprinted by permission of the publishers from *Medieval Romances*, ed. by R. S. and L. H. Loomis. The Modern Library, copyright by Random House, 1957.

At that instant he spied before him in a valley the top of a tower. One might seek as far as Beirut without finding one as noble or as well situated. It was square, built of dark stone, and flanked by two lesser towers. The hall stood in front of the tower, and before the hall an arcade. As the youth descended he confessed that the fisherman had given him good directions, and praised him and no longer called him a treacherous liar, since now he had found harbourage. So he proceeded to the gate, before which there was a lowered drawbridge. As he crossed, four squires came to meet him; two removed his arms; a third led his horse away to give him fodder and oats; the fourth clad the youth in a scarlet mantle, fresh and new. Then they led him to the arcade, and be assured that none as splendid could be found as far as Limoges.

There he waited till the lord of the castle sent two squires to fetch him, and he accompanied them to the square hall, which was as long as it was wide. In the middle he saw, sitting on a couch, a handsome nobleman with grizzled locks, on his head a sable cap, black as a mulberry, with a crimson lappet below and a robe of the same. He was reclining on his elbow, and in front of him a great fire of dry branches blazed between four columns. Four hundred men could seat themselves comfortably around it. The four strong columns which supported the hood of the fireplace were of massive bronze.

The squires brought the youth before his host and stood on either side of him. When the lord saw him approach, he promptly greeted him, saying: 'Friend, do not take it amiss if I do not rise to meet you, but I cannot do so easily.'

'In God's name, sire, do not speak of it, for, as God may give me joy and health, it does not offend me.'

The nobleman raised himself with difficulty, as much as he could, and said: 'Friend, draw nearer; do not be abashed but sit here at my side, for so I bid you.'

As the youth sat beside him, the nobleman inquired: 'Friend, from what place did you come today?'

'Sire, this morning I left the castle called Belrepeire.'

'So help me God,' exclaimed the nobleman, 'you have had a long day's ride. You must have departed before the watchman blew his horn at dawn.'

'No,' the youth answered, 'prime had already been rung, I assure you.'

As they talked, a squire came in at the door, a sword suspended from his neck. He handed it to the rich host, who drew it halfway from the sheath and observed where it was forged, for it was written on the blade. He saw too that it was of such fine steel that it could not break save only in one peril which no one knew but him who had forged and tempered it. The squire who had brought it announced: 'Sire, the fair-haired maiden, your beautiful niece, sends you this gift. You have never seen one lighter for its length and breadth. You may present it to whom you please, but my lady would be glad if you would bestow it where it would be well employed. He who forged it made only three, and he will die before he can make another.'

At once the lord, taking the sword by the hangings, which were worth a great treasure, gave it to the newcomer. The pommel was of the best gold of Arabia or Greece, and the sheath was covered with Venetian gold embroidery. This richly mounted sword the lord gave to the youth, saying: 'Good sir, this was destined for you, and I desire you to have it. Gird it on and then draw it.'

The youth thanked him and fastened the girdle so that it was not too tight. Then he drew out the naked blade from the sheath and, after holding it a little, put it back. Rest assured that it became him well, hanging at his side, and better still when gripped in his fist; and it surely seemed that it would do him knightly service in time of need. Looking about, he noted standing behind him around the brightly burning fire some squires, and he entrusted the sword to the keeping of the one who had charge of his arms. Then he returned to his seat beside the lord, who showed him great honour. The light of the candles was the brightest that one could find in any mansion.

While they were talking of this and that, a squire entered from a chamber, grasping by the middle a white lance, and passed between the fire and those seated on the couch. All present beheld the white lance and the white point, from which a drop of red blood ran down to the squire's hand. The youth who had arrived that night watched this marvel, but he refrained from asking what this meant, for he was mindful of the lesson which Gornemant gave him, warning him

1. *The Grail, Depicted as a Ciborium, the Bleeding Lance, and the Sword on a Bier*
From MS. Bib. Nat. fr. 12577, fol. 74v. Date c. 1325

against too much speech, and he feared that if he asked, it would be considered rude. So he held his peace.

Then two other squires came in, right handsome, bearing in their hands candelabra of fine gold and niello work, and in each candelabrum were at least ten candles. A damsel came in with these squires, holding between her two hands a grail (graal). She was beautiful, gracious, splendidly garbed, and as she entered with the grail in her hands, there was such a brilliant light that the candles lost their brightness, just as the stars do when the moon or the sun rises. After her came a damsel holding a carving-dish (tailleor) of silver. The grail which preceded her was of refined gold; and it was set with precious stones of many kinds, the richest and the costliest that exist in the sea or in the earth. Without question those set in the grail surpassed all other jewels. Like the lance, these damsels passed before the couch and entered another chamber.

The youth watched them pass, but he did not dare to ask concerning the grail and whom one served with it, for he kept in his heart the words of the wise nobleman. I fear that harm will come of this, because I have heard say that one can be too silent as well as be too loquacious. But, for better or for worse, the youth put no question.

The lord then ordered the water to be brought and the cloths to be spread, and this was done by those whose duty and custom it was. The lord and his guest washed their hands with lukewarm water. Two squires brought a wide table-top of ivory, which, according to the story, was all of a piece, and they held it a moment before the lord and the youth, till two other squires came bringing trestles. The wood of which they were made possessed two virtues which made them last forever. Of what were they made? Of ebony. What is the property of that wood? It cannot rot and it cannot burn; these two dangers it does not heed. The table-top was placed on the trestles, and the cloth was laid. What should I say of the cloth? No legate, cardinal, or even pope ever ate on one so white.

The first course was a haunch of venison, peppered and cooked in fat. There was no lack of clear wine or grape juice to drink from a cup of gold. Before them a squire carved the peppered venison which he had set on a silver carving-dish and then he placed the slices on large pieces of bread in front of them.

Meanwhile the grail passed again before them, and still the youth did not ask concerning the grail, whom one served with it. He restrained himself because the nobleman had so gently charged him not to speak too much, and he had treasured this in his heart and remembered it. But he was silent longer than was proper, for as each course was served, he saw the grail pass before him in plain view, and did not learn whom one served with it, though he would have liked much to know. Instead he said to himself that he would really ask one of the squires of the court before he departed, but would wait till the morning when he took leave of the lord and his attendants. So he postponed the matter and put his mind on eating and drinking; in no stingy fashion were the delicious viands and wines brought to the table. The food was excellent; indeed, all the courses that king or count or emperor are wont to have were served to that noble and the youth that night.

After the meal the two passed the evening in talk, while the squires made up the beds for the night and prepared the rarest fruits: dates, figs, nutmegs, cloves, pomegranates, electuaries, gingerbread of Alexandria, aromatic jelly, and so forth. Afterwards they had many draughts of piment without honey or pepper, of mulberry wine and clear syrup. At all this the youth wondered, for he had never experienced the like. At last the nobleman said: 'Friend, it is time to go to bed, and do not take it amiss that I depart to my chamber to sleep. And when you please, you may lie here. Because of my infirmity I must be carried.'

Four nimble and strong servants came out of a chamber, took by the four corners the coverlet of the couch on which the nobleman was lying, and carried him away. Other squires remained with the youth to serve him as was needed. When he wished, they removed his hose and other clothing and put him to bed in white linen sheets.

He slept till break of day, but the household had already risen. When he looked about, he saw no one, and was obliged to get up alone; though he was annoyed, he rose since he must, drew on hose without help, and took his arms, which he found at the head of the dais, where they had been brought. When he had armed himself well he walked past the doors of chambers which he had seen open the night before. But all in vain, for he found them closed. He shouted

*and knocked. No one opened; there was no response. When he had
called long enough, he went to the door of the hall, found it open,
descended the steps, and found his horse saddled and his lance and
shield leaning against the wall. He then mounted and searched about
the courtyard, but saw neither servant nor squire. He rode to the gate
and found the drawbridge lowered, for it had been so left that nothing
should prevent him from passing it freely at any hour. Then he
thought, since the bridge was down, that the squires must have gone
into the forest to examine the nets and traps. So, having no reason
to wait longer, he said to himself that he would follow after them
and learn, if possible, from one of them why the lance bled and
whither the grail was carried. He passed out through the gate, but
before he had crossed the drawbridge, he felt that the feet of his horse
were rising, and the animal made a great leap, and if he had not done
so, both he and his rider would have come to grief. The youth turned
his head to see what had happened and perceived that someone had
raised the drawbridge. He called out, but no one answered.*

*'Speak,' said he, 'you who have raised the bridge! Speak to me!
Where are you, for I do not see you? Show yourself, and I would
ask you a question.'*

*Thus he wasted his words, for no one would reply. So he rode
toward the forest and entered on a path where there were fresh hoof-
prints of horses. 'This is the way,' said he to himself, 'which the
men I am seeking have taken.'*

*Then he galloped through the forest as long as the tracks lasted,
until he spied by chance a maiden under an oak tree, crying and
lamenting in her distress, 'Alas, wretch that I am, in an evil hour
was I born! Cursed be that hour and that in which I was begotten!
Never before has anything happened to enrage me so. Would that
God had not pleased to make me hold my dead lover in my arms!
He would have done better to let me die and let my lover live. O
Death, why did you take his soul rather than mine? When I see him
whom I loved best dead, what is life worth? Without him I care
nothing for my life and my body. Death, cast out my soul that it may,
if his soul deigns to accept it, be its handmaid and companion.'*

*Thus she was mourning over the headless body of a knight which
she clasped. The youth did not stop when he saw her, but approached*

and greeted her. She returned his greeting with head lowered, but did not cease her lament. The youth asked: 'Who killed this knight who lies in your lap?'

'Good sir,' the maiden replied, 'a knight killed him this morning. But one thing I see which amazes me. For people say that one may ride twenty-five leagues in the direction from which you came without finding an honest and clean lodging place, and yet your horse's flanks are smooth and his hide is curried. Whoever it was who washed and combed him, fed him on oats and bedded him with hay, the beast could not have a fuller belly and a neater hide. And you yourself look as if you had enjoyed a night of comfortable repose.'

'By my faith, fair lady,' said he, 'I had indeed as much comfort last night as was possible, and if it appears so, there is good reason. If anyone gave a loud shout here where we are, it would be heard clearly where I lay last night. You cannot know this country well, for without doubt I have had the best lodging I ever enjoyed.'

'Ah sir, did you lie then at the dwelling of the rich Fisher King?'

'Maiden, by the Saviour, I do not know if he is fisherman or king, but he is very rich and courteous. I can say no more than that late last evening I met two men floating slowly in a boat. One was rowing, the other was fishing with a hook, and he directed me to his house and there gave me lodging.'

The maiden said: 'Good sir, he is a king, I assure you, but he was wounded and maimed in a battle, so that he cannot move himself, for a javelin wounded him through the two thighs. He is still in such pain that he cannot mount a horse, but when he wishes to divert himself, he has himself placed in a boat and goes fishing with a hook; therefore he is called the Fisher King. He can endure no other pastime, neither hunting nor hawking, but he has his fowlers, archers, and huntsmen to pursue game in his forests. Therefore he enjoys this place; in all the world no better dwelling could be found for his purposes, and he has built a mansion befitting a rich king.'

'Damsel,' said he, 'by my faith, what you say is true, for last evening I was filled with wonder as soon as I came before him. I stood at a little distance, but he told me to come and sit beside him, and bade me not think that he did not rise out of pride, for he had not the strength.'

'Surely he did you a great honour when he seated you beside him. Tell me, when you were sitting there, did you see the lance of which the point bleeds, though there is no flesh or vein there?'

'Did I see it? Yes, by my faith.'

'Did you ask why it bled?'

'I said nothing about it.'

'So help me God, learn, then, that you have done ill. Did you see the grail?'

'Yes, indeed.'

'And who held it?'

'A maiden.'

'And whence did she come?'

'From a chamber.'

'Whither did she go?'

'Into another chamber.'

'Did no one precede the grail?'

'Yes.'

'Who?'

'Only two squires.'

'What did they hold in their hands?'

'Candelabra full of candles.'

'Who came after the grail?'

'Another maiden.'

'What did she hold?'

'A little carving-dish [tailleor] of silver.'

'Did you not ask anyone where they were going?'

'No question came from my mouth.'

'So help me God, that was worse. What is your name, friend?'

Then he, who did not know his name, divined it and said that his name was Perceval of Wales. He did not know whether he told the truth or not, but it was the truth, though he did not know it. When the damsel heard it, she rose and faced him, saying angrily: 'Your name is changed, good friend.'

'What is it?'

'Perceval the wretched! Ah, unfortunate Perceval, how unlucky it was that you did not ask all those things! For you would have cured the maimed King, so that he would have recovered the use of *his limbs and would have ruled his lands and great good would have come of it! But now you must know that much misery will come upon you and others. This has happened to you, understand, because of your sin against your mother; she died of grief for you. I know you better than you know me, for you do not know who I am. I was reared with you in the house of your mother long ago. I am your first cousin and you are mine. I grieve no less because you have had the misfortune not to learn what is done with the grail and to whom it is carried than because of this knight whom I loved dearly, seeing he called me his dear mistress and loved me as a brave and loyal knight.'*

'Ah, cousin,' said Perceval, 'if what you say is true, tell me how you know it.'

'I know it,' the damsel answered, 'as truly as one who saw her laid in the earth.'

'Now may God of his goodness have mercy on her soul!' cried Perceval. 'It is a sorrowful tale you have told. Now that she is laid in earth, what is there left for me to seek? For I was journeying only to see her. I must now take another road. If you are willing to accompany me, I should be pleased. He who lies dead here can no longer serve you, I warrant. The dead to the dead, the living to the living. Let us go together, for it seems very foolish for you to watch here alone over this body. Let us pursue the slayer, and I promise and swear that, if I overtake him, either he will force me to surrender, or I will force him.'

She, unable to suppress the great woe in her heart, said: 'Good friend, I cannot go with you or leave my lover until I have buried him. If you listen to me, follow this paved road, since it is by this way that the evil, insolent knight who killed my sweet lover departed. So help me God, I have not said this because I wish you to pursue him, though I wish him as much harm as if he had slain me. But where did you get the sword which hangs at your left side and which has never drawn blood and has never been unsheathed in the hour of need? I know well where it was forged and by whom. Do not trust it, for it will betray you in battle and fly in pieces.'

'Fair cousin, one of the nieces of my good host sent it to him last evening, and he gave it to me, and I was well pleased. But you

terrify me if what you have said is true. Tell me now, if you know:
if the sword should break, will it ever be repaired?'

'*Yes, but with much hardship. If one could find the way to the*
lake which is near the Firth of Forth, he could have it hammered,
tempered, and made whole again. If chance should take you there,
go to a smith called Trebuchet, because he made it and will reforge
it; it can be done by no other man.'

'*Surely,' said Perceval, 'if it breaks, I shall be in grievous peril.'*

[Oddly enough, nothing comes of this ominous warning.
Perceval vanquishes a knight in his next combat and sends
him to surrender at Arthur's court. This exploit and others
make so favourable an impression on the King that, when the
young hero arrives by chance in his presence, his welcome is
assured. Two days later a Loathly Damsel, Wagner's Kundry,
makes her appearance at Caerleon, reproves Perceval for his
silence, and launches the knights of Arthur's court on new
adventures.][1]

Great was the joy which the King, the Queen, and the barons
made over Perceval of Wales. They returned that evening with him
to Caerleon, and the rejoicing lasted that night and through the
morrow. On the third day they saw a damsel come riding on a tawny
mule, with a scourge in her right hand. Her hair hung in two black
twisted braids, and, if the book describes her truly, never was there
a creature so loathly save in hell. Her neck and hands were blacker
than any iron ever seen, yet these were less ugly than the rest of her.
Her eyes were two holes, as small as those of a rat; her nose was
like that of a monkey or a cat; her lips were like those of an ass or
an ox; her teeth resembled in colour the yolk of an egg; she had a
beard like a goat. In the middle of her chest rose a hump; her back-
bone was crooked; her hips and shoulders were well shaped for
dancing! Her back was hunched, and her legs were twisted like two
willow wands. Her figure was perfect for leading a dance!

Into the King's presence the damsel urged her mule; never had
such a creature come to a royal court. She gave a general greeting to
the King and all the barons, but, seated on her tawny mule, she

[1] *Percevalroman,* vss. 4603–746.

addressed Perceval alone, in these words: 'Ah, Perceval, Fortune is bald behind, but has a forelock in front. A curse on him who greets or wishes you well, for you did not seize Fortune when you met her. You entered the dwelling of the Fisher King; you saw the lance which bleeds. Was it so painful to open your mouth that you could not ask why the drop of blood sprang from the white point of the lance? When you saw the grail, you did not inquire who was the rich man whom one served with it. Most unfortunate is he who when the weather is fairer than usual waits for even fairer to come. It was you, unfortunate man, who saw that the time and the place were right for speech, and yet remained mute. You had ample opportunity, but in an evil hour you kept silence. If you had asked, the rich King, who is now sore troubled, would have been wholly cured of his wound and would have held his land in peace—land which he will never hold again. Do you know what will happen if the King does not hold his land and is not healed of his wound? Ladies will lose their husbands, lands will be laid waste, maidens, helpless, will remain orphans, and many knights will die. All these calamities will befall because of you!'

Then, turning to the King, she said: 'O King, I depart, and may it not offend you, for this night I must take my lodging far from here. I do not know if you have heard speak of Castle Orgulous; it is there that I am bound to go tonight. In that castle are five hundred and sixty-six knights of fame, and be assured that none but has a lady-love with him, noble, courteous, and fair. I tell you this because no one goes there without finding joust or battle; he who would perform feats of chivalry will not fail of his purpose if he seeks them there. But if any would have the supreme glory of the world, I know the place, the very spot, where he may best win it, if he dares. On the hill which stands below Montescleire a damsel is besieged. Great would be the honour he would win who would raise the siege and deliver the maiden. All praise would be his, and if God grants him that good fortune, he will be able to gird on without fear the Sword with the Strange Hangings.'

After saying all it pleased her to say, the damsel ceased and departed without another word. Sir Gawain then leapt up and vowed that he would go to Montescleire and do all in his power to rescue the lady. Giflet, son of Do, in turn announced that, if God aided him, he would make his way to Castle Orgulous. Kahedin spoke: 'And I will ascend Mount Dolorous, and will not pause till I arrive.'

But Perceval spoke otherwise, and vowed that henceforth he would not lie two nights in the same lodging, nor avoid any strange passage of which he might hear, nor fail to engage in combat with any knight who claimed to be superior to every other, or even two other knights, until he could learn whom one served with the grail, and until he had found the lance that bleeds, and had heard the true reason why it bled. He would not give up the quest for any suffering. Thus as many as fifty arose and swore, one to another, that they would not fail to pursue any adventure or seek any marvel of which they heard, even though it were in the most perilous land.

[Here Chrétien inserted adventures of Gawain, then returned to Perceval.]¹

Perceval, as the story tells, had so lost his memory that he had forgotten God. Five times April and May had passed, five whole years indeed, since he had entered a minster or worshipped God or His cross. But for all that, he did not cease to pursue chivalry, and sought out strange and stern adventures and proved his mettle and undertook no exploit from which he did not emerge triumphant. Within the five years he sent sixty knights of fame to Arthur's court as prisoners. Throughout this time he did not think of God.

Toward the end he was journeying, all armed as was his wont, through a wilderness, when he came upon three knights and ten ladies walking shoeless, in woollen gowns, their heads deep in their hoods. The ladies, who for the salvation of their souls were doing penance on foot for their sins, were astonished to see Perceval coming all armed, holding lance and shield. One of the three knights stopped Perceval and said: 'Dear good sir, do you not believe in Jesus Christ, who wrote the New Law and gave it to Christians? It is surely not right but rather a great sin to bear arms on the day that Jesus Christ died.'

Perceval, who gave no heed to day or hour, answered: 'What day is this then?'

¹ *Percevalroman*, vss. 6217–515.

'What day, sir? Do you not know? It is the holy Friday, the day when every man should adore the cross and weep for his sins, for today He who was sold for thirty pence was hung upon the cross. He who was clean of all sin saw the sins in which the whole world was bound and befouled, and became a man for our sins. In truth He was both God and man, for the Virgin bore a Son, conceived by the Holy Ghost. In Him God received flesh and blood, so that His deity was concealed in human flesh. This is a certainty, and whoever does not believe it will never see His face. He was born of the Virgin Lady and took the form and the soul of man, together with the Holy Deity. On this day He was crucified and delivered His friends from hell. Right holy was that death which saved the living and restored the dead to life. The wicked Jews, whom one should kill like dogs, in their hatred wrought their own harm and our good when they raised Him on the cross. Themselves they destroyed, and us they saved. All who believe in Him ought to spend this day in penitence. Today no man who believes in God should bear arms on field or road.'

'Whence do you now come?' asked Perceval.

'Sir, we come from a good man, a holy hermit, who dwells in this forest, and, so great is his sanctity, he lives by the glory of heaven alone.'

'In God's name, sirs, what were you doing there? What did you ask for or desire?'

'What, sir?' said one of the ladies. 'We asked counsel for our sins and made confession—the highest work which a Christian can do who would draw near to God.'

Hearing them, Perceval was moved to tears, and determined to go speak with the holy man. 'I would go to the hermit,' he said, 'if I but knew the path or the road.'

'Sir,' was the answer, 'whoever would go there should follow this path by which we have come, through this thick, scrubby wood, and let him watch for the twigs which we knotted with our hands as we came. We left such signs in order that no one seeking the holy hermit would lose his way.'

Then they commended each other to God, without further inquiry. Perceval started on the path, sighing from the bottom of his heart because he felt that he had sinned against God and was deeply repentant. So, weeping, he traversed the wood and came to the hermitage. There he dismounted, removed his arms, and tethered his horse to a hornbeam. Entering a little chapel, he found the hermit, a priest, and another ministrant about to begin the highest and the sweetest service that can be celebrated in a church. As soon as Perceval enered the chapel he fell on his knees, and the good man called to him, seeing that he was humble and that the water flowed from his eyes to his chin. Perceval, who greatly dreaded that he had offended God, grasped the foot of the hermit, bent before him, and with joined hands begged for counsel, of which he had great need. The good man bade him make his confession, for unless he were confessed and repentant, he could have no remission.

'Sir,' said Perceval, 'for five years I have not known where I was. I did not love God nor believe in Him, and I have done nothing but evil.'

'Ah, good friend,' said the worthy man, 'tell me why you have done so, and pray God to have mercy on the soul of His sinner.'

'Sir, I was once at the house of the Fisher King, and saw the lance of which the point truly bleeds, but concerning that drop of blood which I saw hanging from the white steel, I did not ask, and ever since I have fared ill. Nor do I know whom one serves with the grail which I saw, and since then I have endured such sorrow that I would willingly have died. I forgot God, and have not implored His mercy and have done nothing, to my knowledge, to obtain pardon.'

'Ah, good friend,' said the worthy man, 'tell me your name.'

The other replied: 'Perceval, sir.'

At this word the worthy man, who recognized the name, sighed and said: 'Brother, a sin of which you know nothing has wrought this harm. It was the sorrow you caused your mother when you left her, for she fell swooning to the earth at the end of the bridge before her gate, and died of that grief. Because of the sin you then committed it came to pass that you failed to ask concerning the lance and the grail. Thus many evils have befallen you, and know that you would not have endured so long if she had not commended you to God. But her prayer had such power that God for her sake has preserved you from death and from prison. Sin cut off your tongue when you saw *before you the bleeding point which never has been staunched, and did not ask the reason. And great was your folly when you did not learn whom one served with the grail. It was my brother; and his sister and mine was your mother. And believe me that the rich Fisher is the son of the King who causes himself to be served with the grail. But do not think that he takes from it a pike, a lamprey, or a salmon. The holy man sustains and refreshes his life with a single mass-wafer. So sacred a thing is the grail, and he himself is so spiritual, that he needs no more for his sustenance than the mass-wafer which comes in the grail. Fifteen years he has been thus without issuing from the chamber where you saw the grail enter. Now will I enjoin penance on you for your sin.'*

'Good uncle,' said Perceval, 'with all my heart will I perform it. Since my mother was your sister, rightly should you call me nephew, and rightly I should call you uncle and love you the better.'

'It is true, good nephew. But now listen: if your soul is seized with pity, you are indeed repentant, and for atonement go to the minster every day before any other place, and it will be for your good. Do not neglect it for any cause, but if you are in any place where there is minster, chapel, or parish church, go there when the bell rings, or earlier if you are already risen. Never will you regret it, but rather will your soul be benefited. If the mass is begun, it will be all the better, and stay until the priest has finished his prayers and chants. If you choose to do so you can still advance in worth and enjoy both honour and Paradise. Believe in God, love God, worship God. Honour good men and good women. Rise in the presence of a priest; it is a service which costs little, and God in truth loves it because it comes from humility. If a maiden asks your help, or a widow or an orphan girl, give it, and yours will be the gain. Such service is the highest. Aid them, and on no account weaken in well-doing. This is what I would have you do to atone for your sins and to recover all the virtues which once were yours. Tell me now if you assent.'

'Yes,' said Perceval, 'right gladly.'

'Now I pray you that you stay two whole days with me and as a penance take only such food as mine.'

Perceval agreed, and the hermit taught him an orison and repeated it till he knew it by heart. In this prayer were many names of our Lord, and they were so great that mouth of man ought not to utter them save in the fear of death. So after teaching the prayer, he forbade Perceval to say it except in great peril, and Perceval said: 'Sir, I will not.' So he remained and heard the service with great delight. After the service he adored the cross, wept for his sins, and repented of them heartily. Thus he meditated, and for supper that night he ate what the holy hermit was pleased to give him, herbs such as chervil, lettuce, and cress, bread of barley and oats, and clear water of the spring, while his horse had straw and a basin full of barley, and was properly groomed and stabled.

Thus Perceval learned how God was crucified and died on a Friday, and on Easter Day he received the communion. Of him the tale tells no more at this point.

Chrétien does not mention Perceval or the Grail again in his unfinished poem, and there is no means of finding out what more he might have read in Count Philip's book, and how he would have solved the knotty problems he had raised about the mysterious vessel. Is it possible, however, by an investigation of the origins of his material to discover reasonable answers to the questions raised by his fascinating and perplexing narrative? In the next chapter I shall attempt this difficult task.

V

The Grail Bearer, the Question Test, and the Fisher King

CHRÉTIEN invested his account of Perceval's meeting with the Fisher King and the mystifying events which followed with exactly the right atmosphere of awe and wonder; it is a masterpiece of 'gothic' narrative. But the discourse of the hermit, far from offering a plausible explanation, cannot but strike the attentive reader with its absurdity. Instead of resolving difficulties, it creates them. The comments of a distinguished French scholar, Albert Pauphilet, are worth quoting.[1]

> The old infirm king, whom a magic question would have cured, was he, after all, not the only lord of the marvellous castle? Nor the only infirm one? For the other lord, his father, whom Perceval did not see, is even more of an invalid than the Fisher King, for he has not left his chamber for fifteen years. Was he also to be healed by Perceval's question? But there is no mention of it. . . . This old man was sustained by a single mass-wafer, brought to him by the Grail, and yet, with every fresh course, the Grail reappears and passes into his chamber; why these repeated servings of a single wafer? Finally, the Host ought not to be placed in any but a liturgical vessel; behold, then, the Grail surreptitiously transformed into a ciborium or chalice, and the strange procession into the commencement of a Christian liturgy. But in that case, what do these unusual accessories signify, this lance, and above all this absence of a priest?

The reader may also be provoked to ask: with what justice could Perceval be blamed for holding his peace when he had received not the slightest intimation of the direful consequences? And the hermit's assertion that Perceval's silence and the calamitous outcome of his visit were due to the sin he had committed in leaving his mother to die of grief seems far-fetched in the extreme. Several commentators have expressed

[1] *Le Legs du Moyen Âge* (Melun, 1950), p. 183.

astonishment that Chrétien assigned to a woman the task of administering the eucharist in violation of the sacramental doctrine of the Roman Church.[1]

His explanation of the uncanny happenings at the Grail castle is therefore incompatible with common sense, common justice, and canonical practice, and it is patently a crude effort, probably not his own, to account for phantasmagoric events which were inexplicable. It is only fair to the poet's art and intelligence to suppose that the responsibility for this explanation—which does not explain—lies with his source, Count Philip's book.

To exculpate Chrétien is obviously to incriminate the author of that book. But the latter was no fool; how, then, could he have been guilty of the absurdities involved in the hermit's discourse? Could he have been following docilely a traditional story which after numberless retellings and through possible misapprehensions had assumed a form something like that which he passed on to Chrétien? In other words, was he the comparatively innocent victim of the confusions and blunders of tradition? Let us find out what we can about the prehistory of Perceval's visit to the castle of the Fisher King.

It has already been pointed out in Chapter III that Irish literature presents us with several stories of a roughly similar type, the *echtra*, in which the mortal hero visits a supernatural palace, is hospitably entertained, witnesses strange happenings, and sometimes wakes in the morning to find that his host and his dwelling have disappeared. One of these which was in existence before 1056, bears a title which, for lack of better English equivalents, has been translated as the *Phantom's Frenzy*. It should be understood that the word 'phantom' does not here denote a spectre or illusion, but a supernatural being, and that 'frenzy' does not mean madness, but a prophetic ecstasy. The relevant portion of the saga may be summarized thus.[2]

King Conn of the Hundred Battles (who reigned in the

---

[1] Frappier, *Chrétien de Troyes*, p. 193. A. C. L. Brown in *PMLA*, xxv (1910), pp. 8–10. J. Marx, *Légende Arthurienne et le Graal* (Paris, 1952), p. 243.

[2] Dillon, *Early Irish Literature*, pp. 107–9.

second century A.D.) lost his way in a mist. A horseman (the phantom) approached, welcomed him, and invited him to his dwelling. Conn, accompanied by a poet of his household, came to a golden tree and a house with a white-gold ridge-pole. Entering, the two saw their host already arrived and seated on a throne. He revealed himself as Lug. A young woman, who wore a golden crown and who was called the Sovranty of Ireland, served Conn with huge ribs of meat. Then, filling a golden cup with ale, she asked Lug, 'To whom shall this cup be given?' 'Pour it,' said Lug, 'for Conn.' When she repeated the question, Lug prophetically named each of Conn's royal descendants. Finally, the phantom and his house vanished, but the cup remained with Conn.

At first glance, the resemblances between Conn's visit to the palace of Lug and Perceval's visit to the Grail castle may seem less striking than the differences. Nevertheless, the following parallels exist.

1. Conn was invited by a former king of Ireland to his home.	1. Perceval was invited by the Fisher King to his home.
2. Conn arrived at a splendid mansion.	2. Perceval arrived at a splendid castle.
3. Conn found his royal host already seated.	3. Perceval found his royal host already reclining on a couch.
4. Conn was served by a crowned damsel with a golden vessel.	4. Perceval saw a damsel with a golden vessel about to serve his host's father.
5. The damsel asked, 'To whom shall this cup be given?'	5. Perceval failed to ask, 'Whom does one serve with the Grail?'
6. The house and the host vanished.	6. The host could not be found.

The judicious reader, even though he may concede that in Irish or Welsh literature one is most likely to find the sources of Arthurian story-patterns, and that considerable changes are likely to occur in transmission, may still be wary of accepting the *Phantom's Frenzy* as a remote source of Perceval's adventure at the Grail castle because of the differences, particularly because of the absence in Chrétien of any trace of Lug's prophetic role.

But Professor Dillon regards the prophecies as a separate element, an interpolation in the story of Lug's entertainment of Conn. 'The form of the *echtrae* [a visit to the Other World] was used by some scholar of the eleventh century ... to introduce a list of the kings of Ireland'; and Dillon refers to the *Phantom's Frenzy* as a 'compilation'.[1] This analysis is, in fact, borne out by the conclusion, which reads: 'So men speak of the "Vision and Adventure [*Echtra*] and the Journey of Conn", and the "Phantom's Frenzy".'[2] Since, then, the prophecies form an addition to the original story, it is only natural that they find no echo in Chrétien's poem. Thus the chief obstacle to the recognition of the *Phantom's Frenzy* as a remote source of Perceval's visit to the Grail castle is removed.

And the more one learns about Lug and the Sovranty of Ireland, the stronger the case for some connexion between the two stories becomes. Lug's spear was one of the four chief treasures of the Tuatha De Danann, the Irish gods.[3] Though it is not mentioned in the *Phantom's Frenzy*, one might expect to see it in Lug's mansion. What better explanation is there for the functionless lance in the Fisher King's castle? Later Chrétien informs us that it will destroy the whole realm of Logres (England)[4]—a prophecy which accords with the origin of the lance in the spear of Lug, noted for its destructiveness. We read that, when it passed into the possession of Celtchar, it would 'kill nine men at every cast, and one of the nine will be a king or crown prince or chieftain'.[5] Further evidence for a connexion between the bleeding lance and the spear of Lug will be found in Chapter VII.

More impressive is the resemblance between the Grail Bearer and the Sovranty of Ireland, for they possessed a remarkable trait in common: they appeared in beautiful and in repulsive forms. Two romances, *Peredur* and *Perlesvaus*, assure us that the bearer of the dish or salver who passed before the hero in his uncle's castle was identical with the ugly damsel

---

[1] Dillon, op. cit., pp. 107 f.   [2] Ibid., p. 109.
[3] Dillon, op. cit., p. 58. *Revue Celtique*, xii. 57 f.
[4] Vss. 6166–71. Marx in *Moyen Âge*, lxiii (1957), pp. 476–8.
[5] *PMLA*, xxv (1910), p. 19.

who appeared later at Arthur's court and complained of the hero's silence.[1] Now Chrétien, though he describes both the beautiful Grail Bearer and the Loathly Damsel, says nothing of their identity, and it is easy to understand why he, or a predecessor, suppressed a notion so fantastic. It is most unlikely that the authors of *Peredur* and *Perlesvaus* hit upon the idea independently, and one must infer a common remote source. Indeed, it is the identity of the two damsels which explains what Chrétien failed to account for, the knowledge which the Loathly Damsel possessed of Perceval's silence in the presence of the Grail and her anger at him.

The most notable trait of the Sovranty of Ireland, likewise, was her transformation from extreme ugliness to radiant beauty. Several Irish tales are concerned with her metamorphosis, and some later retellings, like the *Wife of Bath's Tale*, are attached to the Arthurian cycle.[2] Celtic scholars recognize that this allegorical figure originated as a personification of the land of Ireland itself,[3] and under the name of Ériu (Ireland) she was thus described: 'One time she is a broad-faced beautiful queen [note the crown which the Sovranty of Ireland wears in the *Phantom's Frenzy*] and another time a horrible fierce-faced sorceress, a sharp whitey-grey bloated thick-lipped pale-eyed battle-fiend.'[4] Another description of the Sovranty of Ireland in her ugly phase gives these details:[5] 'Every joint and limb of her, from the top of her head to the earth, was as black as coal. . . . The green branch of an oak in bearing would be severed by the sickle of green teeth that lay in her head and reached to her ears. Dark smoky eyes she had. . . . Her ankles were thick, her shoulder blades were broad, her knees were big.' Now the Welsh author of *Peredur* gives very similar details when he comes to describe the Loathly Damsel at Arthur's court, who, be it remembered,

[1] Loomis, *Arthurian Tradition*, p. 377, n. 6. S. Eisner, *A Tale of Wonder* (Burt Franklin, New York, 1957), pp. 110–14.

[2] Eisner, op. cit., pp. 17–23, 45–61.

[3] *Ériu*, xiv (1943), pp. 14–18. *Folklore*, xxxi (1920), pp. 118–22. *Revue Archéologique*, sér. 4, xxiv (1914), pp. 205–22.

[4] *Revue Celtique*, i (1870–72), pp. 48 f.   [5] Ibid. xxiv (1903), pp. 197.

was identical with the bearer of the salver which corresponds to the Grail.[1] 'Her face and her two hands were blacker than the blackest iron dipped in pitch; ... one eye was mottled grey and glittering, and the other black as jet; ... her teeth were long and yellow . . . Her thighs were broad and bony, and below all was thin, except her feet and knees, which were fat.'

Obviously, the Welshman did not derive his description from Chrétien's account of the Loathly Damsel, but more or less directly from an Irish description of the Sovranty of Ireland, whom we have seen serving Conn with her golden vessel in Lug's palace. Thus we have further evidence that the Sovranty of Ireland, or Ériu, was the prototype of the Grail Bearer, and that Conn's visit to the palace of Lug, in some form uncontaminated by the prophetic list, furnished the original model for Perceval's strange adventures at the Fisher King's castle.

Some readers may be wondering at this point why Irish authors should have laid themselves out to paint so unflattering a portrait of Ériu, the goddess of Ireland, at least in some of her appearances. In the search for an answer to this puzzle, let us recall Ker's statement, quoted in the last chapter, that the land of the Holy Grail was more or less clearly related to mythology; for we must make an excursus into the field of myth in order to understand the dual aspects of the Grail Bearer and her prototype, the goddess Ériu, alias the Sovranty of Ireland.

The oldest account of the two forms assumed by the goddess is a poem written by a poet who died in 1014.[2] At first she is described as thin-shanked, grey-headed, bushy-browed. 'As it were a flash (?) from a mountain-side in the month of March, even so blazed her bitter eyes.' But after her transformation, her countenance bloomed like the crimson lichen of Leinster crags, her locks were like Bregon's buttercups. Her mantle was a matchless green. These details strongly hint that the goddess is the Emerald Isle incarnate, in all the floral beauty

---

[1] Loth, *Mabinogion*, 2nd ed. (Paris, 1913), ii. 103 f. *Mabinogion*, trans. G. and T. Jones, Everyman's Lib., pp. 217 f.   [2] *Ériu*, iv (1910), pp. 103–5.

of spring. And this would be quite in accord with Irish literary tradition. In a tale of the eighteenth century one reads that Finn, on hearing some verses about 'a bright-faced queen, with couch of crystal and robe of green,' said: 'I understand the sense of that poem also. The queen you saw is the River Boyne. . . . Her couch of crystal is the sandy bed of the river; and her robe of green the grassy plain of Bray.'[1]

If, then, Ériu in her lovely form as described by the eleventh-century poet was Ireland in her spring-time glory, what was she in her loathly and monstrous form? Was she not Ireland in the still wintry month of March, before she had been transformed by the caresses of the sun? Though in all these transformation stories the miracle is caused by union with a destined King of Ireland, her rightful husband was one of the early fabulous Kings of Ireland, called Mac Grene, meaning 'son of the Sun'. Many authorities have recognized in him a sun-god, and Joseph Loth suggested that Mac Grene was simply another name of Lug.[2] This is corroborated by a text which refers to Lug's wedding of the kingship of Ireland,[3] and by the *Phantom's Frenzy*, which, as we have seen, introduces the crowned Sovranty of Ireland as a hostess in Lug's palace.

All this converging evidence points to the existence in pagan times of a nature myth which interpreted the miracle of spring by the mating of the sun-god with the land of Ireland. It was probably too clear a survival of heathenism to be preserved in its pristine form, but it can be detected still in fragmentary references and euhemeristic tales of the metamorphosis of the Sovranty of Ireland by union with the successors of Lug to the crown—successors who were presumed to have inherited some of his solar powers.

The demonstration that the Grail Bearer and the Loathly

---

[1] P.W. Joyce, *Old Celtic Romances* (Dublin, London, 1920), p. 187.
[2] *Folklore*, xxxi (1920), pp. 120 f. *Revue Archéologique*, sér. 4, xxiv. 205-22. Eisner, op. cit., pp. 35, 43.
[3] J. Rhŷs, *Lectures on the Origin and Growth of Religion* (London, 1892), pp. 414-16. Gruffydd, *Math Vab Mathonwy*, p. 109.

Damsel were identical and were descended from the two forms of the Sovranty of Ireland leaves little room for doubt that the *Phantom's Frenzy* in an earlier state provided the basic pattern for Perceval's visit to the Grail castle. But there is still one essential element in Chrétien's narrative unaccounted for. Even though the oft-repeated question asked by the Sovranty of Ireland may have suggested the wording of the question which Perceval failed to ask (in fact, it makes more sense in its context than does the question, 'Whom does one serve with the Grail?' in *its* context), yet Conn underwent no test and no momentous consequences flowed from his success or failure. Where can one discover a situation similar to Perceval's and a similar outcome?

The unique example of a question test which I have been able to find, after much searching and after consultation with authorities on story motifs, is a folktale collected on the west coast of Ireland well over a hundred years ago by the Rev. Caesar Otway, and published in 1841. It may be summarized as follows.[1]

There lies off the coast of Erris an enchanted isle, crowned with a lofty castle, which is visible once every seven years. The king of this castle has sometimes been seen on the mainland as a small, royally dressed man of pleasant presence. 'It is supposed that if *rightly* asked, this hide-and-go-seek potentate will tell the questioner where he can find untold heaps of gold, but the querist must be very particular, for if he ask as he should do, the wealth will be obtained by the one, and the enchantment will be removed by the other; but if not, the king vanishes never to return, amidst wild laughter resounding from the ocean wave, at the folly of him who might have wealth, but had not the wit to win it.' A certain drunkard, Watty O'Kelly, invoked the presence of the king, and a dialogue ensued which ended as follows: Wat—, 'Is it any harm to ask you who you are?' King—, 'None in life; I'm King of the three Kingdoms behind. And each of these three times

---

[1] *Sketches in Erris and Tyrawley* (Dublin, 1841), pp. 251-4. See also ibid., pp. 80, 104 f.

larger than Ireland. And that's your share of them, Watty O'Kelly.'

Douglas Hyde, writing in 1936, kindly cautioned me against accepting this dialogue as a reliable translation from the Irish. But it is clear that Watty asked the wrong question; the king vanished and the spell remained on the castle.

Here, then, in Ireland and Ireland alone, do we find the motif of a country laid under a spell which can be lifted only by the asking of a question. Here, too, is the king of the country who appears in friendly fashion to a mortal, and a mortal who through his failure to ask the right question is dismissed with mockery. Can this extraordinary and unique parallel to Perceval's experience be due to mere chance? The odds against such a notion must be hundreds to one. It is entirely possible and even probable that the tale of Watty's adventure with the fairy king is the late descendant of an old Irish *echtra*, orally preserved through the centuries and degraded in the process. A number of Irish sagas recorded in medieval manuscripts were current as folktales in the nineteenth century, and one of them, the saga of the betrayal of Curoi by his wife Blathnat, is included as a folk-tale in Otway's book.[1]

The evidence, therefore, suggests that an *echtra* containing the question test was in existence early enough to combine with the *echtra* of Conn's visit to the palace of Lug, and that the result, after a long period of transmission, is to be found in Chrétien's poem, where the test derived from the first source has curiously incorporated the wording of the question from the second source. However this may be, it is certain that no other country provides such remarkable analogues to Perceval's experiences at the Fisher King's castle as does Ireland.

But the sceptic may properly ask: What of the Fisher King? Except that he invites the hero to his abode, arrives there before him, and later disappears, he betrays no likeness to Lug. What of the Grail itself, which by definition and by its

[1] *Sketches in Erris and Tyrawley*, pp. 39–41.

content, the sacramental wafer, offers a contrast rather than a resemblance to the cup of ale poured out for Conn?

This challenge is not hard to answer if one remembers that such Irish material as reached the French must have passed through Wales, for in Welsh tradition we find the hospitable king who has supplanted Lug, and a vessel of the shape and with the properties of the Grail, which has taken the place of the cup. We even find an explanation of the puzzle presented by the sacramental wafer.

The immediate prototype of Chrétien's Fisher King has been recognized by a long line of scholars[1] as Brân the Blessed, son of Llŷr, the principal figure in the *mabinogi* of *Branwen*, named after his sister and composed probably about 1060.[2] Brân seems to have originated as a god of the pagan Britons. Branodunum, now Brancaster in Norfolk, may have been named after him, just as Camulodunum (Colchester) was named after the god Camulos, Gobannion (Abergavenny) after the smith-god Gobannos, and Lugubalia (Carlisle) after the god Lugus. Brân according to the *mabinogi* was the son of Llŷr; apparently he reminded the Welsh of the Irish deity of the sea, Manannan mac Lir, and like him was believed to dwell on an elysian isle, where old age was unknown and where his company of immortals banqueted without stint and without end. This primitive mythical figure can still be detected in the gigantic Brân of the *mabinogi*, but, as in the case of Lug, the euhemeristic process has transformed him. He has become King of the island of Britain, crowned in London, and has acquired the Christian epithet *bendigeid*, 'Blessed'. He gives his sister in marriage to the King of Ireland. He holds court on the west coast of Wales, at Harlech, Aberffraw, and Caer Seint; and the imaginary feasts of his followers are localized at Harlech and Gwales, that is, the island of Grassholm. He is no longer immortal, but is wounded in battle, his severed head is buried in the White Hill in London, and we

---

[1] Heinrich, Nutt, Martin, Rhŷs, Anwyl, Brown, Dorothy Kempe, Nitze, Helaine Newstead. See Loomis, *Arthurian Tradition*, p. 386, n. 45,

[2] Translated in Loth, op. cit. i. 119–50; *Mabinogion*, trans. G. and T. Jones, pp. 25–40. On date see ibid., p. ix.

are told that this served as a protection of the island against invaders—a superstition of which we find variants attached to the corpses of other British kings.[1]

Unfortunately the *mabinogi* tells much of Brân which has not left its mark on the Grail romances; otherwise his relationship to the Fisher King would have been generally accepted long ago. Such evidence as we possess has been assembled in cogent fashion by Professor Helaine Newstead in *Bran the Blessed in Arthurian Romance*; and below in Chapter X the nexus between *Branwen* and the Grail material in the French romance of *Sone de Nansai* will be demonstrated. Here, however, it must suffice to list five points of resemblance between Brân and the Fisher King.

1. According to Chrétien, Perceval's host was wounded through the thighs or the legs with a javelin in battle. According to the *mabinogi*, Brân was wounded in the foot with a lance in battle. In an old poem in the Book of Taliesin there is a passage referring to the same battle which Dr. Proinsias Mac Cana in his study of *Branwen* translates: 'I was with Brân in Ireland; I saw when "the Pierced (Thick) Thigh" was slain (wounded)'.[2] The words in parentheses are alternative translations, and the words in double quotation marks are taken to be a descriptive title of Brân. The older tradition, therefore, seems emphatic on the point that Brân was smitten in the thigh, just like the Fisher King.

2. According to Chrétien and other romancers, the Fisher King entertained his guests sumptuously. According to the *mabinogi*, Brân dispensed lavish hospitality, and his feasts were proverbial.

3. In the *Didot Perceval* the Fisher King is called Bron.[3]

4. In Robert de Boron's *Joseph*, Bron, called the Rich Fisher,

---

[1] *Folklore Record*, v (1882), p. 14. Faral, *Légende Arthurienne*, i. 126; ii. 224–6; iii. 33, 182, 299. P. Mac Cana, *Branwen Daughter of Llŷr*, pp. 91–98.

[2] Mac Cana, op. cit., pp. 162–4. Referring to this translation, the author remarks that it 'provides a perfect antecedent to the wound in the groin or the thighs . . . which incapacitated Chrétien de Troyes's Fisher King.'

[3] Roach, *Didot Perceval* (Philadelphia, 1941), pp. 150, 207.

was instructed to set out with his followers to the West.[1] The followers of Brân, in the company of his severed head, journeyed to Gwales (Grassholm), the westernmost isle of Wales.

5. In *Perlesvaus* Gawain feasted in the Fisher King's castle with twelve knights, 'aged and grey-haired, and they did not seem to be so old as they were, for each was a hundred years old or more, and yet none seemed to be forty.'[2] Brân's followers passed eighty years in a great hall in the midst of abundance and joy, yet 'none of them perceived that his fellow was older by that time than when they came there'.[3]

Can there be any reasonable doubt that Brân is the immediate prototype of the Fisher King; that he has taken over from Lug the role of the generous, supernatural host; and that this replacement has obscured the connexion between the *Phantom's Frenzy* and the *Conte del Graal*?

To the question, 'Why does the Welsh sea-god turn up in the French poem fishing from a boat on a river?' no certain answer can be given. It is a legitimate surmise, however, that a sea-god would often be conceived as floating on the waters, and that when, as a result of the euhemeristic process, he became a King of Britain, he would be transferred from the sea to a river.[4] Moreover, since there was, and still is, a ruined castle called Dinas Brân, the 'fortress of Brân', perched above the River Dee in North Wales, famous for its fishing, a tradition might easily have arisen which placed Brân, equipped with hook and line, in a boat on the river which flowed below his castle. What neater explanation is there, since Brân was particularly associated with North Wales and was the original of the Fisher King, Bron?

As for the Grail, we have already learned that less than fifty years after Chrétien wrote his poem the monk Helinand

---

[1] Robert de Boron, *Roman de l'Estoire dou Graal*, ed. Nitze (Paris, 1927), vss. 3310–54.

[2] *Perlesvaus*, ed. Nitze, i, ll. 2414–7.

[3] Mac Cana, op. cit. p. 102. Loth, op. cit., i. 148.

[4] H. Newstead, *Bran the Blessed in Arthurian Romance* (New York, 1939), pp. 18–21. Loomis, *Arthurian Tradition*, pp. 391 f.

defined the word *graal* as 'scutella lata et aliquantulum profunda', a wide and slightly deep dish. Even earlier Giraldus
Cambrensis, that observant Welsh author, wrote that his
countrymen were served in 'scutellis latis et amplis', wide and
capacious dishes.[1] Though this correspondence in size and
shape may not prove the derivation of the Grail from Wales,
since large dishes were certainly in use in other countries, it is
a matter of high significance regarding its origin that one of
its outstanding properties (though not mentioned by Chrétien) is attached to a dish described in a Welsh list of the royal
treasures or talismans of Britain. According to Manessier's
Continuation of Chrétien's poem, after the Grail had passed,
'all the tables were provided with delectable viands and so
nobly filled that no man could name a food which he could
not find there.'[2] Similarly, Wolfram von Eschenbach assures
us, on oath, that in the presence of the Grail each man obtained whatever he held his hand out for, hot dishes or cold,
flesh of wild or tame, and his cup was filled with whatever
beverage he might name.[3] The *Queste del Saint Graal* asserts
that, as the vessel passed before the tables, they were instantly
filled at each seat with such food as each person desired,[4] and
in the *Estoire* we read that the vessel brought to the holy in
life 'all the good viands which heart of man could conceive'.[5]
Now this is precisely the magic virtue ascribed in the list
of talismans to the dish of Rhydderch, an historic king of
Strathclyde in the sixth century: 'whatever food one wished
thereon was instantly obtained'.[6]

Could anything be plainer than that the Welsh were familiar
with a talisman of the size, form, and preternatural powers

[1] Giraldus Cambrensis, *Opera*, ed. Dimock, vi (London, 1868), p. 183.
[2] C. Potvin, *Perceval le Gallois* (Mons, 1866–71), vi. 151.
[3] *Parzival*, 238, 8–239, 5.
[4] Sommer, *Vulgate Version*, vi. 13. *Queste*, ed. Pauphilet, p. 15.
[5] Sommer, op. cit. i. 250.
[6] Edward Jones, *Bardic Museum* (London, 1802), p. 48: 'Lliain (neu Dysgl
Rhiganed) Rhydderch Ysgolhaig; y bwyd a chwenychai, fe fyddai arno (neu
ynthi) fo ai caid yn y man.' No other manuscript known to me mentions the
Lliain (table-cloth); all mention the *Dysgl* (platter). On Rhydderch see *Arthurian
Literature*, ed. Loomis, pp. 22–28; *Trioedd Ynys Prydein*, ed. R. Bromwich (Cardiff,
1961), pp. 504 f.

which the continental authors attributed to the Grail? If it be objected that the dish of Rhydderch is not recorded before 1460 and therefore might conceivably have been derived from the Grail legend, the answer is likewise clear: it has no sacred associations such as the Grail had attracted to itself by the fifteenth century, and its possessor bears a name unknown to the Grail romances but renowned in Wales. Therefore, it was not borrowed from the French; rather, it provides the clearest and the most immediate prototype of the Grail. That such a dish should be counted among the possessions of Rhydderch, whose epithet *Hael* proclaims his generosity, is natural enough; it is even more natural that a similar vessel should be the prized possession of Brân, the sea-god, who, like the Irish sea-god, Manannan, was a lavish host, and whose followers feasted without stint for eighty years on the isle of Grassholm; and it is natural that Brân's vessel should be found in the possession of Bron, the Fisher King.

But why, one may well ask, did Chrétien, instead of representing the talisman as a platter of plenty which provided the assembled company with an abundance of food, each to his taste, as in other versions, assert through the mouth of the hermit that the Grail contained but a single consecrated wafer, and that destined for the Fisher King's father alone? It is this statement which involved the poet in the absurdities noted earlier in this chapter, namely, the unsuitability of so large a vessel as the receptacle for so small an object; the uncanonical administration of the sacrament by a woman; the futility of of her repeated passages through the hall when one passage would have sufficed.

Where did Chrétien, or rather the author of his source, find so bizarre a notion? Once more Welsh tradition provides a reasonable and realistic answer. In Chapter III it was pointed out that misunderstandings were inevitable in the transmission of stories from one language and cultural milieu to another, and that they were responsible for irrational and freakish features. Could a misunderstanding, a mistranslation, have been responsible for this, the most irrational and freakish feature in Chrétien's poem?

Now the very list which contains the dish of Rhydderch, close prototype of the Grail, contains also a drinking vessel, the Horn of Brân: 'the drink and the food that one asked for one received in it when one desired.'[1] If one looks for any obvious traces of this miraculous horn in the Grail romances, one is disappointed; instead one finds the wonder-working mass-wafer, the Corpus Christi, in intimate association with the dish. At first glance, it seems preposterous that the Corpus Christi should have been substituted for a horn. But it is a fact that in Old French the nominative case for the words 'horn' and 'body' was identical, *li cors*. The First Continuation of the *Conte del Graal* illustrates the use of *cors* in both senses; in one instance it refers to a magic horn which, according to the manuscripts, bore the name of *Beneïz* or *Beneoiz*, meaning 'Blessed'.[2] Now the French were not too familiar with sacred drinking-horns, but they were familiar in Chrétien's day with the Corpus Christi as a sacred, miraculous food. Caesarius of Heisterbach gives an instance of a woman who was sustained solely by the Body of Christ.[3] Under the date 1180 the chronicler Guillaume de Nangis told of a paralytic young herdswoman of the diocese of Sens who, unable to take other food, was likewise kept alive by the Host; the rumour of this could easily have reached Chrétien if he was living in or near Troyes. In the *Queste del Saint Graal* we read that Perceval saw in an abbey King Mordrain, who had lived for four hundred years so saintly a life that he had tasted no earthly viand but that which the priest elevates in the mass; 'that is, the body

[1] National Library of Wales, MS. Peniarth 77, p. 214: 'Corn Bran galed or gogledd; y ddiod ar bwyd a ofynid a gaid ynddo pan i damunid.' The words 'or gogledd', meaning 'from the North', indicate that Brân son of Llŷr, the euhemerized god, has been equated with Brân son of Dyfnwal, a pseudo-historic figure, who, according to a Welsh version of Geoffrey of Monmouth's *Historia Regum Britanniae*, Jesus College MS. LXI, was allotted the country north of the Humber, the Gogledd. See *Historia*, ed. A. Griscom (London, New York, 1929), p. 276. On the Brâns see *Trioedd Ynys Prydein*, ed. R. Bromwich, pp. 284–6.

[2] Roach, *Continuations of the Old French 'Perceval'*, ii, vss. 12315, 12387.

[3] *Dialogus Miraculorum*, book ix, ch. 47. P. Browe, *Die eucharistischen Wunder des Mittelalters* (Breslau, 1938), pp. 49 f.

(*cors*) of Jesus Christ.'[1] In Mordrain then, we have a close counterpart to the Fisher King's father, and it seems plain that the author of the *Queste* and Chrétien were both reflecting the current belief in the miraculous nutritive virtue of the Corpus Christi.

The misinterpretation of *li cors*, meaning 'horn', as 'mass-wafer' was a natural, almost an inevitable, blunder, and was bound to occur frequently. Once the platter and horn, associated in Welsh tradition, came to be the *graal* and the sacramental wafer of French tradition, no wonder that Chrétien, or rather the author of Count Philip's book, decided that the one must be the receptacle of the other. No wonder that the wafer was assigned the function of sustaining the Fisher King's father. No wonder that, as a consequence, the Grail's original function of feeding a whole company with every delicacy that they could wish was dropped, though the Grail Bearer was still, significantly, allowed to pass through the hall with every course—a relic of her original role.

It will appear more and more clearly in later chapters that the sanctification of the Grail legends was largely due to the ambiguity of the word *cors*. Once the conviction grew and spread that in these tales the word referred to the Body of the Lord, either in its historical or its sacramental sense, and that a vessel somehow associated with it had been seen in Britain in King Arthur's time, French men of letters were offered an irresistible opportunity for imaginative elaboration, and they did not fail to take advantage of it.

A few puzzles remain. Whence came the Fisher King's father, for whom there is no counterpart in the Celtic sources mentioned? Was he invented to serve as a recipient for the holy wafer? However, the Vulgate cycle seems to preserve a tradition, independent of Chrétien, that there were two kings in the Grail castle, one the father of the other;[2] and this

---

[1] Sommer, op. cit. vi. 62 f. *Queste*, ed. Pauphilet, p. 86.

[2] In the *Queste* the castle of Corbenic is the dwelling of King Pelles and the 'roy Peschour', Galaad's great-grandfather. In the *Estoire* the Maimed King, Pelleam, was the father of Pelles. In the Prose *Lancelot* (Sommer, op. cit. v. 303) Pelles asks Bohors if he has seen his father, the Maimed King, in the castle.

tradition may have suggested adding to the Fisher King a second invalid who could serve as the communicant required to consume the miraculous wafer and whose name could supply an answer to the traditional question, 'Whom does one serve with the Grail?'

A similar explanation would apply to the damsel bearing the carving-dish, the *tailleor*. She seems to be a double of the Grail Bearer, derived from a variant version of Perceval's entertainment by the Fisher King. But Chrétien neglected to provide any function for her, and by the time he reached the episode of the Loathly Damsel he seems to have forgotten about her altogether.

Finally, there is the Hermit Uncle, whom Perceval found dwelling in a *desert* or wilderness, and to whom he told the story of his humiliation at the Grail castle. Can a prototype be found for him? Perceval's earlier history, beginning with his father's wounding in battle and including Perceval's upbringing by a woman in a forest, his skill with javelins, and his departure to a king's court, presents a striking similarity, as scholars have long been aware,[1] to the *enfances* of Finn son of Cumal, the hero of a saga cycle which is still remembered by the peasantry of Ireland. There can be little doubt that Chrétien's story of Perceval's parentage and boyhood had its remote origin in the Finn saga. Now, in a twelfth-century text, the *Boyhood Deeds of Finn*, we read that the youth went into Connaught and found his father's brother Crimall, an old man in a desert wood. He told his uncle his story from beginning to end, and how he had killed the man who had wounded his father. He then bade his uncle farewell.[2]

Given the clear parallel between the earlier careers of the two young heroes, Perceval and Finn, this later parallel can hardly be due to mere chance. And it is not difficult to guess how the French story developed out of the Irish through the use of a little reason. Why should Perceval's uncle be living in

[1] See Loomis, *Arthurian Tradition*, p. 335, nn. 1, 2.
[2] T. P. Cross, C. H. Slover, *Ancient Irish Tales* (New York, 1936), p. 365.

a wilderness unless he was a hermit? If so, what more natural than that Perceval should reveal his identity and relate his adventures in the course of a long confession? Why such a long confession unless he had neglected that duty? What more appropriate day for such a confession than Good Friday? In some such fashion, we may reasonably conjecture, the scene which first appears in Chrétien's poem and which indirectly inspired Wagner to compose his Good Friday Spell, came into existence.

It is possible to claim, then, with ample justification that the Celtic hypothesis accounts for nearly every feature, for every important personage, connected with the Grail in Chrétien's poem. It enables us to understand what Chrétien leaves shrouded in mystery; for example, the reason for the Loathly Damsel's monstrous appearance, her intimate knowledge of Perceval's behaviour at the Grail castle, and the motive behind the tongue-lashing which she gives him. It explains realistically, as the result of mistranslation, the most troublesome enigma of all, the Corpus Christi in the Grail.

Some may feel disappointed to learn that there is no higher or lower level of meaning in the *Conte del Graal*, and that the Christian element is due to a blunder. Others may resent an interpretation which explodes Miss Weston's fascinating theory of a lost mystery cult, conveyed by Eastern merchants from the Mediterranean to Britain, and of secret initiation rites enacted in remote ages—a theory also discredited by the absence of any reference to such a cult in the mass of medieval testimony on heresy. Still others would have preferred a demonstration that the Catharists or Albigensians had produced the legend in the caverns of the Pyrenees, and suffused it with symbolism.

But the Celtic hypothesis has great advantages over any rival theory. It accords with historic probability, with the demonstrable origin of the Arthurian legend in Wales. It is based on a comparison between Chrétien's story with Welsh and Irish texts, most of them dated earlier than 1180. Though it may not possess the false fascination of Oriental or Manichaean occultism, it introduces us to a wonderland of adventure and myth no less charming. Even the errors and confusions which it presupposes provided stimuli for the composition of an enthralling and, in some of its branches, a noble literature.

VI

The First Sequel to the *Conte del Graal*: the Corpse on the Bier and the Broken Sword

IF any corroboration be needed for the exegesis of Chrétien's treatment of the Grail story given in the last chapter, it is supplied by the version of Gawain's visit to the Grail castle told by the first continuator of the poem (formerly called by scholars Pseudo-Wauchier), who added some 9,500 verses. As Professor Roach has remarked of this episode, 'nothing resembles the scene described by Chrétien'.[1] Instead we have a visit to an Otherworld castle which resembles in striking ways, not, to be sure, the *Phantom's Frenzy*, but two other Irish *echtrai*. The poet who introduced this Grail adventure into a continuation of Chrétien's work replaced the castle in a valley by a mansion at the end of a causeway far out at sea; replaced the two decrepit kings by a stalwart figure; replaced the Grail, which was borne by a damsel to a hidden invalid, by a Grail which, without visible bearer, served the whole company; and at the same time he credited the hero with restoring fertility to a barren land, of which function Chrétien affords no hint. All these novel elements find analogues in one or both of two Irish *echtrai*, the *Adventure (Echtra) of Art Son of Conn* and the *Adventure (Echtra) of Cormac Son of Art*. To attribute such parallels to mere chance is to defy all laws of probability.

Let us, then, examine the account of what one might call Gawain's *echtra*. The First Continuation has come down to us in a short, a long, and a mixed version.[2] The short one is the original, which later redactors expanded and endeavoured to harmonize with Chrétien. It is distinguished, as noted in

[1] *Colloques Internationaux du Centre National de la Recherche Scientifique*, iii, *Les Romans du Graal dans la Littérature des XIIe et XIIIe Siècles* (Paris, 1956), p. 113.

[2] Roach, *Continuations of the Old French 'Perceval'*, i, pp. xxxiv–xxxix.

Chapter II, by frequent addresses to a knightly audience, and fifty verses before the author announces his intention to reveal the secrets of the Grail, he asks for a drink of wine.[1] Evidently, he was a professional *conteur* with a talent for riming, his repertory included a tale of Gawain's entertainment at the Grail castle, and he set it down on parchment. Either he or a scribe attached it to Chrétien's poem, careless of the fact that it was completely at variance with the account of Perceval's visit.[2] He wrote probably not more than a decade or two later than Chrétien, say between 1180 and 1200, and what he wrote is preserved substantially in a manuscript at the British Museum, Additional 36614. The narrative of the visit to the Grail castle, like Chrétien's, is in the 'gothic' vein, and some readers may feel that it surpasses even the master's work in the creation of suspense, mystery, and an awesome atmosphere.

As the tale begins,[3] Queen Guenevere was sitting in her pavilion at a crossroads, playing at 'tables' with King Urien, when an unknown knight rode rapidly by without pausing to greet her. Annoyed, she sent first Kay and then Gawain to bring him back. The stranger consented at last to return with Gawain when he was assured that Gawain would give him all aid on his secret errand. Just as the two arrived at the Queen's pavilion, the unknown was mortally wounded with a javelin thrown by an invisible enemy. Before dying, he adjured Gawain to don his arms, mount his steed, and give it free rein. Bound by his promise, Gawain obeyed and rode away as night fell, not knowing who the slain knight was, nor what his mission, nor by whom he had been murdered.

It is at this point that the author interjects an appeal to the audience to recite a paternoster for the dead (plural), and to give him a drink of wine.[4] Then we are told how Gawain, overtaken by a thunderstorm, took refuge in a large chapel. A black, hideous hand extinguished a tall candle, there was a wild cry, and Gawain was almost thrown from his saddle by

---

[1] *Colloques Internationaux*, iii. 115–7.

[2] Roach, *Continuations*, i, pp. xx–xxii. Note that this MS. contained at first only Chrétien's poem, and the First Continuation begins with a new hand.

[3] Ibid. iii. 436.　　　　　　　　　　　　　　　　[4] Ibid. iii. 452.

the startled horse. As the storm abated, he rode on till day dawned and he saw that he had crossed the land of Britain. But still he continued through a great forest till the sun had run its course. A translation follows.[1]

He had been awake all night and was so weary that the desire to sleep seized him and he could hardly keep from falling. The steed dragged at the bridle, and Gawain slackened his hold and let it go as it willed. It bore him so rapidly that he came to the sea before nightfall. He could go no farther except by a wide causeway which he found before him, leading far into the sea. It was planted on both sides with cypresses, laurels, ebonies, and olive trees, and the branches met above, covering the causeway, which had a fair and solid surface of hard stones and sand; but it was fearsome to enter because it was dark. Sir Gawain bent low and gazed along the causeway and saw far off a light like a kindled fire. The horse wished to go thither, but the rider would not let it enter the causeway because he heard the sea beating against the trees, and the wind lashed the branches so hard that it came near to breaking them. Then Gawain thought that he would await the dawn before he would proceed on the causeway, but the horse took the bit in its teeth and gave a great leap so that he could not restrain it. Willy nilly he was carried forward at great speed. Abandoning the reins, he gave the animal frequent pricks of the spur, both hard and light, and it dashed on swiftly. He rode till midnight without finding the light though he had thought to reach it earlier. So he hastened on.

Sirs, Gawain followed the causeway till he came to a large hall. There he saw with wonder a great company, and I tell you truly that he was received with much honour as soon as he had dismounted. Never was seen such joy.

'Fair sir,' said they, 'God has brought you to us, and long we have desired your coming.'

They led him before a great fire and speedily disarmed him; they brought a crimson mantle edged with squirrel-fur and wrapped it about him. Then they all looked at him intently and began to take counsel one with another in low tones. When Sir Gawain saw them

[1] Ibid. iii. 456–78, 490–6.

thus in close converse, he was filled with terror and alarm. They all said, 'This is not he', and disappeared from about him. He remained alone in the hall, which was high, long, and wide; never was seen one so large. In the middle was a bier of extraordinary size. Sir Gawain beheld it, raised his hand and made the sign of the cross, like a man terrified. On the bier was spread for honour a great scarlet cloth of Greek samite, with a cross of gold embroidery in the midst. On the breast of the corpse which lay there, sirs, was one half of a sword-blade; the other half was lacking. Never was seen steel so bright as the fragment which lay on the silk. At the head and the feet four large candles were burning; the candlesticks were of silver, and the censers which hung from them without other support were of fine gold. Long did Gawain remain there, fearful and sore perplexed, for he knew not what to do. Much it troubled him that he found no one to speak to.

'O God,' said he, 'whither can I go?'

As he said this, he heard loud lamentation which drew near the door of the hall. He raised his head and saw entering, first of all, a very rich silver cross, adorned with jewels and fine gold; never did treasury contain one more precious. A tall ecclesiastic who bore it had no light task. Over his alb he wore a noble tunic of precious cloth from Constantinople. After him came a great procession of canons, each clad in a rich cope of silk. Then they began the service of the dead in right seemly fashion, and after they had sung the vigil right loudly, they censed the bier with the four censers which hung from the candlesticks. Then the hall filled with people. I can assure you that never have you heard such great dole since the hour you were born as that which they made around the bier. Sir Gawain prayed God to keep him from sorrow and, standing with the other folk, he bore himself as was right and fitting. As soon as the service was ended, the censers were restored to the candlesticks from which they had been taken. At once all those of whom you have heard—those who had made the great dole and the clergy who had sung the service —vanished. The lamentation ceased, the body remained. Gawain could not but cross himself when he beheld the marvel which had taken place. Then, pondering, he sat down, for he had stood a long while, and covered his eyes with his hands.

Anon he heard another large crowd approaching, and, lifting his eyes, he saw in the hall the same folk whom he had seen at first. First he saw twenty servants putting cloths on the tables, and, when they had spread them, there issued from the door of a chamber a tall and stalwart knight of a goodly age, a little grizzled. On his head he wore a golden crown; in his right hand he carried a royal sceptre, and on the same hand there was a large ring, set with a very rich, beautiful ruby. I tell you in truth that there was not in Christendom so fair and courteous a man. Then the attendants cried: 'The King desires water,' and so he washed his hands in basins of fine gold. Then he bade pour the water at once for Sir Gawain, and afterward took him by the hand and seated him at his side for supper.

Then Gawain saw entering by a door the rich grail, which served the knights and swiftly placed bread before each one. It also performed the butler's office, the service of wine, and filled large cups of fine gold and decked the tables with them. As soon as it had done this, without delay it placed at every table a service of food in large silver dishes. Sir Gawain watched all this, and marvelled much how the grail served them. He wondered sorely that he beheld no other servant, and hardly dared to eat. When all had tasted as much of the first course as pleased them, it was promptly removed, and the second was given them. Sirs, I will not tell you all the courses which the grail brought, for to do so would tire you greatly, but I will merely say that they ate at leisure, and you would have seen the grail serving them in the most honourable, fair, and brisk fashion. When the repast was ended, everyone vanished in the twinkling of an eye.

Gawain, who remained alone, covered his face with his mantle; he was greatly troubled and alarmed at the marvel he had witnessed. He knew not what to do, nor what would become of him. Yet, though greatly terrified, he took heart and courage again and uncovered his face. He looked up and down the hall, but saw nothing at all save the bier and a complete lance, fixed perpendicularly in a vessel (orcel) of silver. This lance bled so that the red blood flowed copiously into the silver vessel. All around the shaft appeared the tracks of the drops which fell into the vessel. From there the blood passed through a golden pipe, entered another pipe of green emerald, and so flowed out of the hall. But Gawain did not know what became

*of it, and was abashed at the marvel. He heard the door of a
chamber open, and saw two squires issue from it, holding two lighted
candles. Then the King himself came forth, holding a sword, which
had belonged to the knight, slain at the pavilion, of whom you have
heard me tell. Then the King addressed Sir Gawain, made him
rise from the table where he was sitting, and led him to the bier.
Bitterly he mourned him who lay dead upon it, and exclaimed
with tears:*

'*Ah, noble body, lying here, for whose sake this kingdom is
desolate, may God grant that you may be avenged so that the people
may be glad thereof, and that the land which has long been desolate
may be restored.*'

*Then he drew forth the sword which had been broken in the
middle, and handed it to Gawain, and the good knight took it. Sirs,
the other half was lying on the breast of the dead man, and the king
took it in his hands, and said to Sir Gawain, who was standing
beside him:*

'*Fair sir, if it please God, this sword will be reunited by you.
Take the two pieces which have been broken apart, place them together, and we shall see if they will reunite.*'

Sir Gawain answered: '*Fair dear sir, right willingly.*' *He placed
the two pieces of steel together, but he could in no wise unite them
and so mend the sword. Greatly was the King grieved thereat. He
straightway replaced the piece on the body exactly as it had been;
then he took Sir Gawain gently by the hand and led him into a
chamber. There he found a large company of knights, ladies, and
other folk. The two seated themselves on a precious silk couch-cover,
adorned with a pattern of wheels.*

Then the King said: '*Fair sweet sir, do not be distressed by aught
that I tell you. The task for which you have come hither will not
now be achieved by you. Much greater must be your prowess. But
you should understand that if God will hereafter so increase your
valour that he will let you return, you will be able to achieve the
task. Sir, no one will achieve it unless he has first reunited the
sword. I know well that he who undertook the adventure has remained in your country. I do not know who has kept him there, but
we have eagerly awaited him. Truly you have displayed might and*

hardihood to come here, and if you desire any fair thing which we have in this country, however precious, you shall have it willingly, sir, so help me God. Ask at your pleasure concerning anything that you have seen, and we will surely tell you all that we know of it.'

Sir Gawain had not slept the night before and had tired himself by riding all day, so that great was his yearning for slumber, yet greater far was his desire to hear of the marvels. So he forced himself to stay awake and asked:

'Sir, I saw a bleeding lance, and much have I wondered about it since. Tell me for the love of God whence comes the blood which flows around it, and I ask you also—for I would know—concerning the sword and concerning the bier which stands out in the hall. If it please you, tell me the truth.'

The King replied: 'Never has anyone dared to ask the question which you have put to me. Nevertheless, I will not hide the truth, but will tell you all surely, fair sweet friend. First, I will tell you of the great anguish and sorrow which came from the lance and of the great glory. Rest assured, sir, that by it we are glorified and healed, for it is the very lance with which the Son of God was smitten through the heart on the day when He was hung upon the cross. Ever since it has remained here, and continually it bleeds and will bleed till Doomsday. In this place it will stay by God's decree. I declare to you—I do not lie—that on that day all men shall see their Creator bleeding as freshly as the lance does now. The Jews and the sinners who slew Him through malice may well have cause to dread. Do you know what then will save us? His blood shall ransom us, but not the wicked. That stroke redeemed us from hell and delivered us from torment. But, sir, another stroke has deprived us of so much that no man could tell it—the stroke that was dealt by the sword which could not be reunited a moment ago. Never was so evil and foul a stroke dealt by any sword, for it has destroyed many a king, count, baron, lady, maiden, and high-born damsel. You surely have heard tell at length of the great destruction which caused us to come hither. The realm of Logres (England), the whole country, was destroyed by the stroke of this sword alone. Sir, I will not lie but will tell you who it was who lost his life and who it was who smote him. Never did man hear such a wonder.'

Here a passage of 226 lines has been interpolated, giving the
early history of the Grail—a passage translated in Chapter
XIV, which flatly contradicts the later statement that Gawain
had not learned about the service of the Grail.]

*Then the King began to weep and to tell the story as he wept.
But, sirs, as he was relating the truth of what had happened, he saw
that Sir Gawain was asleep. Unwilling to wake him, he let him
repose and ceased to tell more. Sir Gawain slept till morning, when
he found himself, his horse, and his arms in a field of gorse near
the sea. He was full of wrath and chagrin that he found himself
there and saw no town, house, wall, castle, or tower. He exclaimed:
'This is an evil lodging!' Then he armed himself and mounted.
Well did he know that he had been disgraced by falling asleep,
because by so doing he had lost the chance to hear about the great
wonders. Never had he been so dismayed as he was now for fail-
ing to inquire who was destined to fill the land again with people.
Much was he troubled at heart.*

*'Ah, God,' said he, 'how generously the noble, just, wise, and
courteous King related to me the truth concerning the high secret. It
grieves me that I fell asleep.'*

*Then he said that he would do such deeds of arms and would so
strive that, if God granted him to find the court again, he would reunite the sword, accomplish the task for which he came, and ask
without fear about the fair service of the grail and the bier; and that
he would never return to Britain until he was mightier in arms than
he was now.*

*Then he rode away through the country. Never was a land seen
of eye better garnished with water, wood, and meadows. It was the
waste kingdom, which the evening before had been wholly void of
every good thing. But in the night God had restored the streams to
their proper channels in the country, and all the woods, it seems, had
turned green as soon as he had asked why the lance bled. Sirs, I
assure you that more people would have filled the land if he had
only asked further questions. But those of the country who saw him
ride by blessed him and cried with a loud voice:*

'Sir, you have both slain us and healed us! Thus you should be

glad and joyful for one reason, and sad for the other—glad because of the weal that we now enjoy, for well we know that you are the cause. Yet we should hate you because you did not learn why the grail served. No one could tell the great joy that would have come of asking, but now you must suffer dole and grief.'

VII

Irish *Echtrai*: the Waste Land and the Bleeding Lance

THE tale just translated, though utterly different in content from Chrétien's narrative of the marvels of the Grail castle, resembles it in the uncanny atmosphere it creates. Bruce remarked: 'The air of mystery and the suggestion of the supernatural are well maintained throughout the whole episode.'[1] But, as in Chrétien, there are flaws and incoherences. How is it that if the broken sword had belonged to the knight slain under Gawain's safe-conduct, nothing was said about his carrying the weapon, and how were the pieces transported to the Grail castle? Though Gawain must have traversed a Waste Land before reaching the castle, nothing was said about it before he saw it restored to fertility.

As a sequel to Chrétien's poem, moreover, the adventure of Gawain at the Grail castle is preposterous, for its author, as already said, contradicts his predecessor on every essential point. It is hard to understand how Bruce and other commentators could have believed that he knew and was inspired by Chrétien's account and in 'a legitimate attempt to gain the effect of mystery' produced a scene totally irreconcilable with his model.[2] The effect on readers who remembered Chrétien's story must have been blank bewilderment, for our ancestors were not totally wanting in a sense of continuity and harmony. One can only conclude that Gawain's visit to the Grail castle had a source quite different from Perceval's and combined quite different strands of tradition.

The case for an independent source for the Grail episode in the First Continuation is clinched by the striking analogues to

[1] Bruce, *Evolution*, i. 295.   [2] Ibid. i. 296.

be found in two Irish *echtrai* mentioned at the beginning of the last chapter, the *Adventure of Art Son of Conn* and the *Adventure of Cormac Son of Art*. It would be wrong to describe these sagas as sources of Gawain's entertainment at the Grail castle, since they have come down to us in fourteenth- and fifteenth-century manuscripts, and the first of them seems to be a late combination of two or more stories. Yet the correspondences which both sagas present to the Frenchman's eerie tale afford sufficient evidence of a genetic relationship. The Irish *echtrai* may be regarded more accurately as remote cousins rather than as ancestors of the Grail scene in the First Continuation.

Turning our attention to the *Adventure of Art Son of Conn*, let us note the curious fact, that in spite of the title, the principal figure in the first part of the saga is not Art but his father, King Conn of the Hundred Battles, whom we have met as the hero of the *Phantom's Frenzy*, and that Conn is again described as visiting an Otherworld palace and being entertained by a supernatural host and hostess. It is far from improbable that this originally formed an independent *echtra*, which was later prefixed to the adventures of Art. However this may be, it is an extraordinary and impressive fact that, whereas the experiences of Conn described in the *Phantom's Frenzy* foreshadow the visit of Perceval to the Grail castle, so the experiences of the same Conn related in the *Adventure of Art* adumbrate the visit of Gawain to the Grail castle. Let me summarize the relevant part of the saga.[1]

By his marriage to an evil woman, King Conn brought an enchantment on his kingdom, so that there was neither grain nor milk in Ireland. To restore fertility, he set out in a coracle across stormy seas without guidance till he landed on an island. There he found a hall, thatched with coloured bird's wings, with bronze doorposts and doors of crystal, and near it were wells and hazel-trees dropping their leaves and blossoms into the wells. Within the hall he saw the niece of the sea-god Manannan and her husband Daire. He was tended and led to the fire by invisible agency. Then food-laden boards rose up

---

[1] Dillon, *Early Irish Literature* (Chicago, 1948), pp. 112–14.

before him, and a drinking-horn appeared, though he could not see who fetched it.

Conn's method of ending the food-shortage corresponds in no way to that employed by Gawain, but at last we learn that his evil wife was banished[1] and may infer that the barren earth yielded its crops once more. There are, to be sure, obvious differences between this tale and the visit of Gawain to the Grail castle—the sea voyage instead of the ride along the sea-beaten causeway, and the restoration of fertility by the banishment of an evil woman instead of by the asking of a question. Yet there are no less striking similarities: the Waste Land and its restoration to fertility; the stormy journey; the splendid hall beyond the sea; the supernatural host; and, most noteworthy of all, the provision of food and drink without visible servitors. After all, a complete correspondence is hardly to be expected when the Irish saga and the French poem have followed such divergent paths for centuries.

The case for a relationship, even though remote, is fortified by the fact that another *echtra*, the *Adventure of Cormac in the Land of Promise*,[2] offers correspondences to the *echtra* of Conn on the one hand, and to the adventure of Gawain on the other. King Cormac, grandson of Conn, allowed his wife to be carried off by a warrior, lord of a land where there was no old age, decay, or sadness. Setting out to recover her, he came on a palace described in almost the same terms as the hall of Manannan's niece, with beams of bronze, thatch of birds' wings, and hazel-trees overhanging a spring. He was welcomed by the warrior and a beautiful woman. His feet were washed by invisible hands, and the water was heated by hot stones, which went in and out of themselves. After being entertained lavishly with miraculous food, Cormac was informed by his host that he was Manannan mac Lir. The next morning he woke to find himself on the lawn of Tara, together with his wife, unharmed, and a truth-testing cup.

Despite differences in motivation and in the situation of the

---

[1] Dillon, *Early Irish Literature*, p. 116.
[2] Ibid., pp. 110-12. T. P. Cross, C. N. Slover, *Ancient Irish Tales*, pp. 503-7.

Otherworld palace, there is here a patent resemblance to the adventure of Conn—the palace, the divine occupants, the hospitable reception, and the service by invisible agency. And it is no accidental coincidence that the entertainment of Cormac in the Other World matches the entertainment of Gawain in the Grail castle on four points: the stately royal host, the service by invisible agency, the feasting, and the waking the next morning in the open.

Thus nearly all the major points of difference between the accounts of Chrétien and his first continuator can be neatly explained by the hypothesis that the former was based on an early form of the *Phantom's Frenzy*, while the latter blends features similar to those in the *Adventure of Art* and the *Adventure of Cormac*. Common to both Chrétien and his continuator are the question test and the bleeding lance. It was proposed in Chapter V that the lance originated in the spear of Lug, but Chrétien's description of it provided little evidence for this relationship. But, as described by the continuator, fixed upright over a silver vessel, the lance does resemble in its setting the spear which, according to an Irish saga, came into the possession of Lug.

Chrétien's prophecy that the lance of the Grail castle was destined to destroy the realm of Logres identifies it with a destructive weapon which figures in a prose romance of about 1230, now referred to as the *Suite du Merlin*.[1] Merlin informed the foredoomed hero Balaain (Malory's Balin) that he was destined to strike a blow which would bring great calamity on three realms.[2] Later, Balaain came to the castle of King Pellehan. When attacked by the King, he ran through the hall seeking a weapon. He entered a rich chamber and saw on a silver table a vessel (*orcuel*) of silver and gold, and in it a lance standing without any support, the head below the shaft. Balaain seized the lance, drove it through Pellehan's thighs

---

[1] On this romance, formerly known as the *Huth Merlin*, see Fanni Bogdanow in *Arthurian Literature*, ed. Loomis, pp. 325–35.

[2] *Merlin*, ed. G. Paris, J. Ulrich (Paris, 1886), i. 231. *Roman de Balain*, ed. M. D. Legge (Manchester, 1942), p. 25.

and replaced it. At once the walls collapsed. When with Merlin's help he departed, he found the trees fallen, the crops destroyed, and the inhabitants dead. Thenceforth the kingdom was called the Waste Land.[1]

Three points should be noted about this powerful story. First, it provides a sort of prelude to Gawain's visit to the Grail castle, since it explains how the land came to be waste. Secondly, the lance with which Balaain dealt the dolorous stroke is surely the bleeding lance which Gawain saw in the Grail castle, since Pelleam is the name given in the *Estoire del Saint Graal* to the King maimed in the thighs by a lance,[2] and this same King, according to the *Queste*, awaited the coming of Galaad to the Grail castle to heal him with the blood dripping from the lance.[3] Thirdly, the story of Balaain's use of the lance presents an extraordinary likeness to the story of how the Irish hero Brian obtained the spear of Lug. This forms an episode in the *Fate of the Children of Turenn*, a saga which, though here summarized from a late version, was in existence in the eleventh century.[4]

The three sons of Turenn were compelled by Lug to fetch for him, among other talismans, the spear of King Pisear. They came to his palace and Brian demanded the famous spear. When attacked by the King, Brian killed him and put the courtiers to flight. Then he went with his brothers 'to the room where the spear was kept; and they found it with its head down deep in a cauldron of water, which hissed and bubbled round it. Brian, seizing it boldly in his hand, drew it forth', and departed. The weapon was delivered in due course to Lug.

[1] *Merlin*, ed. Paris and Ulrich, ii. 23–30. *Roman de Balain*, pp. 74–82. Details lacking due to a lacuna in the Huth MS. are supplied from Cambridge University Library MS. Additional 7071, fol. 270v.

[2] Sommer, *Vulgate Version*, i. 290.

[3] Ibid. vi. 191. *Queste*, ed. Pauphilet, p. 271. The MSS. as usual confuse the name with Pelles and Pellinor. See *Mod. Phil.* xvi (1918), pp. 122 f.

[4] Dillon, op. cit., pp. 61 f. P.W. Joyce, *Old Celtic Romances* (Dublin, London, 1920), pp. 54–59, 71–74. Cross and Slover, op. cit., pp. 60–63, 69–71. It has been argued that the late version of the *Fate of the Children of Turenn* was influenced by some such Arthurian story as that of Balaain, but in *Arthurian Tradition*, p. 379, n. 26, I have tried to meet this objection.

Thus a remarkable parallel exists between the lance of the Grail castle and the spear of Lug, a parallel so close as to leave little doubt that the one originated in the other. How the fiery spear of Lug came to possess the mysterious attribute of bleeding, one can only guess; possibly it was suggested by the fact that in two Irish descriptions of what is surely the same spear its head was plunged in a cauldron of blood.[1] The identification, made by the first continuator, of the bleeding lance with the spear of Longinus, which pierced the side of Christ on Good Friday, was natural, but absurd.[2] Just as in Chrétien's poem the traditional question test called for an answer, an explanation of the Grail and the mass-wafer, and prompted the absurd solution based on contemporary legends about the Eucharist, so the continuator was required by the question test to explain the lance. Since Celtic tradition provided no answer, all connexion with the spear of Lug having long since been lost, what more natural than to recall the most famous lance of Christian legend? The absurdity of introducing the lance which pierced the side of Christ as one of the phantasmagoric exhibits in the hall of a British castle does not seem to have disturbed the author, for supposedly authentic relics of the Passion were becoming thick as blackberries in Western Europe. If he knew of a rival relic, the head of the holy spear, which has been studied by Laura Hibbard Loomis, and which the poet of the *Chanson de Roland* placed in the hilt of Charlemagne's sword Joyeuse,[3] or if he had heard of the 'discovery' of the lance, shaft and all, at Antioch in 1098, he was not, apparently, disturbed. What is curious and very significant is his failure to place the weapon in an appropriate setting, a chapel or sacristy. Standing in an unconsecrated hall, it betrays, not its identity with one of the most revered relics of Christendom, but its affinity to the spear of King Pisear, which came into the possession of Lug.

---

[1] *PMLA*, xxv (1910), p. 22.
[2] On Longinus and his spear see R. J. Peebles, *Legend of Longinus in Ecclesiastical Tradition and in English Literature, and its Connection with the Grail* (Baltimore, 1911).
[3] *Romanic Review*, xvii (1950), pp. 241–56. *Speculum*, xxv (1950), pp. 437–56.

Though the experiences of Gawain at the Grail castle may be explained in large measure as a story of the restoration of the Waste Land to fertility as a result of his asking the fateful question, though we can detect elements which had a remote origin in Irish *echtrai*, and though the bleeding lance can be identified as the spear of Lug, there are other elements which seem to belong to a different narrative pattern. Apparently the nameless knight slain at the Queen's pavilion by an invisible foe had been summoned to the Grail castle to fulfil a mission; before expiring he had passed on this task to Gawain without telling him its nature. When Gawain arrived at the castle, the inmates were naturally dismayed that he was not the expected knight. Nevertheless, he was put to the test of the broken sword, which was somehow connected with the corpse on the bier. Having failed in the test, he was judged unfit to accomplish the secret mission, and was firmly, though courteously, dismissed. It is the combination of two distinct patterns—the restoration of the Waste Land, in which Gawain partly succeeded, and the mending of the sword, in which he failed—which was largely responsible for the obscurities which tantalize the reader of the first continuator's powerful story.

We are left to ponder the following questions: What was the mission which the murdered knight was supposed to discharge and which, before dying, he transferred to Gawain? How had the sword been broken, and why was Gawain asked to mend it? Who was the illustrious person whose death had caused so great a calamity?

In Manessier's Continuation of the *Conte del Graal* we find an answer to these questions, and though the effect of mystery is dissipated, the plot is clarified. It is a coherent narrative of murder and vengeance, partly, I believe, invented to serve as a sequel to the First Continuation, but partly derived from the very same traditions of vengeance on which that continuation was based. For in the next two chapters it will appear that the First Continuation, Manessier, *Peredur*, and *Perlesvaus* offer variant versions of a blood-feud of which there are only slight traces in the other Grail romances. And Perceval, whom we have hitherto considered mainly in the role of destined healer of a king and restorer of his land, is assigned the additional role of avenger of the wrongs done to his kinsmen.

VIII

Manessier's Sequel and *Peredur*: the Mission of Revenge

BETWEEN the First Continuation of the *Conte del Graal* and Manessier's sequel stretches a long narrative, formerly assigned to Wauchier de Denain, in which Perceval's adventures, eerie and amorous, are related at length. No virgin, he arrives a second time at the Grail castle, and succeeds where Gawain failed. A squire brings the two fragments of a sword. Perceval joins them, except for a slight crack, and is greeted by the Fisher King as the lord of his house. Apparently the second continuator regarded this as a suitable termination to the career of Perceval. But Manessier realized that much remained to be elucidated, and continued with a complicated story of which the following digest will serve to recall the significant details.[1]

Perceval sat down to a sumptuous feast, and afterwards saw passing before him two damsels, one bearing the Grail and the other the carving-dish. The Fisher King revealed that the first damsel was his daughter and the second his niece, daughter of Boon or Gron, 'roi du désert', that is, King of the Waste Land. This second king, whose name in uncorrupted form we have ample reason to believe was Bron, had been treacherously killed by Partinal, Lord of the Red Tower, with a sword which broke in pieces with the stroke. Bron's body had been sent to his brother's castle, and his daughter had brought the broken brand, informing her uncle that the knight who could repair it would avenge her father's death. The

---

[1] Potvin, *Perceval le Gallois*, v, vss. 34935–45379. Summarized by A. Nutt, *Studies on the Legend of the Holy Grail*, pp. 19–22, and by Wrede, *Fortsetzer des Gralromans Chrestiens von Troyes*, pp. 30–39, See, on date of Manessier, ibid., pp. 151–8.

Fisher King also disclosed that it was while handling the fragments that he had maimed himself through the legs, and that
he could not be cured till he, too, was avenged on the Lord of
the Red Tower. Perceval then undertook the task. After many
irrelevant experiences he came to the dwelling of a smith, who
completely restored the weapon. Perceval rode on, killed the
Lord of the Red Tower, and returned triumphant to the Grail
castle. On hearing of his approach, the Fisher King leaped to
his feet, miraculously cured of his wound. Only then did
Perceval learn that the Fisher King was his uncle (not, as in
Chrétien, his cousin).

If we eliminate from this narrative a few features which are
not matched in other Grail romances and therefore are not
based on tradition, such as the wounding of the Fisher King
by his own carelessness and his cure by the settling of a blood-
feud, there remains a distinct and coherent pattern. And if one
compares it with the first continuator's obscure tale of Gawain's
experiences at the Grail castle, one sees how neatly the motivation is clarified and the questions answered. The secret mission
with which Gawain was charged is furnished with a purpose
—revenge for the illustrious personage lying on the bier. The
breaking and the mending of the sword are harmonized with
this purpose, and the presence of the fragments in the castle
no longer offers a problem. The relation of the dead man on
the bier to the King of the Grail castle and to the hero himself is satisfactorily explained.

That the story of Perceval's revenge on the slayer of his
kinsman was no new invention of Manessier's, of this there
can be little doubt, for the motif turns up, with variations, in
several forms of the Perceval story which could not have been
influenced by Manessier. And it is possible to discover a remote common source. Already in Chapter V we have had
occasion to note that there is a striking parallel between the
enfances of Perceval and an Irish saga, the *Boyhood Deeds of
Finn*, and that the analogy extended to Perceval's meeting
with his hermit uncle in a desert wood and relating his history.
Alfred Nutt, moreover, pointed out long since that the same

tradition of Finn, still current in Ireland and Gaelic Scotland in the nineteenth century, emphasized the young hero's obligation to avenge his father's murder; and that this blood-feud showed a significant resemblance to the vendetta in certain versions of the Grail quest.[1] Nutt did not argue his case cogently enough to convince scholars of the derivation of Perceval's early history from that of Finn. But have we sufficient reason to refer ultimately to the Finn saga the obligation which rests on Perceval to avenge a murdered kinsman, whether it be his father (as in *Sir Percyvelle* and the Prose *Tristan*), his uncle (as in Manessier), or his male cousin (as in *Peredur* and *Perlesvaus*)?[2] There are three reasons:

1. As just stated, in two romances Perceval was charged with the duty of punishing the murderer of his father.[3] So was Finn.

2. It can hardly be a mere coincidence that the colour red is associated with the victims of Perceval's vengeance, while Finn's hereditary enemies were the sons of Daire the Red. The victims are, in Manessier the Lord of the Red Tower, in *Sir Percyvelle* the Red Knight, in *Perlesvaus* the Knight of the Vermeil Shield of the Forest of Shadows, Cahot the Red, and the Red Knight of the Deep Forest. In *Perlesvaus*, moreover, a Red Giant is mentioned who had killed the hero's uncle, Alibran of the Waste City—a very suggestive name and title —and had fatally wounded his father, Alain le Gros.[4]

3. If we glance back at Chapter IV, we find that Chrétien tells how Perceval, on leaving the castle of the Fisher King, came upon a damsel, his cousin, who was mourning her newly slain lover, and how he was put by her on the track of the

---

[1] Nutt, op. cit., pp. 158 f., 189. Nutt placed too much confidence in the antiquity of the Lay of the Great Fool. Miss Sheila J. McHugh proved in '*Sir Percyvelle*': *Its Irish Connections* (Ann Arbor, Mich., 1946) and in *Mod. Phil.*, xlii (1945), pp. 197–211, that the Lay is in part derived from Arthurian romance.

[2] Loomis, *Arthurian Tradition*, pp. 399–401.

[3] W. H. French, C. B. Hale, *Middle English Metrical Romances* (New York, 1930), pp. 553–61. E. Löseth, *Roman en Prose de Tristan* (Paris, 1890), pp. 167–9, 234–8, 241 f. See Pace in *PMLA*, xxxii (1917), pp. 508–604; A. C. L. Brown in *Mod. Phil.*, xviii (1921), pp. 212–19; and Loomis, *Arthurian Tradition*, pp. 403 f.

[4] Ibid., p. 397.

slayer. In *Perlesvaus* we have a cognate version in which the hero meets a damsel, carrying the head of her lover in a rich vessel of ivory, and is instigated by her to avenge the dead man, who turns out to be his cousin, the son of his uncle Brun Brandalis.[1] In these cognate stories we seem to detect the influence of an episode in the *Boyhood Deeds of Finn*, relating how the youth, on the way to visit his uncle, comes on a woman mourning her newly slain son. Finn goes in pursuit of the slayer and kills him, only to learn that he has thus settled scores with the warrior who had sorely wounded his father.[2] In spite of the shifted relationships of the characters, the narrative patterns of the Irish and the French stories are much the same.

The influence of the Finn saga on the Perceval romances being assured, there should not be much doubt as to the ultimate source of the theme of vengeance. It becomes clear also that the tradition of Finn's feud with the sons of Daire the Red was grafted on to certain lost versions of the Brân legend, for how otherwise can one explain the curious fact that in Manessier it was Boon or Gron, King of the Waste Land, who was killed by the Lord of the Red Tower, and in *Perlesvaus* it was Alibran of the Waste City who was killed by the Red Giant, and the son of Brun Brandalis who was killed by the Red Knight of the Deep Forest? Unless these remarkable coincidences in name are deceptive, the vendetta motif, though Irish in origin, was absorbed in the Welsh stage into the complex of stories about Brân son of Llŷr, and thence passed into the Perceval romances.

Some readers, familiar with *Branwen*, may object that there is no trace of such a vendetta in this, the only extensive history of Brân son of Llŷr preserved to us. This would be a formidable objection if the *mabinogi* were regarded by scholars as a complete and canonical collection of the traditions about Brân, and if it were certain that no variant and inconsistent tales had ever existed. But Dr. Proinsias Mac Cana concludes

[1] *Perlesvaus*, ed. Nitze, i, ll. 8678–710, 8825–64, 8985–9036.
[2] T. P. Cross, C. H. Slover, *Ancient Irish Tales*, pp. 364 f.

his book, *Branwen Daughter of Llŷr*,[1] with the statement that
the author's aim was 'to create a piece of literature to be judged
independently on its own merits, and not as some reflection of
the traditions of his forebears'. His book also contains much
evidence for the absorption of Irish materials into the *mabinogi*.
There is therefore no rational ground for rejecting the evidence of the French romances, which points toward the merg-
ing of the Irish Finn legend with the Welsh traditions of Brân.

The motif of the broken sword which the hero is called on
to mend—a motif which occurs not only in all four continuations of the *Conte del Graal*, but also in *Peredur* and the
Queste del Saint Graal (whence it came to Malory)—is also
plausibly derived from the Finn cycle, though in this case the
hero is not Finn but his nephew Cailte. The Irish analogue
was pointed out over thirty years ago by Professor Penning-
ton, and is here briefly summarized from the *Colloquy of the
Old Men*, dated 1142–67.

Cailte and a companion came by chance to a faery palace
and were invited to enter. The host, Fergus Fair-hair, son of
the great god Dagda, asked Cailte to repair a broken sword
which the gods (the Tuatha De Danann) had refused to mend.
Cailte spent a day in performing the task, and also mended
a spear and a javelin. Fergus disclosed that each of these weapons was destined to destroy one of the enemies of the gods.
Cailte announced that it was his destiny to carry out some
deed for which the men of Ireland and Scotland, as well as the
gods, would be thankful. After three days Cailte and two
companions went on their way with the mended weapons,
came to another faery palace, and were entertained by a troop
of beautiful women. The enemies of the gods attacked the
palace, and in the ensuing battle Cailte fatally smote the King
of Norway with the mended spear, and his companions similarly employed the sword and the javelin.

[1] p. 190.
[2] *Mod. Lang. Notes*, xliii (1928), pp. 534–6. For translation see S. H. O'Grady,
Silva Gadelica (London, 1892), ii. 247–9. On dates see R. Thurneysen, *Irische
Helden- und Königsage* (Halle, 1921), p. 48; *Ériu*, x (1926), p. 74.

Though many of the details do not match the story of
Perceval in the Second and Third Continuations, yet there is
an essential sameness. A warrior came to an Otherworld mansion, was welcomed, was asked by his host to repair a broken
blade, did so, was informed by his host that the weapon was
destined to slay an enemy, and that he would earn the grati-
tude of the people. The recurrence of the motif, even in a text
as far removed from the First Continuation as the *Queste del
Saint Graal*, warrants the belief that it was traditional, and no
other literature offers as close an analogue as the Irish. Dates, of
course, as well as other considerations, eliminate the *Colloquy of the Old Men* as a possible remote source; so, as in other
cases, the relationship between the Irish and the Arthurian
tales must be that of cognates with a common ancestor.

This theme of the sword-mending was then linked up with
the other tradition of a blood-feud and served as a test of the
hero's fitness to carry out his obligation to revenge the murder of a kinsman. The combination appears most clearly in
Manessier, but it can also be discerned dimly in Gawain's testing
in the First Continuation. The test alone, without any explicit
relation to the feud, is found in the Second Continuation, the
Queste del Saint Graal, and *Peredur*, where, as we shall presently see, the young hero at his uncle's bidding twice struck an
iron column with his sword, twice broke it and miraculously
rejoined the pieces, but the third time was unable to repair
the fracture. This failure, his uncle declared, showed that the
youth had attained only two-thirds of his strength. And when
we look back at Chrétien's narrative and observe how oddly
inept is the presentation of the handsome sword to Perceval
by the Fisher King—a weapon destined to fly in pieces in
battle—we may well suspect that this is one more instance of
the muddled state in which certain traditions reached the poet.

The feud quest, as Nutt called it, is as important in *Peredur*
as in Manessier, but takes a very different form. The Welsh
romance, written down about 1200, is so very confused that
it must be based on mere memories of various French or

Anglo-Norman romances.[1] But the hero bears the original Welsh name which probably suggested to the French the name Perceval, 'Pierce-valley', on the analogy of such well-attested names as Percehaie, meaning 'Pierce-hedge'.[2] The romance was translated well over a hundred years ago by Lady Charlotte Guest in the *Mabinogion*, and the scenes pertinent to our inquiry which are here translated follow her rendering, with a few corrections.[3]

Peredur rode forward. And he came to a vast and desert wood, on the confines of which was a lake. On the other side was a fair castle. On the border of the lake he saw a venerable, hoary-headed man, sitting on a brocaded cushion, and having a garment of brocade upon him, and his attendants were fishing in the lake. When the hoary-headed man beheld Peredur approaching, he arose and went towards the palace, and the old man was lame. Peredur, too, went forward to the palace, and the door was open, and he entered the hall. There was the hoary-headed man sitting on a cushion, and a large blazing fire burning before him. The household and the company arose to meet Peredur, and disarrayed him. The man asked the youth to sit on the cushion; and they sat down and conversed together. When it was time the tables were laid, and they went to meat. When they had finished their meal, the man inquired of Peredur if he knew how to fight well with the sword.

'I know not,' said Peredur, 'but were I to be taught, doubtless I should.'

'Whoever can play well with the cudgel and shield will also be able to fight with a sword.'

The man had two sons; the one had yellow hair and the other auburn. 'Arise, youths,' said he, 'and play with the cudgel and shield.' So did they.

'Tell me, friend,' said the man, 'which of the youths thinkest thou plays best.'

'I think,' said Peredur, 'that the yellow-haired youth could draw blood from the other if he chose.'

---

[1] On *Peredur* see Foster in *Arthurian Literature*, ed. Loomis, pp. 199–205.
[2] Loomis, *Arthurian Tradition*, pp. 345 f.
[3] For more authoritative translations see Appendix I.

'*Arise, friend, and take the cudgel and the shield from the hand of the youth with the auburn hair, and draw blood from the yellow-haired youth if thou canst.*'

So Peredur arose, and went to play with the yellow-haired youth; and he lifted up his arm and struck him such a mighty blow that his brow fell over his eye, and the blood flowed forth.

'*Ah, friend,*' said the man, '*come now and sit down, for thou wilt become the best fighter with the sword of any in this island; and I am thine uncle, thy mother's brother. With me shalt thou remain a space, in order to learn the manners and customs of different countries and courtesy and gentleness and noble bearing. Leave, then, the habits and the discourse of thy mother, and I will be thy teacher; and I will raise thee to the rank of knight from this time forward. Thus do thou. If thou seest aught to cause thee wonder, ask not the meaning of it; if no one has the courtesy to inform thee, the reproach will not fall upon thee, but upon me that am thy teacher.*'

And they had abundance of honour and service, and when it was time they went to sleep. At the break of day Peredur arose, and took his horse, and with his uncle's permission he rode forth. He came to a vast desert wood, and at the farther end of the wood was a meadow, and on the other side of the meadow he saw a large castle. Thither Peredur bent his way, and he found the gate open, and he proceeded to the hall. He beheld a stately hoary-headed man sitting on one side of the hall, and many youths around him, who arose to receive and honour Peredur. They placed him by the side of the owner of the palace. Then they discoursed together; and when it was time to eat, they caused Peredur to sit beside the nobleman during the repast. When they had eaten and drunk as much as they desired, the nobleman asked Peredur whether he could fight with a sword.

'*Were I to receive instruction,*' said Peredur, '*I think I could.*'

Now there was on the floor of the hall a huge column, as large as a warrior could grasp. '*Take yonder sword,*' said the man, '*and strike the iron column.*'

So Peredur arose and struck the column so that he cut it in two; and the sword broke in two parts also. '*Place the two parts together, and reunite them,*' and Peredur placed them together and they became entire as they were before. A second time he struck the column, *so that it and the sword broke in two, and as before they reunited. The third time he gave a like blow, and placed the broken parts together, and neither the column nor the sword would unite as before.*

'*Youth,*' *said the nobleman,* '*come now and sit down, and my blessing be upon thee. Thou fightest best with the sword of any man in the kingdom. Thou hast arrived at two-thirds of thy strength, and the other third thou hast not yet obtained; and when thou attainest thy full power, none will be able to contend with thee. I am thine uncle, thy mother's brother, and I am brother to the man in whose palace thou wast last night.*'

Then Peredur and his uncle discoursed together, and he beheld two youths enter the hall and proceed up to the chamber, bearing a spear of mighty size, with three streams of blood flowing from the point to the ground. When all the company saw this, they began wailing and lamenting. But for all that the man did not break off his discourse with Peredur. As he did not tell Peredur the meaning of what he saw, he forbore to ask him concerning it. When the clamour had a little subsided, behold, two maidens entered, with a large salver (dyscyl) between them, in which was a man's head, surrounded by a pro-fusion of blood. Thereupon the company of the palace made so great an outcry, that it was irksome to be in the same hall with them. But at length they were silent. When it was time that they should sleep, Peredur was brought to a fair chamber. The next day with his uncle's permission he went his way.

There follows the meeting with a beautiful woman, sitting beside a corpse. She is the hero's foster-sister, not as in Chrétien, his cousin; the incident is dealt with cursorily and nothing is said of the mysterious adventure of the evening before. Not till long after do we read of the arrival of the Loathly Damsel at Arthur's court and her denunciation of the hero. It has already been pointed out in Chapter V that the description of her does not resemble that which Chrétien gives but was evidently copied, directly or indirectly, from a description of the Sovranty of Ireland before her metamor-phosis into a creature of floral beauty. Her words to Peredur were:

'*I greet thee not, seeing that thou dost not merit it. Blind was fate in giving thee fame and favour. When thou wast in the palace of the Lame King, and didst see there the youth bearing the streaming spear, from the point of which were drops of blood flowing in streams down to the hand of the youth, and many other wonders likewise, thou didst not inquire their meaning nor their cause. Hadst thou done so, the King would have been restored to health, and his dominions to peace. Whereas from henceforth, he will have to endure battles and conflicts, and his knights will perish, and wives will be widowed, and maidens will be left portionless, and all this is because of thee.*'

She has more to say to Arthur and his knights. Peredur's only response was:

'*By my faith, I will not sleep tranquilly until I know the story and the meaning of the lance whereof the black maiden spoke.*'

At the end of the romance, after a series of irrelevant encounters with monsters, a battle, an abortive love affair, and other adventures, some of them similar to those in the continuations of the *Conte del Graal*, Peredur arrived at a castle in a river valley.

As he entered it, he saw a hall, and the door of the hall was open, and he went in. There he saw a lame grey-headed man sitting on one side of the hall, with Gwalchmai (Gawain) beside him. Peredur beheld his horse in the same stall with that of Gwalchmai. They made Peredur welcome. He went and seated himself on the other side of the hoary-headed man. Then behold, a yellow-haired youth came and bent the knee before Peredur, and besought his friendship.

'*Lord,*' *said the youth,* '*it was I that came in the form of the black maiden to Arthur's court, . . . and I came with the bloody head in the salver, and with the lance that streamed with blood from the point to the hand, all along the shaft; and the head was thy cousin's, and he was killed by the sorceresses of Gloucester, who also lamed thine uncle; and I am thy cousin. There is a prediction that thou art to avenge these things.*'

With the help of Arthur's war-band Peredur fulfilled the prophecy, killed the sorceresses, and thus avenged his uncle and his male cousin. With this the singularly incoherent narrative ends.

Even the reader inured to the extravagances and confusions of the Grail cycle may be surprised by the number of obvious distortions, errors, and inconsistencies of *Peredur*. Though the author or compiler may not have known Chrétien's poem,[1] he followed a version very similar in certain parts, and confused the Maimed King, who was Perceval's host in Chrétien, with his previous host, Gornemant, who trained the youth in the military art and warned him against loquacity.[2] There are two youths who bear the bleeding spear, but only one is mentioned by the black maiden at Arthur's court, and she forgets to mention the salver at all. The Red Knight, who seems to have been the traditional slayer of Perceval's kinsmen, has been replaced by the sorceresses of Gloucester, for no apparent reason.[3]

Sometimes, however, one can detect how an error occurred. When near the end of the story the yellow-haired youth greets Peredur in the lame man's (the Maimed King's) castle, it seems very odd that he should announce that he had previously appeared as the black maiden (the Loathly Damsel), as the bearer of the salver (the Grail Bearer), and in other female forms. The change of sex calls for an explanation; and there is one. The Old French word for 'high-born maiden', *damoisele*, by which Chrétien designated the Grail Bearer, differs by only a single letter from *damoisel*, the objective case of the noun meaning 'high-born youth'. To mistake one word for the other was easy, either in reading or in hearing.[4] Presumably, then, in the French source of *Peredur* it was a yellow-haired damsel, Perceval's female cousin, who revealed that she had appeared to him on previous occasions in feminine disguises, including those of the Loathly Damsel and the bearer of the head on the salver. Once again we discover

---

[1] On this question see Foster, loc. cit., pp. 192, 199–201.
[2] Mary R. Williams, *Essai sur la Composition du Roman Gallois de Peredur* (Paris, 1909), pp. 54 f.
[3] On the sorceresses of Gloucester see Loomis, *Arthurian Tradition*, pp. 455 f.
[4] Bruce notes in *Evolution*, i. 345, other misunderstandings in *Peredur*.

in mistranslation the cause of the puzzles of Arthurian romance.

We have seen in Chapter V how such an error, the misinterpretation of *cors*, meaning 'horn', as *cors*, meaning 'body', offered the most rational and realistic explanation for the Corpus Christi in the Grail described by Chrétien. What sort of blunder could have led to the introduction of the head of Peredur's male cousin into the salver borne by his female cousin? Her purpose in exhibiting it to him was apparently to rouse his curiosity and spur him to revenge. But there is nothing in Chrétien's narrative which could have suggested this use for the Grail, nor in the First Continuation, nor in the Irish *echtrai* on which these were indirectly patterned. It has been seriously argued that the Welsh author was thinking of Herodias with the head of John the Baptist, but if so, he must have been crackbrained, for John the Baptist was not Peredur's cousin, nor was he killed by the sorceresses of Gloucester.

I believe that the answer to this riddle can be found in the confusion of two originally distinct personages—a phenomenon of which we have already discovered several instances. Two types of female keep appearing in the Perceval romances. One is the true Grail Bearer, whose prototype was the Sovranty of Ireland and whose pristine function was to serve the visitor to the Otherworld palace with her golden vessel.[1] She was not involved in a blood-feud. The other is the damsel whose Irish prototype was the woman whom Finn found mourning her son, slain by one of Finn's hereditary foes. Her function was to send Finn in quest of the murderer, and her more easily recognizable counterparts in Arthurian romance are the damsel in Chrétien's poem whom Perceval found sitting under a tree with her lover's corpse in her arms, and the damsel in *Perlesvaus*, mentioned above, also sitting under a tree, with the head of Perceval's male cousin in a vessel of ivory.[2]

Now Manessier, as we have seen, introduces both these

[1] See Ch. V. [2] *Perlesvaus*, ed. Nitze, i, ll. 8678–710.

types as members of the Fisher King's household. Both were cousins of Perceval, but one, the Fisher King's daughter, had no other office than to bear the Grail; the other, in addition to bearing the *tailleor*, caused the body of her father, King of the Waste Land, and the sword with which he was killed, to be conveyed to the Grail castle, in order that his death might be avenged. Fusion of the two distinct types was almost inevitable. When in *Perlesvaus* the Grail Bearer appears as the Loathly Damsel at Arthur's court, though she has not a word to say of a vendetta, she is carrying in her hand the head of a king.

We can now understand what has happened in *Peredur*. The author has combined in one person the two damsels in the Fisher King's household,[1] so that we are presented with the horrifying spectacle of a vessel, which Chrétien assigned to sacramental purposes and which later romancers identified as one of the most holy relics of the Passion, utilized for the exhibition of a head swimming in blood and for the incitement of the hero to carrying out a family feud.

It is greatly to the credit of Alfred Nutt that as early as 1888 he not only recognized Brân as the prototype of the Fisher King, and found the root of Perceval's *enfances* in the vendetta theme in the saga of Finn mac Cumail, but also perceived that it had been combined with a quite distinct theme, the disenchantment or unspelling of the Waste Land.[2] In 1902 he offered an analysis of the Grail legend which still holds good today.[3]

At an early stage of their development these stories, crystallising as they did round the same hero, would have a tendency to influence each other, to become confused. From out the mass of varying, but only slightly varying narratives, a few main forms would emerge, differentiated by greater or less insistence upon the vengeance or the unspelling theme, but betraying, as a rule, a mixture of both. The unspelling

[1] Bruce expressed much the same idea in *Evolution*, i. 346: 'All that the Welsh author did then was to put on the dish instead of the wafer, the head of Manessier's Goon Desert. . . .' But there is no proof that the author of *Peredur* knew Manessier, though he knew much the same tradition.

[2] Nutt, *Studies*, pp. 181–3.

[3] Nutt, *Legends of the Holy Grail* (London, 1902), pp. 52 f.

conception, as the more definitely mythical of the two, would suffer most change; the more recondite significance of the old mythic talisman of increase and plenty would tend to disappear; its material food-producing properties would subsist, and this characteristic, as a matter of fact, is found in every version in which the Grail appears. . . . What relates to the vengeance conception on the other hand, was retained in comparatively unchanged form; . . . its simply human character commended it as much to men of the twelfth century as to those of an earlier age. In the *Peredur* and in Manessier it has suffered little from contamination, but in Crestien and the remainder of the *Conte del Graal* it is subordinated to the unspelling quest, the Grail and question.

If later scholars, especially those versed in Celtic literature, had taken these penetrating observations more seriously, the great riddle would have been solved decades ago. But unfortunately the good seed fell on stony ground and remained there for forty-seven years.

Today we can probe even more deeply into the causes for the confusion and inconsistency in the Grail stories. As we review some of the findings of the previous chapters, we perceive that there were not only two main themes which tended to combine in bewildering associations, but several subordinate disharmonies contributed to the mystification of both the authors and their readers. There was a wounded King for the hero to cure; there was a slain King for him to avenge. Yet they seemed to bear somewhat the same name. The King's infirmity or death caused his land to be sterile and waste; yet, strange to say, he possessed a talisman of inexhaustible abundance. There were two damsels in the King's household, one whose function was to serve his guests with the talismanic vessel, to assume a monstrous shape when the hero failed in his task of healing the King, and violently to rebuke him; the other whose function was to spur the hero on to avenge a kinsman's death. The task of healing required the hero to ask a spell-breaking question; the task of vengeance required him to unite the fragments of a broken sword. One talisman of plenty, because of the unfamiliarity of the word *graal* to many people, even Frenchmen, was often misunderstood. Another such talisman, a drinking horn, because of the ambiguity of the French word *cors*, was frequently interpreted as 'body' and its nutritive properties were sometimes assumed to be the miraculous power of the mass-wafer, the Corpus Christi, to sustain life.

Is it any wonder that the authors of the Middle Ages produced a literature of the Grail which strikes the modern reader at times as a mystifying muddle? Is it any wonder that scholarly investigators have found it more than a little baffling to interpret?

IX

Perlesvaus: Welsh Talismans and a Welsh Elysium

In the last chapter there was reference to *Perlesvaus*,[1] a French prose romance, which, like Manessier's continuation and *Peredur*, gave prominence to the theme of vengeance. Though far superior in construction to *Peredur* and more richly imaginative than Manessier's version, it is by no means free of flaws and aberrations. Indeed, the author seems at times deranged. Take his opening sentence.[2]

The history of the holy vessel which is called Grail, in which the precious blood of the Saviour was received on the day He was crucified in order to redeem His people from hell: Josephus set it in remembrance by annunciation of the voice of an angel, so that the truth might be known by his writing and by his testimony concerning knights and worshipful men, how they were willing to suffer pain and travail in order to exalt the law of Jesus Christ, which He desired to renew by His death and crucifixion.

What could be more preposterous than the claim that the Jewish historian Josephus of the first century A.D. recorded at the prompting of an angel the sufferings of the knights of King Arthur's court four hundred years later? If the author were living today, one might suspect that he was a victim of paranoia, for he displays several of the typical symptoms. He invokes angelic and therefore heavenly authority; later he displays a savage vindictiveness in the treatment not only of the enemies of God and the Church, but also of the personal enemies of the hero; he has a taste for the gruesome; his

[1] First edited by C. Potvin as the first volume of *Perceval le Gallois* (Mons, 1866–71). The standard edition is that of W. A. Nitze and others (Chicago, 1932, 1937).
[2] Ed. Nitze, i, ll. 1–7. The translations in this chapter owe much to that of Evans.

       H

typology, as we shall see, is confused and frequently absurd. But even if this diagnosis is correct, it is not inconsistent with the possession of considerable imaginative and artistic gifts, as we shall see.

The author makes another statement regarding his source in a colophon, which some have taken more seriously than the first. He professes to have obtained his material directly from a Latin book kept at the holy house in the Isle of Avalon at the head of the Adventurous Marshes—obviously a reference to Glastonbury Abbey.[1] This statement, coupled with the fact that in the body of the text he seems to know Glastonbury as the site of the tombs of Arthur and Guenevere and refers to the Tor, which is so conspicuous in the landscape, as 'la montaigne de la valee', has led some scholars to suppose that he was intimately connected with the famous monastery, and to characterize the romance as Glastonbury propaganda.[2] Moreover, there is a description of the chasm which still separates the parts of the castle at Tintagel in Cornwall,[3] and this suggests that the author had travelled in England. But these two topographical details could have been based on hearsay, and the rest of the geography of the romance is so utterly unrelated to actuality that it is hard to believe that its author was familiar with the country. A comparison with documents emanating from Glastonbury Abbey about the time that *Perlesvaus* was written demonstrates that there is little in common, and there is actual contradiction—a matter to be discussed in Chapter XV. Not only does this fact render it unlikely that the romance was intended as propaganda, but it is also noteworthy that there is no effort to link Joseph of Arimathea or the Grail with Glastonbury. The author's claim to have used a Latin book from the Isle of Avalon deserves as little credence as his other assertion that the story of the Grail was dictated by an angel to the historian Josephus.

What conclusions can we safely draw about the author of

[1] Ed. Nitze, i, ll. 10188–90.
[2] Ibid. i. 16; ii. 45–47. Bruce, *Evolution*, ii. 166, n. 44.
[3] Ed. Nitze, i, ll. 6571–99; ii. 319 f.

Perlesvaus? Since the manuscripts are predominantly written in the dialect of north France,[1] and since an early copy was presented by the lord of Cambrin in Flanders to Jean de Nesle, castellan of Bruges and *bailli* of Flanders and Hainaut,[2] he was presumably resident in this general region. If we take into consideration his pronounced piety and his fairly wide reading in secular literature, we may infer that he was a chaplain or secretary in some noble household of northern France or Belgium. He must have had access to an unusually good library; he was certainly familiar with most of the French Arthurian literature available at the time. As we shall see, he knew Chrétien's *Perceval* and the Second (Wauchier) Continuation.[3] Whether from Robert de Boron or some other source he had learned of the Grail as a receptacle of the Holy Blood, and of Alain the father of the Grail hero,[4] The appearance of Ban of Benoic and Claudas seems to prove acquaintance with the beginning of the Prose *Lancelot*, though perhaps in an early form. If we could fix the dates of these sources, we would have a *terminus a quo* for *Perlesvaus*. Nitze argued for a date of composition soon after 1200, but others would put it about 1225.[5]

Besides the sources that we can tentatively identify, the author must have become acquainted, either through the *conteurs*, whom he mentions in l. 7280, or through French texts otherwise unknown, with a rich fund of traditional matter. His version of the Beheading Test is so different from any other that it must have come from the Irish through a different intermediary;[6] and the same may be said of his versions of the revenge motif. Most surprising is the discovery that this continental romance reflects with extraordinary clearness archaic Welsh traditions which can hardly be detected at all in any other Grail text. Just why or how this remarkable linkage came about, no one can say, but it affords one of the

---

[1] Ibid. ii. 19, 21, 22.   [2] Ibid. ii. 73–81.
[3] Ibid. ii. 90–104.   [4] Ibid. ii. 121–4.
[5] Ibid. ii. 89. Bruce, *Evolution*, ii. 156, n.
[6] Ed. Nitze, i, ll. 2856–923, 6633–733 ; ii. 281–3. G. L. Kittredge, *Study of 'Gawain and the Green Knight'* (Cambridge, Mass., 1916), pp. 52–61.

strongest proofs, as we shall see, of the debt which French Arthurian fiction owed to the Celts.

Of course, *Perlesvaus* also mirrors some of the dominant French ideas and enthusiasms of the time. The establishment of Christianity, that is, 'the New Law', at the point of the sword is a favourite topic, and, to quote Jessie Weston, the hero's 'career is marked by hecatombs of slaughtered pagans'[1] —evidently an expression of contemporary crusading ardour. There is a multiplicity of relics, a vision of the Virgin, and two visions demonstrating the Real Presence of Christ's body in the mass-wafer. Moreover, the amorous hero of Chrétien's *Conte del Graal* and *Peredur* would not do, and is replaced by a virgin Perceval, a counterpart of Galahad. But if one looks for any deep spirituality in the book, one looks in vain; instead one finds the physical trappings of religion and the spectacular marvels.

Also, in accord with the spirit of the times, the author sought to find an occult meaning in names and to attach a typological or allegorical meaning to some of his episodes, even altering the narrative pattern in order to fit the alleged significance. But, far from being a Dante, he betrays in these efforts a defective if not a diseased mind. To judge by two of the best manuscripts, he attached the name Messios to the Maimed King,[2] but if it was his intention to suggest a parallel with Christ, where is the parallel? He gave us no help, and it is rather Perceval, the bearer of the red cross shield, who is the awaited one, the character who most plainly typifies the Messiah.[3]

In the course of our examination of the Grail episodes we shall meet with other examples of grotesque typology, but surely none so crass as the following.[4] The Questing (that is, Barking) Beast is a strange monster in the Arthurian menagerie, whose hybrid origins in William of Malmesbury's *Gesta Regum Anglorum* and in Welsh tradition have been well

---

[1] J. L. Weston, *Quest of the Holy Grail* (London, 1913), p. 22.
[2] Ed. Nitze, i, l. 2788.
[3] J. N. Carman, in *PMLA*, lxi (1946), pp. 50–61.
[4] Ed. Nitze, ii. 139–44. *Zeits chr. f. romanische Philologie*, lvi (1936), pp. 409–18.

elucidated by Nitze.[1] Our romancer describes her as a small white animal, carrying in her womb twelve barking hounds. She runs to Perceval for protection, but finding no welcome, she takes refuge at a cross and is there delivered of her whelps, which thereupon rend her in pieces, but are unable to devour her flesh. This beast, we are solemnly told,[2] signifies Our Lord Jesus, and the twelve hounds represent the Jews, who sacrificed Him on the cross, but were unable to partake of the sacrament of His body! To select a pregnant bitch to signify the incarnate Deity seems the last word in extravagance and bad taste.

But an author must not be judged by his maddest moments, and there is much in *Perlesvaus* that reveals a sense of order and rationality. When the variety of his sources involved the author in inconsistencies, he was aware of the flaw and offered an amusing excuse:[3] 'The quest of adventures would not have pleased the knights so well an they had not found them so different. For, when they had entered into a forest or an island where they had found any adventure, and they came there another time, they found holds and castles and adventures of another kind, so that their toils and travails might not weary them, and also for that God would that the land should be conformed to the New Law [of Christianity].' The fabric of the narrative is intricately knit together by the principle of interlacing.[4] Like Scott and many another novelist, the author of *Perlesvaus* made a practice of dropping one thread of the story to take up another, but he was nearly always careful to take up again where he had left off. By turns, Arthur, Gawain, Lancelot, and Perceval assume the principal role, in a coherent narrative sequence.

When the sources are available to us, it can be shown that our romancer exercised great freedom in his handling, and it can be assumed that he used his other materials in the same

[1] Ed. Nitze, i, ll. 5486–518.   [2] Ed. Nitze, i, ll. 5984–6006.
[3] Ibid. i, ll. 6615–22.
[4] On interlacing, 'entrelacement', see F. Lot, *Étude sur le 'Lancelot' en Prose* (Paris, 1918, 1954), pp. 17–28. See also ed. Nitze, ii. 157–70, on structure of *Perlesvaus*.

independent fashion. When the book begins, Perceval has already visited the Grail castle and failed to ask the fateful question; hence the Fisher King has fallen into a dolorous languor, and his kingdom has been torn with strife. But not till we have read more than a twentieth part of the book do we learn this,[1] and only when we have read two-sevenths does Perceval recover from the illness which overtook him after his failure, and start upon his triumphant career.[2] He never heals the Fisher King, and only after the King dies does Perceval come into possession of the Grail castle, and this he accomplishes not by asking the question, but by conquest. Though one cannot be quite sure, these deviations from tradition seem to be original with the author.

The first person prominent in the Grail tradition to come on the scene is the Loathly Damsel, in whom we have already detected a descendant of Ériu, the divine personification of Ireland.[3] As in Chrétien, she makes her appearance at Arthur's court riding a mule, but she herself and the circumstances attending her arrival are modified in unexpected ways.[4] She has none of the animal features ascribed to her by the poet, and she is, indeed, said to be well shaped. But her visage is plain and her head completely bald, as a result of Perceval's failure to ask whom one served with the Grail. Her locks will not grow again until a knight asks the required question, or conquers the vessel—an alternative which has not been suggested hitherto. In one hand she grasps the head of a king, sealed with silver and crowned with gold. A second damsel, riding astride a horse, accompanies her, brings a hound and a shield with a red cross on it, and holds the head of a queen, sealed in lead and crowned with copper. A third damsel comes afoot and drives the mule and the horse before her with a whip. Outside the hall is a rich cart, drawn by three white stags and containing 150 heads of knights, some sealed in gold, some in silver, some in lead. When the Bald Damsel

---

[1] Ed. Nitze, i, ll. 634–42.   [2] Ibid. i, ll. 2939–42.
[3] See Ch. V.   [4] Ed. Nitze, i, ll. 596–682.

has complained of the silence of Perceval at the hostel of the
Fisher King, she leaves the shield with the red cross for one
who shall conquer the Grail, and then departs with her companions and the stag-drawn cart.

Presently they meet Gawain, and the Bald Damsel en-
courages him to proceed to the Fisher King's court, and, in
order to ensure his success, which means so much to her, as
well as to the King, she tells him precisely what question he
must ask. Escorted by Gawain, the little procession passes
the castle of the Black Hermit. One hundred and fifty-two
knights, all in black, charge out from it and each snatches one
of the heads, those held by the damsels and those in the cart,
and return to the castle.[1]

Later Gawain learns that the Bald Damsel was indeed the
Grail Bearer.[2] Still later he is informed at the Castle of Inquiry[3] that the heads of the king and the queen are those of
Adam and Eve; the heads sealed in gold belong to the New Law
of Christ, those sealed in silver signify the Jews, and those sealed
in lead the false law of the Saracens. The castle of the Black
Hermit represents hell, and its master is Lucifer. The bald
damsel signifies Fortune, who was bald before the Crucifixion,
and did not acquire her hair till Our Lord had redeemed His
people. The cart represents the wheel of Fortune.

It is only near the close of the romance that this strange
narrative is carried to its conclusion. Perceval, having conquered the Grail castle partly by virtue of the red cross shield,
which the Bald Damsel had left for him at Arthur's court,
comes upon her again, and, perceiving that she is no longer
bald, congratulates her on the beauty of her hair.[4] He then
rides, unharmed by the bolts shot at him, into the castle of the
Black Hermit and in a fierce encounter overthrows him. The
Hermit's body is thrown into a stinking pit, and the heads of
the king and the queen and those sealed in gold are delivered
over to the damsel of the cart.[5]

The story of the heads, carried off by the black knights to

[1] Ibid. i, ll. 693–766.   [2] Ibid. i, ll. 1404–11.
[3] Ibid. i, ll. 2160–95.   [4] Ibid. i, ll. 9945–48.   [5] Ibid. i, ll. 9962–95.

their castle and of Perceval's triumph over the Black Hermit is a patently romanticized version of the peopling of hell with the souls of mankind and the release of the righteous souls by Christ after the Crucifixion.[1] In the main the narrative and its significance are clear and well sustained intermittently over a stretch of some 350 pages in Nitze's edition. On the other hand, the bald damsel is a very puzzling figure, since she blends in herself at least two, and perhaps three, Celtic prototypes, and has been endowed by the author with two inconsistent allegorical roles. It is a fascinating game to disentangle the several strands of Celtic tradition and scholastic reinterpretation which are intertwined in her story.

First, since we are told that the Bald Damsel is the Grail Bearer, she must, in part at least, be derived from Ériu, the goddess who represents Ireland. To be sure, the loss and the later restoration of her hair bear only the remotest resemblance to the transformation of the Sovranty of Erin from a deformed monster to a paragon of beauty. But luckily Chrétien and *Peredur* have provided us with the means of proving the descent of the Grail Bearer, and hence of the Bald Damsel, from Ériu.

Secondly, the fact that the Bald Damsel holds the head of a king, makes it apparent that she belongs also to the category of females whose original function was to urge the hero on to avenge the death of a kinsman. In this respect, she has a double in *Perlesvaus* itself, who, as already mentioned, appears in ll. 8678–710 carrying in a rich vessel of ivory the head of the hero's cousin, the son of his uncle Brun Brandalis; later this cousin's death is duly avenged.[2] The closest Irish prototype of these damsels, we remember, is the woman who sent Finn in pursuit of the warrior who had killed her son and had sorely wounded Finn's father.

Thirdly, there is the richly equipped cart, drawn by three stags, which accompanies the Bald Damsel. It is unique in Arthurian literature, has no precise counterpart in Christian

---

[1] Ed. Nitze, ii. 231–33. Carman in *PMLA*, lxi (1946), pp. 42–44.
[2] On this double see Ed. Nitze, ii. 213 f.

symbology,[1] and bears no resemblance to the wheel of Fortune as generally conceived.[2] The only plausible explanation
of the vehicle[3] is that it preserves a reminiscence of the cart
drawn by two stags in which rode the Irish mermaid Liban,
daughter of the god Dagda, as described in the *Death of Eochaid
Mac Maireda*.[4] This surmise is confirmed by the fact that in
the *Wasting Sickness of Cúchulainn* Liban summons the hero
to the aid of her sister against her foes,[5] much as Chrétien's
Loathly Damsel enlisted Gawain for the deliverance of the
maiden of Montesclaire; and the Loathly Damsel is identical
with the Bald Damsel of *Perlesvaus*.

Three strains of Irish influence, therefore, can be detected
in the composition of this hybrid personage. What did the
French author proceed to make of her, and with what
motives?

First, he eliminated the grotesque animal features which
Chrétien attributed to her, apparently because, knowing her
identity with the Grail Bearer, he considered them unsuitable
to her lofty function.

Secondly, he seems to have been struck by the speech which
Chrétien put in the mouth of the Loathly Damsel: 'Ah,
Perceval, Fortune is bald behind but has a forelock in front. A
curse on him who greets you or wishes you well!' By some
capricious impulse he decided to equate his Loathly Damsel
with Fortune, made her completely bald, and offered the
clumsy explanation of her cart as signifying the wheel of
Fortune (ll. 2191–5). But, in spite of this explicit indication
of the damsel's allegorical nature, he makes nothing more of
it. There is no other attribute or action of hers in the rest of
the book to remind us that she is the fickle goddess.

[1] The chariot drawn by a single griffin, described by Dante in *Purgatorio*, canto
xxix, offers no parallel, either in the concrete details or the symbolic meaning.

[2] Professor Howard Patch, however, shows in *The Goddess Fortuna* (Cambridge,
Mass., 1927), p. 169, n. 3, that there are a few instances where the wheel of Fortune
is conceived as a vehicle.

[3] R. S. Loomis, *Arthurian Tradition*, pp. 297–9, and n. 26.

[4] S. H. O'Grady, *Silva Gadelica* (London, 1892), ii. 269.

[5] *Serglige Con Culainn*, ed. M. Dillon (Columbus, Ohio, 1951), p. 33. A. H.
Leahy, *Heroic Romances of Ireland* (London, 1905), i. 61 f.

Thirdly, the author assigned to her another and quite a inconsistent allegorical role. She is, when bald, a personification of the Old Law, the Old Testament dispensation.[1] She holds the head of Adam; the second damsel holds the head of Eve, and the 150 heads in the cart are those of mankind, divided into three groups—Jews, Saracens, and, by anticipation, Christians. As a result of the Fall, all the heads are carried off to the castle of the Black Hermit, hell. When Perceval conquers the Grail castle, an act which Professor Carman has interpreted as the Redemption of mankind by the Crucifixion,[2] the Bald Damsel recovers her hair;[3] and when Perceval triumphs over the Black Hermit—a re-enactment of Christ's descent into hell—the heads of Adam and Eve and all the heads sealed in gold are delivered over to her. She is now, surely, the New Law, the New Testament dispensation, in other words, the Church.

What could have prompted the imposition of this second allegorical role on a personification of Fortune? I believe the clue is to be found in the *Sermons on the Canticles* of Gilbert of Holland (a district in Lincolnshire, not to be confused with the Netherlands), a work which seems to have enjoyed a considerable circulation as a sequel to the sermons of the great St. Bernard of Clairvaux on the same topic. The twenty-third sermon is a commentary on the Vulgate Latin text, Canticles, vi. I, which may be translated:[4] 'Thy locks are like flocks of she-goats which ascended from Mount Galaad.' Now the Song of Solomon had been accepted from early Christian times as an allegory of spiritual love, and it was Gilbert's task to interpret the text in accord with this basic assumption. After explaining that Mount Galaad signified Christ, he continued in this remarkable style:[5]

This mount is the head of the Church. Do not drop away from this mount if thou art a hair. Why dost thou threaten to separate from us, and, as if torn out, to depart from the flock of remaining hairs? Will

[1] Ed. Nitze, i, ll. 2186-93. [2] *PMLA*, lxi. 44-47.
[3] See above p. 103, n. 4. [4] Migne, *Patrologia Latina*, clxxxiv, col. 119.
[5] Ibid., cols. 119 f.

thy fall bring about the baldness of the Church? She knows not how to be bald, for her very hairs are all numbered. That punishment was inflicted on the Synagogue in the Prophet (Isaiah, iii. 24): 'There shall be baldness instead of curling hair.' Curling are the tresses of the Church, ever returning to her head, winding about it in loving rings, seeking to enter into the very secret places of the head. Therefore her tresses do not drop off but ascend from Mount Galaad, always heaping up the greater works of Christ as examples for her to imitate.

Here, then, the Synagogue or the Old Law is imagined as a bald woman, and the Church or the New Law as a woman adorned with luxuriant tresses. It is next to certain that this passage inspired the author of *Perlesvaus*; the same sermon, as we shall find in Chapter XII, suggested the adoption of the name Galaad for the Christ Knight by the author of the *Queste del Saint Graal*.

How strangely erratic were the workings of the mind which produced the composite figure of the Damsel of the Cart! Taking a hint from the Loathly Damsel's reference in Chrétien's poem to the partial baldness of Fortune, the author of *Perlesvaus* completely decapillated the damsel herself and equated her with Fortune! But then he remembered that the commentator on the Canticles attributed baldness to the Old Law and abundant curls to the Church, and proceeded to work out an elaborate allegory based on this new and inharmonious concept of the damsel's character. He identified the head which she carried with that of Adam, added that of Eve and one hundred and fifty other heads to represent all the souls born under the Old Law. He invented the Black Hermit's castle to represent hell, in which these souls were imprisoned; he eventually restored the damsel's hair to signify the change from the Old Law to the New after the Crucifixion, and brought Perceval to the Black Hermit's castle to deliver the souls of the righteous, and to commit them to the care of the Damsel of the Cart, now a type of the Church. What a curious mingling of the maladroit and the adroit is the handling of this complex figure! What a bizarre culmination to the career of a pagan goddess personifying Ireland, to become a personification of the universal Church!

Let us turn our attention back to the point in the romance where Gawain, after escorting the Bald Damsel on her way, and being directed by her to the Grail castle, came to a hermitage and was astonished to learn that the hermit, unnamed, though he looked no older than forty, was indeed over seventy.[1] This the hermit attributed to the fact that he had often served in the chapel of the Grail, for all who served the Fisher King were immune from the signs of senescence.[2] Later when Gawain arrived at the Grail castle and was welcomed by the Fisher King, he was led into the hall and sat down with twelve grey-haired knights, who were over a hundred years of age, though they looked as if they were forty. Let me quote.[3]

Thereupon Gawain was led into the hall and found twelve ancient knights, all grey-haired though they seemed to be not so old as they were, for each was a hundred years of age or more, and yet none of them seemed as if he were forty. They set Sir Gawain to eat at a right rich table of ivory and seat themselves all round about him. . . . Then a loin of venison is brought in and plenty of other game, and on the table there were rich vessels of silver and large cups with covers, and a rich candelabrum of gold, in which big candles were burning.

A marked parallel to this scene has been pointed out in Chapter V as part of the evidence that the prototype of the Fisher King was Brân son of Llŷr. Brân's followers and his brother Manawydan betook themselves to the isle of Grassholm off the coast of Pembrokeshire.[4] 'They went into the hall . . . and that night they were without stint [of food and drink] and joyful . . . . There they passed eighty years so that they were not aware of having ever spent a time more joyous and delightful . . . nor did anyone perceive that his fellow was

---

[1] Ed. Nitze, i, ll. 893–900.   [2] Ibid. i, ll. 939–47.
[3] Ibid. i, ll. 2414–23.
[4] Loth, *Mabinogion*, i. 148. I. Williams, *Pedeir Keinc y Mabinogi* (Cardiff, 1930), pp. 46, 220. P. Mac Cana, *Branwen Daughter of Llŷr* (Cardiff, 1958), p. 102.

older by that time than when they came there.' It seems that, like the hospitality of the Irish sea-god Manannan son of Ler, who entertained King Cormac in his palace and who instituted the feast where the partakers were ever after free from sickness, decay, and old age,[1] the hospitality of Brân son of Llŷr conferred the same immunity on his guests.

The hermit who surprised Gawain by appearing to be only forty years old when he was over seventy is but one of many hermits encountered in the pages of *Perlesvaus*. Gawain, still seeking the Grail castle, happened on a venerable man in the garb of an anchorite, sitting before his house, where, as we learn, Perceval was recuperating from his illness.[2] Later this man is identified as Pelles, King of the Short Folk (*Basse Gent*), who has adopted the eremitic life.[3] He is the brother of the Fisher King and the uncle of Perceval on his mother's side. Since we are told that Perceval made his confession to this Hermit King after his failure at the Grail castle,[4] we cannot avoid equating him with Perceval's Hermit Uncle in Chrétien, who performed the same function. Therefore, his ultimate prototype, if the argument in Chapter V holds good, must be the uncle whom Finn found in a desert wood and to whom he told his story from beginning to end. But, though there is no reason to abandon that hypothesis, for it alone offers a likely prototype for Chrétien's figure, other elements in the account of Pelles given in *Perlesvaus* and in the Vulgate cycle, where he is even more prominent, must have been derived from another traditional figure. In other words, King Pelles is a compound personality, like the Bald Damsel. Derived in part from Finn's uncle, Crimall, he must have had another prototype also to account for his name and title.

Nothing in Chrétien's *Perceval* accounts for the name Pelles

---

[1] P. Joyce, *Old Celtic Romances* (Dublin, 1920), p. 457.

[2] Ed. Nitze, i, ll. 1652–86.

[3] Ibid. i, ll. 36–38, 1639–48, 2926–32. For evidence that *Basse Gent* means 'Short Folk' see Loomis *Arthurian Tradition*, pp. 142 f. On Pelles see V. J. Harward, *Dwarfs of Arthurian Romance and Celtic Tradition* (Leiden, 1958), index.

[4] Ed. Nitze, i, ll. 2926–30.

or the title King of the Short Folk, but in his earlier poem, *Erec*, Chrétien introduced a very noble king of the dwarfs, Bilis.[1] His realm was the Antipodes, the lower hemisphere. Though a dwarf himself, he was accompanied to Arthur's court by his tall brother, Brien or Brihan. Can Bilis have the same origin as Pelles, King of the Short Folk? Can his brother Brien represent the gigantic Brân son of Llŷr, prototype of the Fisher King?

If we scrutinize the literature of Wales and Cornwall, we discover scattered references which, however inconsistent in many ways, consistently point to a prototype of Bilis, the diminutive King of the Antipodes. Giraldus Cambrensis in his *Itinerary of Wales* tells of a noble and hospitable king of the dwarfs, whose realm is the nether hemisphere, the Antipodes, and is reached by a tunnel.[2] Walter Map, a contemporary of Giraldus, describes a dwarf king of a similar subterranean realm, whose servants provided a bounteous banquet in vases made of precious stones and vessels of gold and crystal—a banquet which exceeded the desires and the requests of all.[3] In the Welsh *Bruts*, translated from Geoffrey of Monmouth's *History of the Kings of Britain*, we find a King Beli and his brother Brân. Of Beli we learn that never was there such abundance of gold and silver as there was in his time;[4] of Brân that he gave food and drink to all who came, and no door was shut against them.[5] In the *mabinogi* of *Branwen*, as we already know, the principal figure is Brân, famed for his hospitality, and he has a grandfather or uncle on the mother's side (the text is inconsistent on this point) named Beli son of Mynogan.[6] This same Beli appears in another Welsh text,

---

[1] *Erec*, ed. W. Foerster (Halle, 1909), vss. 1993–2000.

[2] Giraldus Cambrensis, *Opera*, ed. J. F. Dimock, vi. 75 f. R. S. Loomis, *Wales and the Arthurian Legend* (Cardiff, 1956), pp. 65 f.

[3] Loomis, *Wales*, p. 73. Map, *De Nugis Curialium*, ed. M. R. James (Oxford, 1914), pp. 13 ff.

[4] Geoffrey of Monmouth, *Historia*, ed. Griscom, p. 291. On Beli as 'ancestor deity' see R. Bromwich in *Studies in Early British History*, ed. M. K. Chadwick (Cambridge, 1954), pp. 131 f.

[5] Geoffrey of Monmouth, op. cit., p. 284.

[6] *Mabinogion*, trans. G. and T. Jones, Everyman's Lib., pp. 25, 38. See J. Rhŷs, D. Brynmor-Jones, *Welsh People* (1909), pp. 39, 41–43.

Lludd and Llevelys, as King of Britain, and enjoys the title *Mawr*, meaning 'Great'. In Welsh poetry the sea is referred to as Beli's liquor and the waves as Beli's cattle.[1] An earthwork in north-eastern Cornwall, called Kair Belli in the twelfth century, was described as 'fatale castrum', a faery castle;[2] and we are aware that a typical faery castle was abundantly supplied with costly vessels and delicious food, and was the scene of joyous revels.

What does all this mean? It seems that Beli was a famous figure, in origin a god of the Underworld and of the sea; that, like Brân son of Llŷr, he was a bountiful provider; that he came to be regarded as a kinsman of Brân; that in the euhemeristic stage he, like Brân, was converted into a King of Britain and acquired the title *Mawr*, though a supernatural atmosphere still hovered about the earthwork which bore his name. No Welsh text states that Beli was a dwarf, but if one combines Giraldus's testimony about a dwarf king of the lower hemisphere with Chrétien's description of Bilis, the dwarf King of the Antipodes, one can scarcely doubt that such a tradition existed. And this would explain why Pelles, the hermit, was King of the Short Folk.

The transformation of the Welsh name Beli into Bilis and Pelles is easy to understand. The final *s* in the French names is clearly the nominative termination. Just so the Welsh name Bleddri became in French Bleheris. The initial of Pelles is also explicable, for the Welsh, even as late as Shakespeare's day, were notorious for pronouncing *b* as *p*, as readers of *Henry V* will recall; for example, Fluellen referred to Falstaff as 'the fat knight with the *pelly*-doublet'. So to French ears Beli sounded like Pelli, and Beli Mawr like Pellimor, and this would account for the confusion in some prose romances between Pelles and Pellinor.[3] Brugger and Bruce agreed that the two names were related, but could offer no satisfactory explanation.[4] That they were derived respectively from Beli and Beli Mawr

[1] J. A. MacCulloch in Hastings, *Encyclopaedia of Religion and Ethics*, iii. 290.
[2] *Revue Celtique*, iii. 86.
[3] *Modern Philology*, xvi (1918), pp. 337–46.
[4] Ibid., p. 340, and n. 2.

seems fairly obvious when one considers that Pelles was King of the Short Folk, and Belinor was the name of a dwarf in the romance of *Escanor*.[1]

Pelles, then, as he is depicted in *Perlesvaus*, plays a dual role. The role of hermit and confessor of the hero he inherited through Chrétien from Finn's uncle, Crimall. The role of King of the Short Folk and brother of the Fisher King he inherited from the Welsh tradition of Beli, the dwarf king, brother of Brân. Why the combination of roles? The most plausible guess is that Beli, in the Grail tradition, was an uncle of the hero, as Crimall, in Irish tradition, was an uncle of the hero of the Vengeance Quest. When the two traditions merged, so did the two uncles.

From the Hermit King Gawain learns that a knight (Perceval) lies within the hermitage, grievously ill, and that he is of the lineage of Joseph of Arimathea, but, unable to learn more, Gawain rides on his way.[2] After long wanderings, not recounted in detail, he approaches a very strong castle, descries on the walls many men in religious garb, and is informed that it is the castle of the Grail, but that in order to gain admittance he must fetch and deliver into the hands of the Fisher King the sword with which John the Baptist was decapitated, and later he learns that it is now in the possession of a pagan king, Gurgaran.[3] When he arrives at Gurgaran's castle, the King promises to give him the sword if he will rescue the King's son, who has been carried off by a giant. Gawain rides up a high mountain, interrupts the giant in a game of chess with his captive, and cuts off his right arm. Thereupon the giant strangles the King's son with his left hand, and attempts to carry off Gawain. But Gawain thrusts his sword into the monster's heart, cuts off his head, and returns with it and the body of the youth to Gurgaran. The pagan king then causes the body to be boiled, cut into small pieces, and distributed to

---

[1] Loomis, *Arthurian Tradition*, p. 143. Gerard d'Amiens, *Escanor*, ed. H. Michelant (Tübingen, 1886), vs. 19254.
[2] Ed. Nitze, i, ll. 1664–87.   [3] Ibid. i, ll. 1690–743.

his people to eat. He then asks for baptism and commands Gawain to cut off the heads of all who refuse to believe in God![1] Gawain receives the sword which severed the head of John the Baptist and which has the peculiarity that when the blade is drawn from the sheath at midday, it is covered with blood.[2] In due course it is brought by Gawain to the Fisher King's castle and takes its place with the other holy relics.

This fantastic story is doubtless intended to provide a previous history for the traditional sword which keeps reappearing in accounts of the Grail castle, and it is possible to discern in it four elements, two of them possibly drawn from Welsh tradition. There is an obvious resemblance to the rescue of the three sons of a baron from the giant Harpin of the Mountain in Chrétien's *Ivain*,[3] and this poem may be in fact the direct source. The strangling of the King's son and the eating of his flesh seem to have been taken over from the lost common source of Marco Polo's and Odoric of Pordenone's descriptions of the cannibal practices of an Asiatic people.[4] The sword of Gurgaran may possibly have two prototypes in Welsh tradition. There is the sword of Wrnach the Giant in *Kulhwch and Olwen*, which the hero procured, but there are obvious differences in the attendant circumstances.[5] There is the sword of Rhydderch, listed among the Thirteen Treasures of the Isle of Britain, which include, as we know, the platter of Rhydderch, counterpart of the Grail. This same Rhydderch possessed a sword which, if anyone drew it except himself, burst into flame from the cross to the point.[6] To be sure, a flaming sword is not a bloody sword, but, on the other hand, Gurgaran, owner of the bloody sword, is said to be King of Albanie, Scotland, and Rhydderch, possessor of the flaming sword, was an historic King of Strathclyde. And that the author of *Perlesvaus* was drawing ultimately on Welsh

---

[1] Ibid. i, ll. 1985–2071.   [2] Ibid. i, ll. 2008 f., 2143–5.
[3] Ibid., ii. 249. *Yvain*, ed. Foerster (1926), vss. 3851–4247.
[4] *Travels of Marco Polo*, Everyman's Lib., p. 343. *Voiage and Travayle of Syr John Maundeville*, Everyman's Lib., pp. 248 f. *Romania*, lxxxi (1960), pp. 495 f.
[5] Loth, *Mabinogion*, i. 317–21.
[6] C. Guest, *Mabinogion*, Everyman's Lib., p. 328. Loomis, *Wales*, pp. 158–60.

tradition for the talismans of the Grail castle is proved by his inclusion among them not only of the Grail itself but also of the magic chess-board which is the first object which Gawain sees on entering the castle.

After obtaining the sword and encountering various adventures, Gawain crosses three perilous bridges, passes a horrible-looking but harmless lion, and enters a great hall. There he espies a chess-board, resting on a couch. This incongruous object has a border of gold, encrusted with precious stones; and the squares are coloured gold and blue.[1] After he has been entertained, has seen the Grail and the lance, has failed to ask the crucial question, and is left alone, he again notices the chess-board and observes that the pieces of gold and ivory are set to play. 'Sir Gawain began to move the pieces of ivory, and those of gold moved against him and mated him twice. At the third time, when he thought to avenge himself and saw that he had the worse, he broke up the game, and a damsel issued from a chamber and caused a page to take the board and the pieces and carry them away.'[2]

Professor Weinberg has pointed out in the passages concerned with this board verbal borrowings from the Second (Wauchier) Continuation of Chrétien's *Conte del Graal*,[3] but this does not rule out the possibility of another source which placed the talisman, as Wauchier did not, in the Grail castle. Whether the author of *Perlesvaus* was following a second source, or was himself responsible for introducing this incongruous object in the sacred edifice, is impossible to determine. But certain it is that just such a precious board belongs to medieval Welsh tradition and was even considered a standard appurtenance of those palaces of the Celtic gods from which the Grail castle was derived.

The list of the Thirteen Treasures of the Isle of Britain which, as we have seen, offers several counterparts to the

---

[1] Ed. Nitze, i, ll. 2287–341. I adopt the readings of MSS. Br and P, which give *orle* and *dazur*.   [2] Ed. Nitze, i, ll. 2457–64.

[3] *PMLA*, l (1935), pp. 25–35. *Didot Perceval*, ed. W. Roach (Philadelphia, 1941), pp. 52–56.

talismans of the Grail castle, contains the *gwyddbwyll* of Gwenddoleu.[1] *Gwyddbwyll* was a game, played on a board like chess, and Gwenddoleu was one of the kinglets of the North, like Rhydderch, and was his contemporary. When the men were placed on the board, they would play of themselves. The board was of gold and the men of silver. Moreover, a similar game-board of costly materials seems to have been an indispensable feature of the elysian palaces described in medieval Irish and Welsh literature. In the Irish saga *The Death of Fergus Mac Leite* a dwarf king boasts of the splendour of his palace:[2] 'Golden are its candelabra, holding candles of rich light and gemmed over with rare stones. . . . None that belongs to it feels sorrow now; a retinue is there that ages not. . . . There every man is a chess-player, good company is there that knows no stint.' Likewise in the *Adventure of Laegaire* the hero describes the pleasures of a faery palace at the bottom of a lake:[3] 'Fine plaintive faery music, . . . drinking mead from bright vessels, talking with the one you love. We play with men of yellow gold on chess-boards of white bronze.' The Welsh *Dream of Maxen* describes an Otherworld castle thus:[4] 'The roof of the hall he thought to be all of gold . . . . Golden couches he saw in the hall, and tables of silver. On the couch facing him he could see two auburn-haired youths playing at *gwyddbwyll*. A silver board he saw for the *gwyddbwyll*, and golden pieces thereon.'

It seems manifest that the Celtic Other World, where every desire was satisfied and no pleasure was wanting, would not fail to provide amusement for the long hours between bouts of feasting, fighting, and love-making; and, accordingly, there would be chess-boards and chessmen of costly metals. Such a concept must have been the ultimate cause for the presence of the magic chess-board in the castle of the Fisher King.

[1] Loth, *Mabinogion*, i. 215, n. 2; ii. 114 f.

[2] T. P. Cross, C. H. Slover, *Ancient Irish Tales* (New York, 1936), p. 479. O'Grady, *Silva Gadelica*, ii. 277.

[3] *Speculum*, xvii (1942), p. 385. See M. Dillon, *Early Irish Literature*, pp. 116–18.

[4] Loth, *Mabinogion*, i. 215. *Mabinogion*, trans. G. and T. Jones, Everyman's Lib., p. 80. Though this castle is localized at the site of the Roman ruins of Segontium, it has all the splendours of the Celtic OtherWorld; see Loomis, *Wales*, pp. 6 f.

Turning back to the point where Gawain, on entering, first spied the precious board, we read that he was escorted by knights into a chamber where the royal invalid lay on a couch.[1] The description of the Fisher King's costume and surroundings is more elaborate than in Chrétien's account and quite different except for one detail, the cap of sable fur with a silken cover. A pillar of copper, which supports an angel holding a piece of the true cross, has taken the place of the four copper pillars which sustained the hood of the fireplace—a drastic change emphasizing the sanctity of the King and the castle. When he receives from Gawain the sword with which John the Baptist was beheaded, he kisses the relic and entrusts it to his niece. Here the change from Chrétien's version, in which the King, on being presented with a sword sent by his niece, entrusts it to Perceval for use in battle, seems to have been dictated by the novel concept of the weapon as a hallowed relic, to be preserved in the Grail castle.

Though the influence of Chrétien has been obscured by changes up to this point, it is fairly clear in the passage describing the procession of the Grail and lance through the banquet hall before Gawain and the ageless knights. Let me quote:[2]

Lo, two damsels issue from a chapel, and one holds in her two hands the most holy Grail, and the other the lance of which the point bleeds into it, and they walk side by side and come into the hall where the knights and Sir Gawain are eating. So sweet and so holy an odour accompanies the relics that they forget to eat. Sir Gawain gazes at the Grail and it seems to him that there is a chalice within it, albeit there was none at that time. And he sees the point of the lance from which the red blood drops, and he seems to behold two angels who bear two candelabra of gold with lighted candles. The damsels pass before Sir Gawain and go into another chapel. Sir Gawain is lost in thought, and such great joy fills his mind that he thinks of nothing but God. The knights are all downcast and doleful and look at him.

Lo, the two damsels issue from the chapel and come again before Sir Gawain, and he seems to behold three angels where before he had

[1] Ed. Nitze, i, ll. 2358–78.   [2] Ibid., ll. 2424–57.

beheld but two, and he seems to behold in the midst of the Grail the form of a child. The Master of the knights calls on Sir Gawain. Sir Gawain looks before him and sees three drops of blood fall on the table, and is so astonished that he says not a word. Then the damsels went out, and the knights are filled with fear and look at each other. Sir Gawain cannot withdraw his eyes from the three drops of blood, and when he would fain pick them up,[1] they elude him; wherefore he is very doleful, for he cannot put his hand out to them nor anything within his reach.

Lo, the two damsels come again before the table, and it seems to Sir Gawain that there are three, and he looks up, and it seems to him that the Grail is wholly in the air. He looks and there appears aloft a man nailed to a cross, and the spear was fixed in his side. Sir Gawain sees him and has great pity for him and can think of nothing else but the pain which the King suffers. The Master of the knights calls on him again to speak, and says that if he delays longer, he will never again have the opportunity. Sir Gawain is silent, not hearing the knight but gazing upward. But the damsels return to the chapel and take away the most holy Grail and the lance, and the knights cause the table-cloths to be removed, and rise from meat and go into another hall and leave Sir Gawain all alone.

It is then that Gawain plays the chess-game and is checkmated thrice. Weary, he sleeps on a couch till dawn.[2] He would fain have taken leave of his host but finds the doors bolted. A damsel enters, however, and informs him that a service is being held in a chapel in veneration of the sword which he had given the King, but that he could not be admitted because he had failed to speak the word which would have brought joy to the castle. A voice then warns him to depart, and Gawain leaves the hall, finds his horse and arms, and rides away.

The similarity of this narrative to Chrétien's is sufficient to leave little or no doubt of his influence. But the differences also are striking: the absence of the Fisher King from the hall during the Grail scene, the presence, instead, of the twelve

---

[1] I adopt here the reading of MS. O, 'baillier', instead of 'baisier' of MS. P.
[2] Ed. Nitze, i, ll. 2464-91.

knights, the prompting of the Master, the substitution of angels for the squires, the omission of the damsel with the *tailleor*, the passage of the Grail, not into a chamber, but into a chapel. The hovering of the Grail in the air may have been suggested by the First Continuation. Robert de Boron, who in his *Joseph* equated the Grail with a chalice, may have inspired the curious statement that Gawain beheld a chalice in the Grail, though there was none. All these deviations from Chrétien seem to be examples of the author's independence.

The three drops of blood and the trance which they induced seem to illustrate again the same habits of imaginative association revealed in the author's treatment of the Bald Damsel of the Cart. According to MS. H of Chrétien's *Perceval*,[1] which may well have resembled that followed in *Perlesvaus*, three drops of blood (not one drop) flowed from the lance-head down the shaft to the squire's hand; and these drops may have recalled to the author of *Perlesvaus* the love-reverie later induced in Perceval by the three blood-drops shed by a wounded wild goose.[2] The three drops may also have reminded the author of a vision related in the *Liber Miraculorum* of Gregory of Tours.[3] While a priest was celebrating mass, he saw three drops, of surpassing whiteness, fall on the altar. No one dared to touch them, but another priest tried to collect them in a silver paten; whereupon they flowed into it and, uniting, formed a single beautiful jewel—a demonstration of the unity of the Trinity.

As the repetition of the number three in the Grail scene reveals a preoccupation with the Trinity, so the visions of the infant and the crucified man disclose an equal, if not a greater, interest in the doctrine of the Real Presence.[4] These visions of the Christ Child or of the crucified Saviour, appearing at the moment of consecration in place of the eucharistic wafer, go back in literary history to the Lives of the Desert Fathers.

---

[1] *Perlesvaus*, ed. Nitze, ii. 272.
[2] Chrétien, *Roman de Perceval*, ed. W. Roach (Paris, 1959), vss. 4184–212.
[3] *Perlesvaus*, ed. Nitze, ii. 273.
[4] On this doctrine see Lizette A. Fisher, *Mystic Vision in the Grail Legend and in the* Divine Comedy (New York, 1917), pp. 9–26.

Their ultimate inspiration came, of course, from the words of the Lord as He broke bread and gave it to the apostles on the evening before the Crucifixion: 'This is my body which is broken for you.' There were those who took the words figuratively, and those who took them literally, maintaining that after consecration by the priest the Host was God's physical body under the species of bread. The controversy came to a head in the twelfth century, and in 1215, not far from the date of *Perlesvaus*, the Fourth Lateran Council pronounced in favour of the Real Presence.

Professor Roach has given the subject particular attention.[1] He cites from a life of Bishop Hugh of Lincoln a tale that at the elevation of the Host, the divine clemency deigned to open the eyes of a cleric and showed him Christ in the form of a little infant, most reverently handled by the pure fingers of the saintly officiant.[2] The Cistercian monk Caesarius of Heisterbach gives several instances in his *Dialogus Miraculorum*. At the monastery of Hemmenrode a monk during the celebration of mass saw in the hands of the celebrant the Saviour in the form of a man, while at another time an infant of great beauty was seen mounting from the hands of the priest to the top of the cross, and then assuming the form of bread and becoming the Host which the priest communicated. At another monastic house, as the brethren were prostrating themselves according to custom, one of them saw the infant Jesus, not as one newly born, but as if He had been crucified; from all His wounds the blood flowed into the chalice. Similar was the vision vouchsafed to Gawain.

Professor Frappier accords high praise to the account of Gawain's visit to the Grail castle:[3] 'It is a beautiful idea to contrast the obstinate silence of the visitor with the promptings, more and more urgent, of the twelve old knights and their master.' 'In *Perlesvaus* at last the decisive change is made which was demanded by the separate origins of the holy lance and the Holy Grail; at first introduced in succession or even

---

[1] *Zeitschr. f. rom. Phil.*, lix (1939), pp. 10–56.   [2] Ibid., p. 52.
[3] *Lumière du Graal*, ed. R. Nelli (Paris, 1951), pp. 219 f.

without any connexion, they are now brought in together. The damsels—no longer a squire and a damsel, perhaps for an effect of symmetry and harmony—walk side by side. Into the Holy Grail, the vessel of eternal redemption, flows forever the blood of the lance, of the eternal sacrifice.'

One may gladly agree with these tributes to the artistry of *Perlesvaus*, but it is not so easy to accept Frappier's opinion that the author has provided a happy solution for the question test. Was it a felicitous idea to combine it with the miracle of transubstantiation? Was Gawain depicted in Arthurian romance or in *Perlesvaus* itself as so saintly a character that he should be rewarded with a vision reserved for holy men? Was it not, in fact, a blunder to make this mystic experience the cause of his failure to fulfil his mission, the restoration of the Fisher King to health and of his land to peace?

After Gawain's turn to visit the Grail castle it was Lance-lot's.[1] Unlike his predecessor, Lancelot first came on three grey-haired knights in a boat, one of whom was fishing with a rod of gold. With them was a damsel holding the head of a knight. (Previously three other damsels, including the Bald Damsel and her companion, have been introduced carrying a similar gruesome object, and there are three more to come. Is this macabre obsession another symptom of an abnormal mentality?) Lancelot was directed to the Fisher King's castle, on his way made confession to a hermit, and was rebuked for his love of Guenevere, but refused to renounce her. Warned that because of this mortal sin, he could not see the Grail, Lancelot nevertheless proceeded. The bridge offered no diffi-culty, and he passed unharmed between two lions. He found the Fisher King lying on a bed, and delighted him with news of his nephew Perceval, but informed him for the first time that it was this same Perceval, who by his silence had caused the King's infirmity. Somewhat hurriedly we are told that Lancelot was served at table with costly vessels, but the Grail did not appear, and he departed the next morning.

[1] Ed. Nitze, i, ll. 3626–759.

The author seems to have combined here a recollection of Chrétien's account of the meeting with the Fisher King at the river with a much abridged version of his own account of Gawain's visit to the Grail castle. He interpolated the confession to the hermit and omitted the vision of the Grail, because he was cognizant of Lancelot's passion for the Queen, as it was elaborated in the Vulgate *Lancelot* or in some earlier treatment, and realized that an unrepentant sinner was disqualified from such lofty experiences.

When the author came to treat Perceval's triumphant return, after his long illness, to the castle of the Fisher King, he broke with all precedent—so far as we know—by abandoning the question test, for which he himself had prepared in his account of the visits of Gawain and Lancelot, and by substituting a conquest of the castle by a sort of white magic. Previously the Fisher King has died, his castle has been seized by his evil brother, the King of Castle Mortal,[1] the inmates have fled, and the Grail has ceased to appear. After accomplishing numerous missions of vengeance and destroying 1,500 worshippers of a copper bull (an incident which seems based on a local tradition of Dinas Brân, preserved in the romance of *Fouke Fitz Warin*),[2] Perceval comes to the cell of his uncle, Pelles, receives from him a mule and a banner, and through their magic power and with the aid of a friendly lion discomfits or kills twenty-seven knights who guard the nine bridges at the entrance of the Grail castle. In terror the evil king commits suicide by leaping from the battlements, and Perceval enters into possession. The Grail once more appears, not in the hall but in the chapel, where the other relics are kept. We read nothing, however, of the Grail Bearer's resumption of her office.

[1] On the King of Castle Mortal see Loomis, *Arthurian Tradition*, pp. 246–8.

[2] The two episodes of the Knight of the Dragon and the Copper Bull (ll. 5803–965) seem to be an elaboration and a splitting of the adventure of Payn Peverel at Chastiel Bran as described in *Fouke Fitz Warin*, ed. L. Brandin (Paris, 1930), pp. 3–7. Nitze was mistaken in assuming that in this context *tor* was a feminine noun meaning 'tower'. See *Romanic Rev.* ix (1918), pp. 178 f.; *PMLA*, lxi (1946), p. 57, n. 32; H. Newstead, *Bran the Blessed in Arthurian Romance* (New York, 1939), pp. 95–106.

This narrative of Perceval's success is so different from any other which we know that it seems to furnish another example of the author's originality. Professor Carman has interpreted it as symbolic of the Crucifixion,[1] and I know of no better explanation, but the parallelism, if intended, is hard to discern.

After the lapse of some time Perceval receives a visit from Arthur and Gawain, and shows them the costly tomb of the Fisher King, from which a sweet savour issues.[2] We are informed that the castle is encircled by a river which flows from the Earthly Paradise, that it has three names, Edein, the Castle of Joy, and the Castle of Souls, and that the last name signifies that the souls of all who die within the edifice enter Paradise. If the author meant by this that the Grail castle symbolized the Church, he failed to elaborate the idea. Hermits arrive to sing the mass, and the Grail appears in five forms, the last of which is a chalice. Note, again, the implication that the Grail was not in its proper form a chalice. This was the first time that such a vessel was used in Britain for the consecration of God's body (*cors*). One of the hermits, who reveals that he is the converted pagan, King Gurgaran, brings a bell, cast by Solomon, which is to serve as model for all the bells employed in the service of God and His sweet Mother. Perceval, being summoned to rescue his sister from an abductor, departs from the castle, and Arthur and Gawain go their ways.

In due course Perceval slays the persecutor of his sister and mother and the murderer of King Pelles, and avenges the death of his cousin, the son of Brun Brandalis, on the Red Knight of the Deep Forest.[3] At last, we find him in a ship, alone except for a steersman, sailing across the sea. There follows one of the most charming passages in all Arthurian romance, describing Perceval's visit to the isle of the ageless elders.[4]

Perceval leaves the land behind so that he beholds only the sea....
The ship has sped so far by day and by night, as it pleased God, that
they saw a castle on an island of the sea.... They came near the

[1] *PMLA*, lxi, pp. 44–47. [2] Ed. Nitze, i, ll. 7178–279.
[3] Ibid. i, ll. 8662–92. [4] Ibid. i, ll. 9541–664.

castle and heard four trumpets sound at the four corners (aux .iiii. chies) *of the walls very sweetly.* .... *They issued from the ship and went by the seaside to the castle, and within there were the fairest halls and the fairest mansions that one has ever seen. Perceval looks beneath a very fair tree, which was tall and broad, and sees the fairest and clearest fountain that anyone could describe, and it was all set about with rich golden pillars, and the gravel seemed to be of precious stones. Above this fountain two men were sitting, whiter of hair and beard than new fallen snow, and they seemed young of face. As soon as they see Perceval, they rise to meet him, and bow and adore the shield which he bears at his neck and kiss the cross and then the boss in which the relics were enclosed.*

'*Sir,*' *say they,* '*marvel not at that which we do, for we knew well the knight who before you bore the shield. Many a time we saw him before God was crucified.*'

Perceval marvels much at what they say, for they speak of a far-off time. '*Sirs, do you know the name of him who bore it?*'

'*His name was Joseph of Arimathea. There was no cross on the shield before the death of Jesus Christ, but he had it put there after the Crucifixion for love of the Saviour, whom he greatly loved.*'

Perceval removes the shield from his neck, and one of the worshipful men leans it against the tree, which is blooming with the fairest flowers in the world. Perceval looks beyond the fountain and sees in a beautiful place a cask (tonel) *made as it were all of glass, and it was so big that there was inside a knight all armed. He peers into it and sees that he is alive. He speaks to him many times, but the knight will never answer him at all. Perceval gazes at him in wonder and returns to the worshipful men and asks them who this knight is, and they tell him that he cannot know as yet.*

They lead him to a great hall, and he brings his shield with him, for which cause they make great joy and honour him. He sees that the hall is very rich, for never had he beheld one so beautiful. It was hung about with very rich cloths of silk, and in the midst of the hall was depicted the Saviour of the world in His majesty, and His apostles about Him. Within were folk who were full of great joy and seemed to be of great holiness; and so they were, for had they not been good men, they could not have remained there.

'Sir,' say the two masters to Perceval, 'this mansion, which you see here so rich, is a royal hall.'

'By my faith,' Perceval says, 'so should it be, for never have I seen any so costly.'

He looks around and sees the richest tables of gold and ivory that he has ever beheld. One of the masters sounds a bell three times, and thirty-three men come into the hall in a group. They were clad in white garments, and not one of them but had a red cross on his breast, and they all seemed to be of the age of thirty-two years. As soon as they enter the hall they adore Our Lord with a pure heart and beat their breasts crying 'Mea culpa'. Then they went to wash at a rich golden laver, and then to sit at the tables. The masters caused Perceval to sit at the chief table by himself. They were served there right gloriously and right piously. Perceval looked about him more gladly than he ate.

While he was thus looking, he perceived above him a golden chain descending, adorned with precious stones; and in the midst was a crown of gold. The chain descended with great precision, and it held on to nothing but the will of Our Lord. As soon as the masters saw it being lowered, they opened a large, wide pit which was in the midst of the hall, so that one could see the hole plainly. As soon as the entrance of this pit was uncovered, there issued the greatest and most dolorous cries that anyone ever heard. When the worshipful men of the place heard them, they stretched out their hands toward Our Lord and began all to weep. Perceval hears that dolour and marvels much what it can be. He sees that the chain descends in that direction and that it stops over the hole until the meal is almost ended. Then it withdraws itself into the air and goes aloft, but Perceval does not know what becomes of it. The masters covered the pit again, which was very hideous to look at, and piteous to hear were the voices which issued from it.

The worshipful men rose from the tables when they had eaten and rendered thanks right sweetly to Our Lord, and afterwards returned thither whence they had come. 'Sir,' say the masters to Perceval, 'this golden chain which you have seen is very rich, and the crown likewise. But you can never go forth from here unless you promise that you will come back as soon as you see the ship with the sail bearing a red cross; otherwise you cannot depart.'

'*Tell me,*' says Perceval, '*concerning the chain and the crown, what it may be.*'

'*We will tell you,*' says one of the masters, '*if you promise us what I say.*'

'*Surely, sir,*' says Perceval, '*I promise you faithfully that as soon as I have done what is necessary for my lady my mother and for another I will return hither if I am alive and if I see your ship such as you describe it.*'

'*Yes, do not fail, and you shall have the crown of gold on your head as soon as you return, and you will be seated in the chair, and you will be king of an island that is near to this, very abundant in all good things, for there is nothing in the world lacking there which is needful for man and woman. For a right worshipful man has been King of it and has thus supplied it. Because he proved himself so well in that kingdom and the people who dwell on the island praised him, he has been chosen to reign in a greater realm. Now they desire another worshipful man as King who will do for them as well as he; but take heed that, when you are their King, the island is well supplied, for if you do not provide for it well, you will be placed on the Island of Suffering, of which you heard the cries even now in this hall. . . .*'

'*Sir,*' says Perceval, '*tell me of the knight all armed who is in the cask of glass, who he is and what is his name.*'

'*You may not know*', says the master, '*until your return. But tell me tidings of the most holy Grail, which you reconquered from your uncle. Is it still in the holy chapel which was the Fisher King's?*'

'*Yes, sir,*' says Perceval, '*and the sword with which John the Baptist was beheaded, and other relics in great plenty.*'

'*I saw the Grail,*' says the master, '*before the Fisher King. Joseph [of Arimathea], who was his uncle, collected in it the blood which flowed from the wounds of the Saviour of the World. I know well all your lineage and from what folk you are descended. For your good knighthood and your chastity and your good valour have you come hither, for this was Our Lord's will. Take heed that you are prepared to return hither when the time comes and you see the ship in readiness.*'

'*Sir,*' says Perceval, '*I will return very gladly, and I would not*

have asked to depart had it not been for my lady my mother and my
sister, for I have never seen a place that pleased me so much.'

He was well cared for that night, and in the morning before he
departed he heard a holy mass in one of the fairest chapels that he had
ever seen. The master came to him after mass and brought him a
shield, white as new fallen snow. Then he said:

'You will leave your shield here with us as pledge of your return,
and take this one.'

'Sir,' says Perceval, 'as you please.'

He took his leave and departed from the rich manor and found his
ship all ready and heard the trumpets sound at his going as at his
coming. He entered the ship, and the sail was hoisted and he left the
land behind.

This account of the isle of the ageless elders is remarkable
for its pictorial charm and its moving and tantalizing dialogue,
but it is even more remarkable as bringing together in vivid
form several features of the Celtic Other World mentioned in
three very old Welsh texts.[1] The fountain, the chain mysteriously suspended in the air, and perhaps the golden laver are
to be met in the *mabinogi* of *Manawydan*, dated about 1060.[2]

The young hero Pryderi discovered a lofty castle and, entering, 'beheld a fountain with marble work round it, and on
the margin of the fountain a golden bowl fastened to four
chains, and that upon a marble slab, and the chains ascending
into the air, and he could see no end to them.'

The fountain, the ageless inhabitants, and the situation of
the castle on an island are referred to in a poem of a still earlier
period. The bard Taliesin is conceived as speaking:[3]

> Perfect is my seat in the Faery Fortress (*Caer Siddi*).
> Neither plague nor age harms him who dwells therein.
> Manawydan and Pryderi know it . . .
> And around its corners are ocean's currents.
> And the fructifying spring is above it.
> Sweeter than white wine is the drink in it.

---

[1] *PMLA*, lvi (1941), pp. 889–91, 925–30. Reprinted in Loomis, *Wales*, pp. 134–6, 165–72.

[2] *Mabinogion*, trans. G. and T. Jones, Everyman's Lib., p. 46. Loth, *Mabinogion*, i. 160.   [3] J. Rhŷs, *Celtic Folklore, Welsh and Manx* (Oxford, 1901), ii. 678.

The four corners of the faery castle, the lamentations of the prisoners in the pit, the warrior who would not respond to Perceval's questions, all occur in another archaic poem, *The Spoils of Annwn*, likewise conceived as the work of Taliesin.[1]

> Perfect was the prison of Gweir in the Faery Fortress (*Caer Siddi*);
> Before the spoils of Annwn dolefully he chanted. . .
> In the Four-cornered Fortress, the isle of the strong door, . . .
> Bright wine was their drink before their retinue. . .
> It was difficult to converse with their sentinel.

Even the cask (*tonel*) of glass in which the silent knight is enclosed is accounted for by the fact that in the same poem *Caer Siddi* is also called the Fortress of Glass (*Caer Wydyr*), and it seems likely that *tonel* represents a corruption of *torele*, 'little tower', an hypothesis strengthened by the fact that Nennius, writing about A.D. 800, mentioned a 'turrim vitream in medio mare', 'a glass tower in the midst of the sea', and described men on the tower who would not reply to those who sought to speak to them.[2]

That the verses describing *Caer Siddi* depict a typically Celtic Other World comes out clearly when we compare their content with a passage from the *Adventure* (Echtra) *of St. Columba's Clerics*, a pious saga which Manus O'Donnell incorporated in his biography of the Apostle to the Picts.[3]

For a long time they [the clerics of St. Columba] were without sight of land until at last they beheld an island. In this wise was that island: a dwelling fair and well adorned in the midst thereof, . . . and a man in holy orders in golden apparel before every altar. The household of Columba entered then, and a right courteous welcome was given them. Whilst they were there, a beautiful golden cowl was let down upon the floor of that royal hall. . . . They were richly served and had

---

[1] *PMLA*, lvi. 889–91. Reprinted in Loomis, *Wales*, pp. 134–6.

[2] F. Lot, *Nennius et l'Historia Brittonum* (Paris, 1934), pp. 156 f. Heinzel in *Denkschriften der kaiserlichen Akademie der Wissenschaften*, phil.-hist. Kl., xl, Abth. 3, p. 174, guessed that the knight in the glass cask was Joseph of Arimathea. Not only is the guess unfounded, but it is also contradicted by the fact that the corpse of Joseph was seen by Perceval in its coffin (ll. 6120–5) before he visited the island of the elders, and was removed to a new coffin after the visit (ll. 10150–4) and placed in the ship in which Perceval sailed away.

[3] M. O'Donnell, *Life of Columcille*, ed. A. O'Keller, G. Schoepperle (Urbana, Ill., 1918), p. 399. *Revue Celtique*, xxvi (1905), p. 165.

great cheer that night, and they were given well brewed ale, so that they were drunken and merry.

The cowl of gold lowered to the floor of the royal hall is so obviously by an ecclesiastical adaptation of the crown of gold lowered by the mysterious chain over the royal hall of the ageless elders that one cannot doubt that a common tradition accounts for the similarity. That the tradition was originally a secular one is proved by the unseemly revels in which the clerics indulged. The island must have been the pagan Elysium, like the land described by the Irish god Mider in the ninth-century saga, *The Wooing of Etain*.[1] 'Intoxicating is the ale of Inisfail (Ireland); more intoxicating is the ale of the great country. There rivers run with wine. There old age is unknown.' The correspondences between the *echtra* of the clerics of St. Columba and the adventure of Perceval on the island of the youthful-seeming elders is due to a common heritage of ultimately pagan Irish tradition.

There are also correspondences, as Heinzel and Nitze observed, between *Perlesvaus* and the *Navigatio Sancti Brendani*, the *Voyage of St. Brendan*, another pious Irish *echtra* in Latin form, which enjoyed a prodigious circulation throughout western Europe from the tenth century on. Let me briefly summarize the relevant part of the *Navigatio*.[2] The saint and fourteen monks took ship and, after touching at several islands, disembarked at one where they found two springs. An aged monk ran up and threw himself at Brendan's feet, but to all questioning he answered not a word. The visitors arrived at an abbey more beautiful than any below the throne of God, and enjoyed a delicious, though simple, meal in the refectory. Then they proceeded to the church, a bell was sounded, the canonical hour was chanted. The abbot informed the visitors that his community consisted of twenty-four monks, and that they had lived there for eighty years since the death of the

[1] *Ériu*, xii (1938), p. 181. A. H. Leahy, *Heroic Romances of Ireland* (London, 1905), i. 169.

[2] Benedeit, *Voyage of St. Brendan*, ed. E. G. R. Waters (Oxford, 1928), pp. 36–39.

founder. (Note these numbers.) They had suffered during this time no bodily infirmity, and God himself had supplied them with food. Though Brendan declared that he knew of no place where he would rather abide, the abbot bade him return after three weeks to Ireland, and the saint did so.

Of the correspondences between the *Navigatio* and *Perlesvaus* some may be ascribed to a common tradition, for they are paralleled in other Celtic visits to the Other World. They are: the voyage, the island, the fountains, the uncommunicative resident of the island, the beautiful buildings, the hospitable reception, the delicious meal, the longevity of the inhabitants. The specific number of years, eighty, which they had lived on this blissful island, free from adversity and bodily infirmity, is exactly the period which, as we know, the followers of Brân son of Llŷr spent on the island of Grassholm in the midst of abundance and joy; so this feature also in the *Navigatio* was presumably traditional. But a few correspondences between the *Navigatio* and *Perlesvaus*, such as the sounding of a bell in the course of an entertainment on an Otherworld island, seem to be due to the direct influence of the earlier work on the later. And I feel sure that the number of the island monks who entertained St. Brendan, namely twenty-four, was misread by some scribe, and as a result the number of holy men who joined Perceval at the repast was copied as thirty-three. For the Roman numeral xxxiii differs only by the substitution of an x for an i from xxiiii. And the latter number, a multiple of twelve, would be in harmony with the number of members in a monastic community, which from the time of St. Benedict on was not infrequently set at twelve, as we shall see in the next chapter and in Chapter XIV.

My impression that the author of *Perlesvaus* wrote 'xxiiii' instead of 'xxxiii' as the number of holy men, and had the authority of the *Navigatio* for doing so is confirmed by the fact that he had a good Latin authority for the apparent age of these same men. Like the *Navigatio*, the spurious letter of Prester John, describing the wonders of the East, was standard reading in the early thirteenth century, and catered to much the same literary appetite. The letter credits the Fountain of Youth with restoring those who bathed in it to the bodily condition they possessed at the age of thirty-two, precisely the apparent age of the holy men.[1]

I think we may be safe in concluding from this ample evidence that the main source for the description of Perceval's visit to the isle of the ageless elders was a French text reproducing with remarkable fidelity and fullness the pagan Welsh concept of the Other World, as it is fragmentarily preserved to us in *Branwen, Manawydan,* and the *Spoils of Annwn.* Probably this lost French text had taken on a monastic cast before it came into the hands of the author of *Perlesvaus.* At any rate, he could not help noticing the extraordinary resemblance it presented to the episode in the *Navigatio Sancti Brendani,* summarized above, and accordingly, as I have argued, he set the number of the holy men at twenty-four. Similarly, noting that they, as well as the two masters, were much older than they looked and that there was a splendid fountain within the precincts, he guessed that this was the Fountain of Youth[2] and transferred from the letter of Prester John to his own pages this very precise indication as to their appearance.

After telling of the departure of Perceval from the island, the author recounts other adventures of his and brings him back to the Grail castle. The coffins of Nicodemus, Joseph of Arimathea, and the Fisher King are placed in the holy chapel with the other relics.[3] At last, as Perceval was there at his devotions, a voice announced that the relics must now be distributed among the hermits of the neighbourhood. It also

[1] J. K. Wright, *Geographical Lore of the Time of the Crusades* (New York, 1925), pp. 204 f. *Abhandlungen der königlichen sächsischen Gesellschaft der Wissenschaften,* phil.-hist. Kl., vii (1879), p. 912.

[2] Prof. Carman remarks in *PMLA,* lxi, pp. 59 f., that the isle of the ageless elders 'is but a patent version of the Earthly Paradise'. Some descriptions place the Fountain of Youth in the Earthly Paradise, and the two masters bear a vague resemblance to Enoch and Elijah, the most notable inhabitants. See especially G. G. Coulton, *Mediaeval Garner,* p. 467; H. R. Patch, *The Other World* (Cambridge, Mass., 1950), p. 159; *Études Celtiques,* viii (1959), pp. 420–8.   [3] Ed. Nitze, i, ll. 10116–25.

declared: 'The Holy Grail shall appear here no longer, but within a short time you will know well where it will be.' Perceval disposed of the relics as he had been instructed, and in after times churches and monasteries were built to enshrine them.[1]

One day he heard a trumpet blow, and, looking out from a window toward the sea, he descried a ship drawing near with a red cross on a white sail. The fairest men in priestly garments came ashore, bringing with them the richest coffins of gold and silver; and to these they transferred the holy bodies mentioned above, as well as that of Perceval's mother. The new coffins and their hallowed contents were taken aboard the vessel. Perceval then, bidding farewell to Joseus, the son of King Pelles, who remained behind in the castle, sailed away. The author declares that never did earthly man know what became of Perceval and that the history speaks of him no more.[2] But, of course, he has already informed us of Perceval's destination, namely, the isle of the ageless elders, and has intimated clearly that there he will find the Grail, which is to appear no more in the castle of the Fisher King.

A brief but effective conclusion deals with the fate of this hallowed edifice.[3] After the death of Joseus the castle began to crumble away.

Many folk of the lands that were nearest to it wondered what could be in it. Many were seized with a desire to go and see what was there. They went there but never did they return, and no one knew what became of them. The tidings spread through the lands, and no one dared to enter the place again, save two Welsh knights who had heard speak of it. They were right fair youths and gay. Each pledged the other that he would go there. They entered, light of heart, but they remained a long time, and when they came forth, they led the life of hermits, wore hair shirts, and wandered through the forests. They ate only roots and led a very hard life, but it rejoiced them greatly. When they were asked why they were so happy,

---

[1] Ibid. i, ll. 10134–44.   [2] Ibid. i, ll. 10146–64.
[3] Ibid. i, ll. 10167–83.

they said to those who inquired: 'Go where we have been and you will know why.'

Rarely in Arthurian literature does one encounter the device of tantalizing reticence employed so fittingly to convey the effect of awe and mystery. What beatific visions did the Welsh knights behold in the ruinous castle of the Fisher King?

Though one must accord high praise to the author of *Perlesvaus* for his sensitive handling of the fates of his hero, the Grail castle, and the holy vessel itself, the narrative material was not of his own devising. For he was following, as Professor Carman has pointed out,[1] what is, broadly spreaking, the same pattern as that we find in the conclusion of the *Queste del Saint Graal*. There we read that the Grail, after long being preserved in the castle where dwelt the Maimed King, was transferred to a land across the seas; that the Grail hero (in this case Galahad) took ship, was wafted by God's will to the same land, and was crowned king.

We have already observed in earlier pages of this book that the Welsh situated the abode of Brân, the original of the Fisher King or the Maimed King, at two different places, and that each site had its own distinct cluster of associations. As noted in Chapter V there was, and still is, a ruinous castle in North Wales called Dinas Brân, the fortress of Brân, crowning a hill above the River Dee. According to the thirteenth-century romance of *Fouke Fitz Warin*,[2] which shows great familiarity with the Welsh border, this castle was burnt and laid waste. Many came there to see the wonders, but none escaped alive save one knight who dared the adventure. The ruins of Dinas Brân on the Dee were therefore in the thirteenth century the subject of a legend similar to that which we find in the conclusion of *Perlesvaus* attached to the ruins of the Fisher King's castle, which, Lancelot was informed, was encircled by a river. That this Welsh tradition could actually have become known to the French author through his literary

[1] J. N. Carman, *Relationship of the 'Perlesvaus' and the 'Queste del Saint Graal'* (Lawrence, Kansas, 1936), pp. 46–48.
[2] Ed. L. Brandin (Paris, 1930), pp. 3–6.

sources is no mere surmise, for it was noted several pages back that he included an incident about the worshippers of a copper bull which is obviously an elaborated form of the legend of Dinas Brân as told in *Fouke Fitz Warin*, though he could not, for chronological reasons, have read of it there. Moreover, as we shall see in Chapter XI, the Prose *Lancelot* includes in its account of the nocturnal perils of the Grail castle other elements from the legend of Dinas Brân as preserved in *Fouke Fitz Warin*.

While there was, on the one hand, this Welsh tradition of a ruinous castle, formerly the abode of Brân, so dangerous to enter that all but one or two knights had lost their lives, there was, as we know, the rival tradition, preserved in *Branwen*, which represented the followers of Brân, including his brother Manawydan, as dwelling for eighty years on an island of the sea, free from every sorrow, supplied without stint and growing no older in appearance. It is this latter tradition which is reflected so clearly, along with other features of Welsh origin, in the description of the isle of the ageless elders. If anyone remains sceptical of the connexion between the brief account in *Branwen* of the joyous sojourn of Brân's followers on the isle of Grassholm and the elaborate description in *Perlesvaus* of Perceval's visit to the elysian isle, he is invited to read on through the next chapter, where the corroborative evidence of *Sone de Nansai* clinches the matter.

There were, then, two distinct localizations of the fortress or palace of Brân, one on a river in North Wales, the other on an island off the south-west coast. The former tradition represented the edifice as deserted and decayed and fatal to the adventurous visitor; the other conceived it as an Otherworld dwelling of great magnificence, where there was perpetual feasting without stint and where old age and sorrow were unknown. Apparently the Welsh must have reconciled these traditions by representing the hero of the Grail quest as visiting the mainland castle of Brân before it was abandoned and ruinous, and then taking ship and sailing to an island of elysian plenty, where he is crowned King. Presumably, Brân's vessel of plenty, the Grail, was transferred from the first castle to the second when the hero passed from one to the other. This pattern of events, so vividly described in accordance with Welsh tradition in *Perlesvaus*, is also followed, though less faithfully, in the *Queste del Saint Graal*. Nothing is said of the fate of the Grail castle of Corbenic, and the land of Sarras, of which Galahad is crowned king, is no Elysium. Professor Carman has argued that the *Queste* copied this pattern from *Perlesvaus*,[1] and his view of the relationship is certainly preferable to the opposite one. But since the correspondence is limited to the bare outline, I prefer the opinion of M. Frappier[2] that neither romance influenced the other. Each must have drawn through different literary channels on the same reservoir of Welsh legends about Brân son of Llŷr, his vessel of plenty, and his two traditional abodes.

Quite apart from its peculiar interest for the scholarly detective as one of the most intricate of puzzles furnished by Arthurian romance, and in spite of serious blemishes of taste and lapses in coherence, *Perlesvaus* will always attract the lover of belles-lettres by its graphic brilliance and its charming, easy style.

---

[1] See above, p. 132, n. 1.
[2] See Frappier in *Lumière du Graal*, ed. Nelli, p. 215.

X

Sone de Nansai and the *Mabinogi* of *Branwen*

ONE of the most surprising pieces of literature bearing on the mysteries of the Grail is the little-known French poem, *Sone de Nansai*,[1] which has just been mentioned. Ostensibly it is a realistic, historical romance, set in the period of the Crusades, without any connexion with Arthur and his court; yet under careful scrutiny it reveals a debt to lost Grail traditions and a closer connexion with the Welsh *mabinogi* of *Branwen* than any strictly Arthurian romance displays. Evidently, the scholars, Jessie Weston, Singer, Bruce, and Professor Helaine Newstead,[2] who have argued that *Sone de Nansai* preserves important Arthurian matter not derived from extant French texts, were not far astray.

Still, one can understand why these arguments have been neglected or lightly dismissed by superficial critics. *Sone de Nansai*, composed in the second half of the thirteenth century, probably by a poet of Brabant,[3] is widely separated in general tone and content from any other Grail story. Its hero is conceived as an historic personality, probably from Nambsheim in Alsace,[4] who after many adventures, amorous and military, at last became emperor and made war on the Saracens of southern Italy. Its author had a general knowledge of geography, including that of the British Isles. His imagination tended to realism. Even the ten artificial leopards mounted on the walls of the Grail castle, which uttered harmonious sounds when

---

[1] See previous chapter, p. 133.
[2] Weston, 'Notes on the Grail Romances', *Romania*, xliii (1914), pp. 403 ff. S. Singer, 'Über die Quelle von Wolframs *Parzival*', *ZdA*, xliv (1900), p. 330. *Historia Meriadoci and De Ortu Walwanii*, ed. J. D. Bruce, *Hesperia*, Ergänzungsreihe, 2 Heft (Göttingen, 1913), p. xxxiv. H. Newstead, *Bran the Blessed in Arthurian Romance* (New York, 1939), pp. 93–95, 131, 134, 173, 193, 195.
[3] U. T. Holmes, *History of Old French Literature* (Chapel Hill, 1937), p. 276.
[4] Ibid.

the wind blew, were turned by mechanical means, 'par engien', and had actual counterparts in the pneumatically operated singing birds of the Byzantine empire.[1] The strange creatures which haunt the forest near the Grail castle are not imaginary but have been identified by modern zoologists with wolverenes (*heles*) and with diver-ducks (*galices*).[2] Moreover, though the author was familiar with Arthurian romance, he made no mention of Arthur and his court, and sent no Perceval or Gawain in quest of the sacred vessel. These peculiarities, combined with the comparatively tardy composition of the poem, and its borrowing from the *Estoire del Saint Graal*, have naturally led hasty commentators to suspect that when the author deviated from earlier extant treatments of the Grail, its location, the Fisher King, and the Waste Land, he was merely exercising his inventive powers. But a close analysis of the relevant passages proves that, though invention played its part, much of the material was derived from lost sources, and reveals a kinship to *Perlesvaus*, the *mabinogi* of *Branwen*, and Geoffrey of Monmouth's *Historia Regum Britanniae*. Let me summarize the pertinent passages, introducing occasional quotations.[3]

Attracted by the news of an invasion of Norway by the Irish and the Scots, Sone took service with the Norwegian army, and in the course of a battle killed the Irish king. He then undertook a single combat with a gigantic champion of the King of Scotland. In order to win the favour of Heaven, he took a boat in company with Alain, King of Norway, to an island off the coast, inhabited by a monastic community, there to pray for victory. Disembarking, Sone and Alain were welcomed by the monks to their castle. It was built on a rock, surrounded by battlemented walls; there were four towers at the angles, and in the midst a larger round tower, which contained the great hall.

This was a hundred feet in diameter; there was a central

---

[1] *Speculum*, xxix (1954), pp. 477–87.
[2] K. Nyrop, '*Sone de Nansai* et la Norvège', *Romania*, xxxv (1906), pp. 555–69.
[3] Vss. 4241–5514.

fireplace with a hood supported by four pillars, much as in Chrétien. Around the walls were paintings of the Annunciation to Mary, the life of Christ, and the Descent into Hell. After the King had disclosed the purpose of their coming, he and Sone were invited, midday having passed, to join the monks at a banquet. The table was set in a little meadow, walled with marble, and overlooking the sea. On the walls were mounted the musical leopards already mentioned. If one looked in the opposite direction from the sea, one beheld a forest with a variety of trees, including such tropical species as the almond tree and the olive. There one could observe deer, swans, peacocks, and diver-ducks, the last described with identifying detail. Three streams met at the castle and plunged into the sea, and at this spot great schools of fish gathered. Nowhere could one discover a castle so mighty and so well supplied with every good thing.

The King and the abbot sat at the high table, and Sone on a bench near by. They had plenty to eat, and so much food was brought them that it was an arduous task for those who served. That afternoon Sone made his confession, and the next morning he and King Alain heard mass chanted by the abbot. This was followed by the abbot's discourse on the history of the abbey and of the relics it contained, which began with the rather odd words:[1] 'Lord King, give ear, and those whom you have with you. Wit ye well, the holy body [of Joseph of Arimathea], whose holy vessel ye see reposing there, founded this castle. Wherefore it is a wonder that no one in the land which he ruled dares to do wrong but he loses his mind and life thereby. When the holy man lay down on his bed on the day he died, he gave orders to write down his life.'

Thereupon the abbot went on to relate briefly the early history of the Grail substantially as we have it in the Vulgate *Estoire del Saint Graal*. But, after telling how Joseph of Arimathea discovered the spear-head with which Longinus pierced the side of Christ, as He hung on the cross, the abbot gave a quite unexpected account of Joseph's later career—one

[1] Vss. 4555-65.

without close parallel in the Grail romances. Custodian of the Grail and the spear-head, Joseph did not stay in Syria, but, finding an empty boat near Askalon, he entered it by the command of God and was wafted away without mast or sail to Gaeta near Naples. After a sojourn there, he arrived finally in Norway and killed the heathen King, but made the mistake of yielding to the charms of his lovely daughter. He had her baptized and married her, but she hated him as the slayer of her father and remained a pagan at heart. Chosen King of Norway, Joseph led a pious life, fostered the Church, and built an impregnable castle on an island off the coast. God, to try his faith, wounded him in the thighs and below, so that he was unable to walk; every day after mass he was wont to go fishing in a boat by way of diversion. Hence he was called the 'Fisher King'.[1] At last he was healed by a knight, resumed his martial exploits, and founded a community of twelve monks and an abbot which occupied the island castle and which was now playing host to Sone and King Alain.

But so long as Joseph was maimed, the kingdom of Logres (England) lay under a spell. 'Neither peas nor wheat were sown, no child was born to man, nor did maiden have husband, nor did tree bear leaf, nor meadow turn green, and neither bird nor beast had young.'[2] Later the name of the kingdom was changed to Norway. When the abbot had finished his narrative, he blessed Sone and King Alain.

Then he opened a vessel of ivory, which was carved with many stories, and took out of it the holy Grail. The entire land was illuminated by it. Then you could see the monks weeping and chanting loudly as they wept: 'Te Deum laudamus; there is no other such vessel!' The holy man, whom God loved, placed it on the altar next to the cross. Then he went and brought the holy spear-head of which you have heard me speak. The abbot and the monks wept so sorely that they seemed to melt in tears. The spear-head was beautiful and shining, and at the point hung a drop of red blood, which was a marvel to many people. The abbot showed them the coffins in which

---

[1] Vs. 4823.   [2] Vss. 4846–53.

the bodies of Joseph and his son Adan reposed. Joseph had only two children. The other was called Josephus, the first ordained bishop. The abbot was supplied with holy bodies, and he served them right well, God first and the relics after; he and the monks were zealous in this. When the abbot had displayed everything, he removed the vestments in which he had chanted. He took the youth [Sone] by the hand and said: 'Come, friend, you have fasted too long. The midday bell has been rung. Give heed to the refreshment of your body, for you have good need of it.' The monks led the king to the repast, for it was ready. The abbot and the king washed and then mounted to the high table. Sone ate with a cleric, who told him much about the place. The meal lasted a long time and the courses came very frequently. But the king, who had had enough, said to the abbot that he wished to depart, and the abbot would not delay him, for there was need of him elsewhere.

Thus King Alain and Sone returned to the mainland, and the abbot sent after them the sword with which Joseph had guarded the land. In the combat with the gigantic champion of the King of Scotland, Sone used the weapon to strike off his head. King Alain's daughter was smitten with love for Sone, and gave him the cup from which the Fisher King had been wont to drink. The name of the island castle was Galoche —a corruption of the French feminine adjective *galesche*, meaning 'Welsh'.

The reader of this summary cannot but be reminded of *Perlesvaus*. The strangeness and the glamour of the early romance have been replaced by a trite realism, but who can doubt that there is a relationship? For the two stories have in common: the visit of the hero to a quadrangular castle on an island; the prolonged banquet which he enjoyed there as the guest of a community of holy men; the languishment of the Fisher King; a collection of relics in what had been the Fisher King's castle, including the Grail, the bleeding spear, a mighty sword, and a coffin containing the body of Joseph of Arimathea. It is impossible to attribute the correspondence to chance, and equally impossible for chronological reasons to derive the material in *Perlesvaus* from *Sone*. There is good reason, moreover, for rejecting the third possibility, the derivation of *Sone* from *Perlesvaus*, since this would not account for the highly significant name Galoche, for the wounding of the Fisher King as the cause of the Waste Land, for the name of the land, Logres, and for the curious identification of Joseph of Arimathea with the Fisher King—figures who in *Perlesvaus* are represented as uncle and nephew. Once more, then, we are forced to assume a common source, more or less close, to explain the common features.

This was doubtless written in French. But our study of *Perlesvaus* has revealed that some of the features had their origin in Welsh tradition, namely, the four-cornered fortress on an island and the prolonged and plenteous banquets of which the followers of Brân there partook. And it is Welsh tradition, preserved in the latter part of *Branwen,* which accounts in remarkable fashion for the strange story of Joseph of Arimathea after he left Syria for the West—a story which has no close counterpart in any other Grail romance.

Turning once more to the *mabinogi,* what do we find?[1] Brân was a king of Britain, 'exalted with the crown of London'. He led an expedition to a foreign land and was victorious. Nevertheless, he was wounded in the foot with a poisoned javelin, and, though no causal nexus is mentioned, the islands of Ireland and Britain were rendered desolate. Brân commanded his followers to cut off his head and to travel with it, first to Harlech and then to the island of Grassholm. Obeying his commands, they spent seven years at Harlech, regaling themselves with meat and drink. Then, setting out for Grassholm, they found there a fair royal place, a great hall, overlooking the sea. That night they spent there without stint, and we may infer that they continued to feast, as they had at Harlech, for eighty years, in the company of the uncorrupted head of Brân. This was called the Hospitality of the Wondrous Head.[2]

There are, of course, many differences between the eleventh-

[1] J. Loth, *Mabinogion* (Paris, 1913), i. 119–49.

[2] On the word *yspydawt*, translated 'hospitality', see ibid., p. 390; Ifor Williams, *Pedeir Keinc y Mabinogi* (Cardiff, 1930), pp. 220 f.; P. Mac Cana, *Branwen Daughter of Llyr* (Cardiff, 1958), pp. 144–6.

century *mabinogi* and the thirteenth-century French romance. But let us note the resemblances between what we learn of Brân and what we learn in *Sone* of Joseph of Arimathea, alias the Fisher King.

1. Brân was King of Britain, crowned in London. The Fisher King's realm had been called Logres, i.e. England.

2. Brân led an expedition to a foreign land and was victorious. Joseph sailed to a foreign land and conquered it.

3. Brân was wounded in the foot and thereafter Britain was desolate. The Fisher King was wounded in the thighs and below, and, as a consequence, England was waste.

4. Brân ordained that after his death his followers should dwell for eighty years on an island off the coast of Wales. The Fisher King founded a community which after his death occupied an island called Galoche, i.e. Welsh.

5. Brân's followers feasted without stint in a royal hall overlooking the sea. The Fisher King's community feasted sumptuously in a walled meadow overlooking the sea.

6. Brân's followers carefully preserved his head on an island off the coast of Wales. The Fisher King's community preserved his body in the island castle of Galoche.

When one recalls that in the *Didot Perceval* Bron is the name of the Fisher King, and that Robert de Boron's Bron is called the Rich Fisher and many tales are said to be told of him, can one doubt that *Sone* gives us, in much modified form, the story of Brân and his followers as told in the latter part of *Branwen*?

And it is not hard to account for some of the striking differences between the *mabinogi* and the French romance. The absence from *Sone* of any reference to the severed head at the feast may be accounted for by the supposition that this feature in the *mabinogi* was a misconception due to the ambiguity of the Welsh word *pen*, which could mean either 'chief' or 'head'. Thus both *Perlesvaus* and *Sone* by omitting from the banquet scenes this gruesome object show that they derive from a Welsh tradition which was free from this misconception.

Another point on which *Sone* does not harmonize with *Branwen* is in the number of monks who held their feasts in the island castle of Galoche as compared with the number of Bran's followers who feasted for eighty years on the island of Grassholm without showing any signs of age. There were twelve monks and their abbot; there were only seven followers of Brân. On this point *Sone* is amply corroborated by two Grail romances. For according to *Perlesvaus*, as we saw in the last chapter, Gawain was seated at table in the Grail castle with twelve knights, who, though they were a hundred years old or more, seemed less than forty.[1] And in the *Queste del Saint Graal*, as we shall see, twelve knights assembled in the castle where dwelt the Maimed King, and were served from the Grail by Christ himself.[2] The substitution of the number seven in *Branwen*, as Dr. Mac Cana recognizes,[3] was due to a muddled tradition that all but seven of Brân's army were killed in the battle at which he himself was wounded in the foot. That before this slaughter Brân was wont, by tradition, to surround himself at table with twelve trusted warriors, just as did King Conchobar of Ulster in the saga of *Bricriu's Feast*,[4] seems a warranted conclusion from the French texts.

When so much of the Grail portion of *Sone* is more or less clearly derived from Welsh tales of Brân, what of the astonishing statement that Joseph of Arimathea, before he became known as the Fisher King, had come to Norway and married the king's daughter? This, of course, is in violent disagreement with any other account of Joseph of Arimathea, or the Fisher King, or Brân son of Llŷr; it is also inconsistent with the implications of the poem itself that the Fisher King's land was Logres, i.e. England, and that his island castle was Welsh. Was it, then, an arbitrary fancy of the French poet, designed to extend the range of Sone's exploits?

But here again, though such whimsies cannot be altogether

[1] *Perlesvaus*, ed. W. A. Nitze and others (Chicago, 1932), i, ll. 2414–17. The numeral 'xxii' of the Oxford MS. is an error for 'xii'. Ibid. ii. 266.

[2] *Queste del Saint Graal*, ed. A. Pauphilet (Paris), pp. 270 f.

[3] Mac Cana, op. cit., pp. 146 f.

[4] *Fled Bricrend*, ed. G. Henderson (London, 1899), p. 5.

discounted, the author seems to have been inspired by still another legend of Brân. For in a Welsh translation of Geoffrey of Monmouth's *Historia*, where Brân's name replaces Geoffrey's Brennius, we read that 'then Brân was goaded to rage by these words and went to Llychlyn to marry the daughter of the King of Llychlyn', and that in fact he did so.[1] Since Llychlyn translates Geoffrey's *Norwegia*, Brân's marriage matches that of the Fisher King in *Sone*. This is an extraordinary coincidence.

There are, nevertheless, reasons for caution. There is no further correspondence between the two marriages and their consequences. Moreover, this Brân was the son of Dyfnwal and brother of Beli,[2] not the son of Llŷr and brother of Manawydan, as was the prototype of the Fisher King. Furthermore, his career, as related in the Welsh text, is translated from Geoffrey's pseudo-chronicle, and though the latter contains many genuine Welsh elements, they are notoriously garbled.[3] Thus it seems hazardous to rest any argument on the parallel between the Welsh translation of the *Historia* and *Sone*.

Yet, further investigation discloses at least two bits of evidence that Geoffrey attached to Brennius genuine traditions of Brân son of Llŷr. For the author of *Branwen* relates briefly the victory of the son of Beli over the son of Brân,[4] and this feud reappears in Geoffrey's *Historia* as a highly elaborate narrative of the wars between Brennius and Belinus, in which Belinus was victorious.[5] Moreover, Geoffrey attributes to Brennius a reputation for lavish hospitality which, as we know, was an outstanding characteristic of Brân son of Llŷr. We read of Brennius that 'he was generous in giving food, shutting his door to no man';[6] whereas the banquets provided by Brân seem to have become proverbial as the 'Hospitality of Brân' or the 'Hospitality of the Wondrous Head'.[7]

---

[1] Geoffrey of Monmouth, *Historia Regum Britanniae*, ed. A. Griscom (London, New York, 1929), p. 277.   [2] Ibid., pp. 273, 276.
[3] *Arthurian Literature in the Middle Ages*, ed. R. S. Loomis (Oxford, 1959), pp. 82–85.   [4] Loth, op. cit. i. 146 f.
[5] Geoffrey of Monmouth, op. cit., pp. 277–81.   [6] Ibid., pp. 283 f.
[7] See p. 140, n. 2, and H. Newstead, op. cit., p. 19.

If we grant, then, that Geoffrey's Brennius and the Brân of the Welsh translation each represents a sort of trinity, in which there are features of the Gaulish chief Brennus, who sacked Rome in 390 B.C.,[1] of a probably historic Brân son of Dumngual Moilmut, mentioned in a tenth-century Welsh genealogy,[2] and of the euhemerized sea-god Brân son of Llŷr, then it is entirely possible that in Geoffrey's brief treatment of Brennius's marriage to the King of Norway's daughter, he introduced an authentic legend of Brân son of Llŷr. If so, there is no difficulty in understanding how the same tradition turns up in *Sone*, which preserves so clearly other vestiges of his legendary history.

How the tradition of Brân's marriage to the King of Norway's daughter originated no one can say for certain, but it is interesting to observe that the Welsh word for Norway is Llychlyn, and that Rhŷs asserted that the original meaning of Llychlyn was 'the fabulous land beneath the lakes or waves of the sea'.[3] If that be so, it would not be unnatural for Brân, the sea-god, to wed a princess of Llychlyn, nor is it at all improbable that such a legend survived in Geoffrey's *Historia* as the marriage of Brennius with the daughter of the King of Norway, and in *Sone de Nansai* as the wedding of the Fisher King with the same lady.

Two features of the Grail story in *Sone de Nansai* are most likely to strike the modern reader with amazement: first, the equation of the Fisher King with Joseph of Arimathea, the one derived from pagan Welsh tradition, the other from the Holy Scriptures and the early Christian apocrypha; second, the survival in a romance such as *Sone* of so primitive a superstition as the sympathetic relation between the health of the King and the fertility of his kingdom. For the first of these strange features an explanation will be offered at the end of Chapter XIV, dealing with Joseph of Arimathea. The second feature,

---

[1] J. A. MacCulloch in Hastings, *Encyclopaedia of Religion and Ethics* (London, 1911), iii. 288. E. Faral, *Légende Arthurienne* (Paris, 1929), ii. 135 f. Newstead in *Romanic Review*, xxxvi, pp. 15–17.

[2] Loth, op. cit., ii. 335.

[3] J. Rhŷs, *Studies in the Arthurian Legend* (Oxford, 1891), p. 11.

as we have noted already, seems to reflect the account in *Branwen* of the wounding of Brân in the foot and the subsequent desolation of two islands. But, whereas the early Welsh text mentions no causal nexus, the late French text makes this heathenish concept quite plain. That the tradition was Welsh is confirmed by the description in *Lludd and Llevelys* of a plague which, though from a different cause, fell upon Britain. 'The men lost their colour and their strength, and women the infants in their wombs. . . . Animals, trees, the earth, the waters, all remained sterile.' This spell matches the enchantment which, we remember, afflicted Logres when the Fisher King was maimed in the thighs and below.

It is clear, moreover, that this is a euphemism for sterilization, as Jessie Weston first proposed and as Brunel has proved.[1] In fact, a rationalized version of the belief in a nexus between the vital forces of a ruler and those of a realm is recorded in the twelfth century by the Welshman Walter Map:[2] in the parish where a certain Alan, King of Brittany, was castrated no animals could bring forth young, but when ripe for bearing they went outside the parish to deliver their offspring.

What conclusion can one draw from all this but that the late, realistic, and pious romance of *Sone de Nansai* preserves what, in some ways, is the most faithful and primitive version of the legends of Brân son of Llŷr?[3]

---

[1] J. L. Weston, *The Quest of the Holy Grail* (London, 1903), p. 80. *Romania*, lxxxi (1960), pp. 31–43.

[2] *De Nugis Curialium*, trans. F. Tupper and M. B. Ogle (London, 1924), p. 242.

[3] See above, pp. 56, 138, 141, and below, pp. 216, 248.

XI

The Prose *Lancelot*: Combat and Scandal in the Castle of King Pelles

As was pointed out in Chapter I, the *Lancelot* and the *Queste del Saint Graal* form the third and fourth parts of a huge cyclic work in prose which, because of its popularity as indicated by the number of surviving manuscripts and of redactions in other languages, is known as the Vulgate cycle. Dante and Chaucer were both familiar with the *Lancelot*, reacting to it in quite different ways, and printed editions were brought out as late as the sixteenth century. The whole vast corpus was probably composed between 1215 and 1230, perhaps in the same county of Champagne which gave us our first Lancelot romance and our first quest of the Grail, the poems of Chrétien de Troyes.

The statements in the manuscripts of the Vulgate *Lancelot*, *Queste*, and *Mort Artu* that Master Walter Map was the author is something of a puzzle.[1] He was indeed a man of learning, partly of Welsh blood, was employed as a clerk of Henry II's court, and died in 1209. Some scholars have held, on the basis of rather slender evidence, that he was the author of a lost romance about Lancelot which the author of the Prose *Lancelot* used as one of his sources; thus, it is suggested, Map's name was erroneously attached first to the *Lancelot* and then carried over into the *Queste* and the *Mort Artu*. But even if this hypothesis be accepted and some of Map's work may be embedded in episodes of the prose romance of *Lancelot*—as indeed is much of Chrétien's *Chevalier de la Charrette*—it is certain that the Vulgate cycle was composed on the Continent, and that is only one of several strong reasons for ruling Map out.

---

[1] On Map's connection with the Vulgate cycle see Bruce, *Evolution*, i. 368–73.

This grandiose work was evidently composed over a number of years by several authors; differences in outlook and interest and artistic capacity are very clear. Still, Ferdinand Lot was able to show that the *Lancelot*, *Queste*, and *Mort Artu* were elaborately held together by forecasts to the future, throwbacks to the past, and cross-references.[1] The three books, though they form the conclusion of the cycle, were the first to be written, and they developed as a dominant theme the absorbing passion of Lancelot for Guenevere, its effect on his quest for the Grail, and its consequence in the downfall of King Arthur and the order of the Round Table. Interwoven with this main pattern is a version of the Grail legend very different from any of those previously studied, so different, in fact, that it must have been derived largely from other branches of Grail tradition. It is the version best known to British and American readers since Malory included a felicitous and abridged translation of a large part in his book, and so passed this form of the Grail legend on to Tennyson.

It is a very curious fact that though the *Lancelot* and the *Queste* provide a fairly consistent story of the Grail, beginning with the adventure of Gawain at the Grail castle and ending with Galahad's death in the land of Sarras, and though this story would seem to have taken shape in a single mind, it is split between the two romances, and reveals a wide cleavage in artistry, clarity of purpose, and religious fervour between the two parts. To this particular problem of diversity in unity a solution will be offered in the next chapter dealing with the *Queste*. Our immediate concern is with the episodes in the *Lancelot* which prepare us for the *Queste*, and which, scattered between miscellaneous combats, imprisonments, abductions, and rescues, can be assigned to one of the inferior authors who worked on the Vulgate cycle.

The Prose *Lancelot* recounts five visits to the Grail castle. Of these the first is Gawain's and ends with his humiliating expulsion; the second is Lancelot's, and is the occasion of his begetting Galahad on the Grail King's daughter; Bors on a

---

[1] *Étude sur le Lancelot en Prose* (Paris, 1918).

first visit has much the same experience as Gawain but comes through triumphant, and on a second visit makes the acquaintance of the infant Galahad; Lancelot, rendered insane by the jealous anger of Guenevere, returns by chance to the castle of the Grail and is cured by its magic virtue. Let us now take up the adventures of Gawain, the first to visit the holy castle.

We find him riding at vespertide up the chief street leading to the great tower.[1] A damsel, sitting in a scalding bath, implored him to lift her out, but his strength was unequal to the task—a forewarning of his subsequent failures. Nevertheless, he was received in the hall with joy by squires and knights as soon as he disclosed his name. Let me now quote from Jessie Weston's translation,[2] with a few borrowings from Sommer's edition and some corrections.

There came forth from a chamber a knight, who led with him many other knights; and he was the fairest man that Sir Gawain had beheld since he left his own land, and had the semblance of one of noble birth. When they who were within saw him coming, they spoke to Sir Gawain, saying, 'Behold the King!' Sir Gawain rose to his feet and bade him welcome, and the other returned his greeting with a right fair countenance and bade him sit beside him; and he asked him who he was, and he told him the truth. Then was the King right joyful, for greatly did he desire to see Sir Gawain; so they spoke together.

While they spoke thus, Sir Gawain beheld and saw a white dove, which bore in its beak a censer of the richest gold. As soon as it came there, the hall (palais) was filled with the sweetest odours that heart of man might conceive, or tongue of man tell. All that were there became mute and spoke never a word more, but kneeled down as soon as they beheld the dove. It entered a chamber, and at once the folk in the hall ran and set the tables and the cloths on the dais; and they sat them down, the one and the other, and never a man of them spoke a word. Sir Gawain marvelled greatly at this adventure, but he sat him down with the others, and beheld and saw how they were all in prayers and orisons.

<hr/>

[1] Sommer, *Vulgate Version*, iv. 343–7.
[2] *Sir Gawain at the Grail Castle* (London, 1903), pp. 54–67.

*Then there came forth from the chamber where the dove had en-
tered a damsel, the fairest he had beheld any day of his life. Her hair
was cunningly plaited and bound, and her face was fair to look upon.
She was beautiful with all the beauty that pertaineth unto a woman,
none fairer was ever seen on earth. She came forth from the chamber
bearing in her hands the richest vessel that might be beheld by the eye
of mortal man. It was made in the semblance of a chalice, and she
held it on high above her head, so that all those who were there saw
it and bowed.*

*Sir Gawain looked on the vessel, and esteemed it highly in his
heart, yet knew not of what it was wrought; for it was not of wood
nor of any manner of metal; nor was it in any wise of stone, nor of
horn, nor of bone, and therefore was he sore abashed. Then he looked
on the maiden, and marvelled more at her beauty than at the wonder
of the vessel, for never had he seen a damsel with whom she might be
compared; and he mused so fixedly upon her that he had no thought
for aught beside. But as the damsel passed before the knights, the
holy vessel in her hand, all kneeled before it; and forthwith were the
tables replenished with the choicest meats in the world, and the hall
filled with the sweetest odours.*

*When the damsel had passed the dais once, she returned into the
chamber whence she came, and Sir Gawain followed her with his
eyes as long as he might, and when he saw her no more, he looked on
the table before him, and saw naught that he might eat, for it was
void and bare; yet was there none other but had great plenty, yea, a
surfeit of viands, before him. When he saw this he was sore abashed,
and knew not what he might say or do, since he deemed well that he
had in some point transgressed, and for that transgression was his
meat lacking to him. So he withheld him from asking till the tables
were taken away. But then all gat them forth from the palace, so that
Sir Gawain wist not what had become of them, and knew naught
but that he was left alone; and when he himself would have gone
forth into the courtyard below, he might no longer do so, for all the
doors were fast shut.*

*When he saw this, he leaned him against one of the windows of
the hall and fell into deep thought. Then there came forth from
a chamber a dwarf, bearing a rod in his hand, and when he saw*

Sir Gawain, he cried upon him: 'What is this evil knight, for by ill chance are ye leaning at our windows? Flee ye from hence, here may ye not remain, for in you is much vileness. Go, get ye to rest in one of these chambers that none behold you here!' Then he raised his rod to smite Sir Gawain, but he put forth his hand and took it from him. When the dwarf saw this, he cried, 'Ha! sir knight, it will avail you nothing, for ye may not escape hence without shaming!'

Then he gat him into a chamber; and Sir Gawain looked toward the head of the hall, and saw there one of the richest couches in the world, and he made haste towards it, for there would he lie. But even as he sat him down, he heard a maiden cry upon him, 'Ha! sir knight, thou diest if thou liest there unarmed, for it is the Couch Adventurous, but look, yonder lie arms, take them, and lie down if ye will.'

Sir Gawain ran swiftly where he saw the armour and armed himself as best he might, and when he was armed he sat him down straightway. But scarce had he set him down when he heard a cry, the most fell he had ever heard, and he thought well that it was the voice of the Fiend. Then there came forth swiftly from a chamber a lance of which the blade was all afire, and it smote Sir Gawain so hardly that despite shield and hauberk it pierced his shoulder through and through. He fell swooning, but anon he felt how someone drew out the lance, yet he saw not who laid hand to it. Then was he much afeard, for the wound bled sorely, yet would he not rise up from the couch, but said within himself that though he died for it yet would he behold more of the marvels—yet he knew well that he was sore wounded.

Gawain next saw a huge dragon which cast five hundred young dragons out of its mouth, and, after fighting with a leopard, killed its own young. There followed a procession of twelve lamenting maidens, who made their orisons before the chamber where the dove had entered, and then departed. A big knight, all armed, engaged Gawain in combat till both fell in a swoon on the floor. Celestial music was heard.

Then Sir Gawain saw come forth from a chamber the damsel who the evening before had borne the holy vessel before the table. Before her came two tapers and two censers. When she came even to the middle of the hall, she set the holy vessel before her on a table of silver. Sir Gawain beheld all around censers to the number of ten, which ceased not to give forth perfume. All the voices began to sing together more sweetly than the heart of man might think or mouth speak. All said with one voice, 'Blessed be the Father of Heaven.'

When the song had endured a long time, the damsel took the holy vessel and bore it into the chamber whence she had come, and then were the voices silent as if they had departed thence, and all the windows of the hall opened and closed again, and the hall grew dark so that Sir Gawain saw naught, but of this was he well aware that he felt hale and whole as if naught had ailed him, nor might he feel aught of the wound in his shoulder, for it was right well healed. Then he arose joyous and glad at heart, and went seeking the knight who had fought with him, but he found him not.

Then he heard as it were a great folk that drew nigh him, and he felt how they laid hold on him by the arms and the shoulders, and the feet and the head, and bore him forth from the hall, and bound him fast to a cart that was in the midst of the court, and forthwith he fell asleep.

In the morning when the sun was risen Sir Gawain awoke, and lo! he was in the vilest cart in the world, and he saw that his shield was bound on the shaft before him, and his steed was made fast behind. But in the shafts was a horse so thin and so meagre to look at that it seemed scarce worth twopence. When he found himself in such a sorry case he made sore lament, for it seemed to him that no man was ever so sorely shamed, and he would rather be dead than living.

Then came towards him a damsel, bearing a scourge in her hand, and she began to smite the steed and to lead it swiftly through the town. When the minstrels saw the knight in the cart, they followed shouting and crying, and they threw at him dung, old shoes, and mud in great plenty. Thus they followed him forth from the town, pelting him with all the muck that they could find.

Even to the most casual reader, it is obvious that the long story of Gawain's eerie experiences at the Grail castle differs widely from any account of a visit which we have previously

considered, and it is a logical inference that the author must
have drawn on different traditional sources. To be sure, the
handsome King who led the knights into the hall may have
been taken over from the First Continuation of the *Conte del
Graal*; the precious vessel in the hands of a beautiful maiden is
already familiar; and the appearance of viands on the table as
the maiden passed is a feature found also in Manessier's continuation. But the vessel is now specifically, though mistakenly, described as a chalice, and has acquired a new property. It
denied food to Gawain, because, as he was informed after his
expulsion from the castle, he failed to display suitable humility
at the passing of the vessel. And one may reasonably surmise
that it was this same failure to show reverence to the relic
which was supposed to justify the suffering and ignominy
which he had to endure. Whence did the Grail acquire this
power of discriminating between the worthy and the unworthy? It is not attached to the *Dysgl* of Rhydderch, the
Welsh counterpart of the Grail, but something like it is ascribed
to another vessel in the list of the Thirteen Treasures of the
Isle of Britain, the Cauldron of Tyrnog. 'If meat were put
in it to boil for a coward, it would never be boiled, but if
meat were put in it for a brave man, it would be boiled forthwith.'[1] This must have been an ancient tradition since in the
archaic poem, *The Spoils of Annwn*, cited in Chapter IX, when
the question is put concerning the nature of the Cauldron of
the 'Head of Annwn' (probably the title of Brân son of Llŷr),
the answer is, 'It will not boil the food of a coward.'[2] Of
course, a chalice is not a cauldron and Gawain was no coward,
but the faculty of discrimination was evidently a common
property of Welsh talismanic vessels and was likely to be
attracted, sooner or later, to the Grail.

What of the other startling innovations, especially those
which seem so incongruous with the sanctity of the Grail
castle and which remind one of the gloomy, spectre-haunted

[1] Guest, *Mabinogion*, Everyman's Lib., p. 328. Loomis, *Wales*, p. 157. *Trioedd
Ynys Prydein*, ed. R. Bromwich (Cardiff, 1961), pp. 240, 242, 246.
[2] Loomis, *Wales*, pp. 135, 156–8.

edifices beloved of the Gothic novelists, such as the castles of Otranto and Udolpho? An analysis of Gawain's nocturnal experiences reveals that they are made up of two originally separate narrative patterns: the first a local legend about the ruins of Dinas Brân near Llangollen, which, as we saw in Chapter IX, seems to have inspired the eerie ending of *Perlesvaus*; the second a recurrent Arthurian tradition about the Couch Adventurous or the Perilous Bed, which, originating in Ireland, must have passed through Wales, and so found its way into the French romances. The two narratives formed a natural combination since both dealt with a knight who in spite of warnings dared the nocturnal perils of a castle.

The Dinas Brân legend must have enjoyed a considerable circulation, for not only was it recorded in the Anglo-Norman romance of *Fouke Fitz Warin*, not only did it affect the conclusion of *Perlesvaus*, but it was incorporated in the form of two consecutive episodes in *Perlesvaus*, with Perceval as the hero.[1] So one should not attribute too lightly to coincidence the resemblance between the nocturnal experiences of Gawain in the *palais* (great hall) of the Grail castle and those of Payn Peverel in the *palais* of Chastiel Bran. Payn, fully armed, entered the *palais*, and when night fell, the weather became foul and black, and a wild tempest of thunder and lightning arose. A devil in the form of a giant assailed him with a club, and was subdued only after a fierce fight.[2] The essential features, then, of the Dinas Brân legend reappear in Gawain's visit to the Grail castle, and Dinas Brân, we have already seen, must have been a traditional site of the Grail castle. We must admit that there is nothing diabolic about the big knight who attacked Gawain, but this discrepancy is understandable; such infernal attributes could not be tolerated in a denizen of a castle consecrated by the presence of the Grail.

The experiences of Gawain, not paralleled by those of Payn Peverel and not accounted for by familiar Grail tradition, are

[1] H. Newstead, *Bran the Blessed in Arthurian Romance* (New York, 1939), pp. 97–99. *Romanische Forschungen*, xiv (1931), pp. 88 f. See above, p. 121, n. 2.
[2] *Fouke Fitz Warin*, ed. L. Brandin (Paris, 1930), pp. 3–7.

neatly explained by the addition of a stock adventure of the
Matter of Britain, the adventure of the Perilous Bed.[1] Chrétien gave a very brief version of it in his *Lancelot* and a longer
form in the *Conte del Graal*. The first of these corresponds to
the Prose *Lancelot* on several points: a splendid bed set up in
the hall; a warning damsel; occupancy of the bed by a hero in
spite of a damsel's warning; the descent of a flaming lance at
night.[2] The second of Chrétien's versions corresponds to the
Prose *Lancelot* on the following points: Gawain as hero; the
setting a *palais*; the time, night; the rich bed; the discharge of
missiles with a crashing sound.[3] By a happy chance a much
fuller version of the Perilous Bed adventure is preserved in the
fourteenth-century romance of *Artus de la Petite Bretagne*,[4]
and this, on examination, discloses its origin in an episode of
the eighth-century saga, *Bricriu's Feast*, which has long been
recognized as close to the source of other Arthurian tales,
especially the Beheading Test.[5] Twelve marked resemblances
link the account of Artus's testing in the castle of the Perilous
Bed adventure to the account of Cuchulainn's testing in the
seat of watch in Curoi's castle. To present in detail the evidence for this connexion would take us too far from our main
concern with the Grail castle and its occupants, but it is available in two of my books and in *PMLA* for 1933, for the
curious reader to consult.[6] Moreover, he will discover that
the adventure in its archaic Irish form is steeped in mythology;
it represents the test of a hero in the revolving home of a sky-
god. But of this primitive pattern the Prose *Lancelot* retained
only vestiges—the hero who essays alone the nocturnal perils
of a castle in the absence of its lord, the shaft discharged at him,
and the appearance of monsters.

The three cognate French versions of the Perilous Bed adventure just mentioned do not place it in the castle of the

[1] Loomis, *Arthurian Tradition*, pp. 205–9.
[2] Chrétien de Troyes, *Karrenritter*, ed. W. Foerster (Halle, 1899), vss. 399–538.
[3] Chrétien de Troyes, *Percevalroman*, ed. A. Hilka (Halle, 1932), vss. 7676–937.
[4] *Livre de Petit Artus*, in New York Public Library, fols. 18 r, 21 v, 50 r, 52 v–61 v.
[5] R. Thurneysen, *Irische Helden- und Königsage*, pp. 449, 458–60
[6] See above, n. 1. *Celtic Myth and Arthurian Romance* (New York, 1927), pp.
158–75. *PMLA*, xlviii, pp. 1000–18.

Grail, but it would seem that the author of the *Lancelot* was not the first to do so, nor the first to conclude it with the ignominious departure of the hero. For in the First Continuation of the *Conte del Graal*[1] we read that Gawain's brother, Guerehes or Garahes, entered one of the richest castles in the world, finding not a soul within, and passed into a chamber with three magnificent beds, and rested on one of them for a moment. He entered a second room with two rich beds, and then a third room with a single bed. Descending into a garden he found in a tent a tall wounded knight, lying on a couch and being fed by a dwarf and a damsel. The tall knight was furious at Guerehes's intrusion, and presently a tiny knight on a small horse rode in. Guerehes mounted, but in the ensuing combat was hurled from his saddle by the midget. He yielded and was permitted to depart on condition that he would return at the end of a year. As he rode away through the street of the town, the butchers and fishmongers pelted him with offal.

Without much doubt this narrative must have grown out of the same composite story of the humiliation of a knight in the Grail castle as did the adventures of Gawain related in the *Lancelot*, but the various elements are given a very different treatment. Six beds are described in impressive detail, which suggests that they have some function, but they are promptly forgotten. The tall wounded knight, fed by a maiden from a hanap, is presumably the Maimed King, but his couch is placed in a garden, not in a hall, and he is anything but a hospitable host. The aggressive dwarf of the *Lancelot*, whom Gawain easily disarms, is changed into a formidable antagonist. Gawain's exit in the cart is more ignominious than Guerehes's exit on horseback. Nevertheless, a cognate relationship between the two stories can hardly be denied.

The author of the Prose *Lancelot* was not responsible for the infelicitous introduction of nocturnal combats into the setting of the Grail castle; they seem to have come to him ultimately from the local traditions of Dinas Brân. But he can be blamed for preluding the adventures of Gawain at the castle with the

---

[1] W. Roach, *Continuations of the Old French 'Perceval'*, iii. 548–71.

completely irrelevant struggle to rescue the damsel from the scalding bath. He attempted to impose a certain unity and meaning on the series of experiences by representing them as tests which reveal the unworthiness of Gawain and which forecast the failures which await him in the *Queste del Saint Graal*. But most readers will feel that the attempt was itself a failure.

The same ineptitude characterizes the treatment of Lancelot's first visit to the Grail castle. After illustrating Lancelot's superiority to Gawain by his deliverance of the damsel from the scalding bath—the situation of which T. H. White has given a delicious burlesque in *The Ill-made Knight*, (incorporated in *The Once and Future King*)—the author proceeds to relate Lancelot's arrival at the castle, and here we may quote from Malory's abridged and somewhat altered version.[1]

> *Therewithal came King Pelles, the good and noble knight, and saluted Sir Lancelot, and he him again. 'Fair knight,' said the King, 'what is your name? I require you of your knighthood, tell me!'*
>
> *'Sir,' said Lancelot, 'wit you well my name is Sir Lancelot du Lake.'*
>
> *'And my name is,' said the King, 'Pelles, King of the foreign country, and cousin nigh unto Joseph of Arimathea.'*
>
> *And then either of them made much of other, and so they went into the castle to take their repast. And anon there came in a dove at a window, and in her mouth there seemed a little censer of gold. And therewithal there was such a savour as all the spicery of the world had been there. And forthwithal there was upon the table all manner of meats and drinks that they could think upon. So came in a damsel passing fair and young, and she bare a vessel of gold betwixt her hands; and thereto the King kneeled devoutly, and said his prayers, and so did all that were there.*
>
> *'O Jesu,' said Sir Lancelot, 'what may this mean?'*
>
> *'This is,' said the King, 'the richest thing that any man hath living. And when this thing goeth about, the Round Table shall be*

---

[1] Book xi, chs. 1–3. See Sommer, *Vulgate Version*, v. 106–11.

broken; and wit thou well,' said the King, 'this is the holy Sank-greal that ye have here seen.'

So the King and Sir Lancelot led their life the most part of that day. And fain would King Pelles have found the mean to have had Sir Lancelot to have lain by his daughter, fair Elaine [who is in fact the Grail Bearer]. And for this intent: the King knew well that Sir Lancelot should get a child upon his daughter, the which should be named Sir Galahad, the good knight, by whom all the foreign country should be brought out of danger, and by him the Holy Grail should be achieved. Then came forth a lady that hight Dame Brisen, and she said unto the King: 'Sir, wit ye well Sir Lancelot loveth no lady in the world but all only Queen Guenevere; and therefore work ye by counsel, and I shall make him to lie with your daughter, and he shall not wit but that he lieth with Queen Guenevere.'

'O fair lady, Dame Brisen,' said the King, 'hope ye to bring this about?'

'Sir,' said she, 'upon pain of my life let me deal.' For this Brisen was one of the greatest enchantresses that was at that time in the world living.

Then anon by Dame Brisen's wit she made one to come to Sir Lancelot that he knew well. And this man brought him a ring from Queen Guenevere like as it had come from her, and such one as she was wont for the most part to wear; and when Sir Lancelot saw that token, wit ye well he was never so fain.

'Where is my lady?' said Sir Lancelot.

'In the castle of Case,' said the messenger, 'but five miles hence.'

Then Sir Lancelot thought to be there the same night. And then this Brisen by the commandment of King Pelles let send Elaine to this castle with twenty-five knights unto the castle of Case. Then Sir Lancelot against night rode unto that castle, and there anon he was received worshipfully with such people, to his seeming, as were about Queen Guenevere secret. So when Sir Lancelot was alit, he asked where the Queen was. So Dame Brisen said she was in her bed; and then the people were avoided, and Sir Lancelot was led unto his chamber. And then Dame Brisen brought Sir Lancelot a cupful of wine; and anon as he had drunken that wine he was so assotted and mad that he might make no delay, but without any let *he went to bed; and he weened that maiden Elaine had been Queen Guenevere. Wit you well that Sir Lancelot was glad, and so was that lady Elaine that she had gotten Sir Lancelot in her arms. For well she knew that same night should be gotten upon her Galahad, that should prove the best knight of the world; and so they lay together until undern of the morn; and all the windows and holes of that chamber were stopped that no manner of day might be seen. And then Sir Lancelot remembered him, and he arose up and went to the window. And anon as he had unshut the window, the enchantment was gone; then he knew himself that he had done amiss.*

There are several curious points in this narrative which will not have escaped the attentive reader. Malory by his use of both 'the Sankgreal' and 'the Holy Grail' in reference to the vessel borne by King Pelles's daughter illustrates that confusion between *Sang Real* (royal blood) and *Saint Graal* which was noted in Chapter III—a confusion encouraged by the mistaken belief that the Grail took the form of a chalice.

King Pelles himself is not the wounded or languishing king who appeared as lord of the Grail castle in most of the narratives we have studied; in fact, he later mentions the Maimed King, the Fisher King, as an unseen occupant of the castle,[1] and this latter does turn up eventually in the *Queste del Saint Graal* to be healed by Galahad. The name Pelles, moreover, is derived from Beli, as was shown in Chapter IX, whereas the name of the Fisher King, Bron, was derived from Brân. Here Pelles has lost the title 'King of the Short Folk', which he bore in *Perlesvaus* and which linked him to Bilis, King of the dwarfs; he is not confused with Perceval's Hermit Uncle, and he plays his original part as lord of a faery castle, 'castrum fatale', Kair Belli, mentioned by John of Cornwall.[2]

The substitution of Pelles for the Maimed King was due, therefore, not to any mere whim of the author but to the existence of a rival tradition, probably originating in Wales and Cornwall, which attributed to Beli a role similar to that of Brân as a host to wandering knights in his castle of wonders. This conclusion is neatly corroborated by the fact that an

[1] Sommer, *Vulgate Version*, v. 303.   [2] See above, p. 111.

exactly corresponding substitution has taken place in the character of the Grail Bearer. King Pelles's daughter, Elaine, never appears in a repellent aspect at Arthur's court to upbraid a visitor to the Grail castle for his failure, as does the Grail Bearer in *Peredur* and *Perlesvaus*. She is not the hero's cousin who is concerned with his wreaking vengeance on his kinsman's murderer, as are the damsels of the Grail castle in Manessier and *Peredur*. She cannot be descended, therefore, from the same Irish prototypes as are the damsels we have previously considered.

To determine her origin let us see what more we can learn of her in the *Lancelot*. In the course of Gawain's visit her vessel displayed a property which we have not observed before; it healed Gawain of the wound in his shoulder, and later it cured Lancelot's madness.[1] Elaine herself was involved in a liaison with Lancelot, as we have seen, and bore him a son of matchless prowess in arms, Galahad, who, when grown up, fought with his father incognito. She nursed a vain passion for Lancelot and provoked the anger of Guenevere. She dwelt for a time with her maidens on a winterless Isle of Joy.[2]

Surprising as it may seem, in all these respects she has a counterpart in either Morgan le Fay or Morgan's sister Morcades. There is no attribute of Morgan's better authenticated than her power of healing.[3] Morcades was involved in a liaison with Lot and bore a son, Gawain, who in early tradition was the nonpareil of Arthur's knights and who fought with his father incognito.[4] Morgan nursed a vain passion for Lancelot and earned the hatred of Guenevere.[5] Morgan and her maidens dwelt on the winterless Isle of Avalon.[6] Can there be any doubt that Elaine, whose story differs so radically

[1] Sommer, *Vulgate Version*, v. 400.   [2] Ibid., p. 403.

[3] Geoffrey of Monmouth, *Vita Merlini*, ed. J. J. Parry (Urbana, 1925), vss. 918–21. Hartmann von Aue, *Erek*, ed. M. Haupt (Leipzig, 1871), vss. 5213–5. A. Graf, *I Complementi della Chanson d'Huon de Bordeaux*, i, *Auberon* (Halle, 1878), vss. 1221–6. Chrétien de Troyes, *Erec*, vss. 4218–28; *Ivain*, vss. 2952–5.

[4] *Romania*, xxxix (1910), pp. 19–23; Sommer, *Vulgate Version*, ii. 317.

[5] Sommer, op. cit. iv. 123–8; v. 193, 215 f.

[6] L. A. Paton, *Studies in the Fairy Mythology of Arthurian Romance* (Boston, 1903; New York, 1959), pp. 45 f.

from that of the other Grail Bearers, is modelled on Morgan le Fay and her sister? She must, therefore, have the same prototype.

The casting of Morgan in this unexpected part of Grail Bearer was not due to the author's wild caprice; it was based on tradition; in fact, on the same tradition which replaced Bron, the Maimed King, by Pelles. Over a hundred years ago Lady Guest pointed out that the Welsh counterpart of Morgan was Modron[1]—a statement strangely overlooked by later scholars, but amply substantiated by the fact that Morgan's father was Avalloc, and her son by Urien was Ivain (Morgan being no monogamist), whereas an authentic Welsh triad says explicitly that Modron, daughter of Avallach, bore in her womb Owain son of Urien.[2] And who was the father of Avallach? Beli.[3] Modron was therefore the granddaughter of Beli, while her counterpart and inferentially her literary descendant, Morgan, appears in Malory as Elaine the daughter of Pelles.

Unfortunately Welsh literature tells us even less about Modron than about Beli; probably their heathenish origin was remembered, as was that of Gwynn ap Nudd. But all the linguistic experts agree that her name is a regular Welsh development from that of the great goddess Matrona, worshipped by the Celts from Cisalpine Gaul to the lower Rhine.[4] Knowledge of Morgan's divine descent carried right down through the Middle Ages, since three medieval authors refer to her respectively as *dea*, *gottine*, and *goddess*.[5] One French manuscript offers a rationalistic explanation.[6] 'It was true that Morgan, the sister of Arthur, knew much of enchantment and spells, surpassing all women; and by reason of the great attention she gave to them she left and forsook the company of folk and spent day and night in the great, deep, and lonely (*soutaines*) forests, so that many folk, of whom there were

---

[1] Guest, *Mabinogion*, Everyman's Lib., p. 357, n. 3.

[2] Loth, *Mabinogion*, ii. 284. Loomis, *Arthurian Tradition*, pp. 91, 269–72.

[3] Loth, ii. 336. J. Rhŷs, *Studies in the Arthurian Legend* (Oxford, 1891), pp. 335–7.   [4] Loomis, *Wales*, pp. 128 f.

[5] Paton, op. cit., p. 35, n. 2. Hartmann von Aue, *Erek*, vs. 5161. *Gawain and the Green Knight*, vs. 2452.

[6] *Zeitschrift für französische Sprache und Literatur*, xxxi (1907), p. 252.

numerous fools throughout the land, said that she was not a
woman, but they called her Morgan the goddess (*déesse*).'

Morgan naturally inherited certain characteristic roles and
powers from the Celtic goddess, and so did King Pelles's
daughter. Like Morgan she possessed supernatural therapeutic
power, for she healed the wounds inflicted on Gawain in the
palais of Corbenic by the fiery lance and the big knight. The
Isle of Joy, where she later dwelt with her maidens, is easily
recognizable, like Morgan's Isle of Avalon, as a pagan Elysium,
such as the Isle of Women in the Irish voyages.[1] Her union
with Lancelot out of wedlock and her bearing him a glorious
son not only match the role of Morcades as the mistress of Lot
and mother of Gawain, but may also have their remote origin
in the pagan Irish tradition of the mating of the goddess
Dechtire with the god Lug, which resulted in the conception
of Cuchulainn, the hero of the Ulster cycle.[2] There is ample
evidence—in fact, too much to reproduce here—that Lug was
the Irish original of both Lot and Lancelot,[3] and Cuchulainn
the original of Gawain.[4] It is a logical conclusion that Morcades and King Pelles's daughter, as the respective mothers of
Gawain and Galahad, have inherited the unsanctified role of
the goddess Dechtire, Modron being the intermediary.

If one accepts, then, the hypothesis that King Pelles's
daughter is a figure immediately derived from Morgan and
more remotely from Modron and Dechtire, and if one
realizes how powerful was the tradition behind her composite
story, one can readily understand how difficult was the position in which the author of the *Lancelot* was placed. He had
to adjust that traditional story to two other well-established
données. Chrétien de Troyes had made it impossible to think
of Lancelot otherwise than as the utterly faithful paramour of

[1] T. P. Cross, C. N. Slover, *Ancient Irish Tales*, p. 595. Dillon, *Ancient Irish Literature*, pp. 106, 128. *Romania*, lix (1933), pp. 557 f., 560–2.

[2] Cross and Slover, op. cit., pp. 133–6.

[3] *Bulletin Bibliographique de la Société Internationale Arthurienne*, No. 3 (1951), pp. 69–73. Ulrich von Zatzikhoven, *Lanzelet*, trans. K. G. T. Webster (New York, 1951), pp. 15–18.   [4] Loomis, *Arthurian Tradition*, pp. 147–53.

Guenevere; hence he could be brought to lie with King Pelles's daughter only through deception and only in the belief that he was lying with the Queen. Even more difficult to reconcile with the role of Pelles's daughter as the unmarried mother of a bastard—to use plain language—was the fact that the Grail, with which her healing vessel had been identified, had come to be regarded as a relic of the Passion and every person connected with it, including her father and her son, was surrounded by an aura of holiness.

A man of far greater ingenuity than the author of the *Lancelot* would have been baffled to find a satisfactory way of harmonizing three such stubbornly irreconcilable traditions. His solution, as we have seen, was crude, even offensive. He brought Lancelot to the bed of Elaine, but in doing so he debased King Pelles, that 'good and noble knight', to the point of authorizing the deception of Lancelot and acting as pander to his own daughter. As for her, she readily enters into the scheme and seems to think it right and proper to fornicate, in anticipation of the fact that her son is destined to achieve the Holy Grail! The author was not unaware that some of his readers might censure her conduct; he declared her unfit to continue in her office of Grail Bearer and took pains to point out that if the flower of her virginity was spoiled it was recompensed by the birth of that flower of virginity, Galahad.[1]

The notion of divinely ordained and eventually beneficial sins was familiar, of course, to the author. There was Jacob's deception of his father Isaac, and Judah's lying with his daughter-in-law; and, supreme example, there was the *felix culpa*, the disobedience of Adam and Eve, without which original sin there would have been no Redeemer, no Divine Sacrifice. Indeed, the parallel between the conception of Christ, the Messiah, and the conception of that messianic figure, Galahad, must have been at least vaguely present in the author's mind, and Bruce went so far as to accuse him of parodying the most sacred of all subjects.[2] That he had any such blasphemous intention is not to be conceded, but it must

---

[1] Sommer, op. cit. v. 111.   [2] Bruce, *Evolution*, i. 260.

be granted that he lent himself to the charge. For the modern thoughtful reader there can be few passages in Arthurian romance as distasteful and as repellent to reason as the sanctimonious plotting that went into the begetting of Galahad. But the responsibility was not wholly the author's. He undertook an impossible task.

The story of Lancelot, King Pelles's daughter, and Galahad is continued, though with many irrelevant interruptions, to the end of the Prose *Lancelot*, and has been skilfully summarized by Malory. Bors, Lancelot's cousin, twice visits the Grail castle, and on the second occasion sees the child Galahad, learns the secret of his birth, and, like Gawain, undergoes the perils of the adventurous hall, but without the final humiliation of the cart.[1] Brisen a second time dupes Lancelot into lying with Elaine under the impression that he has Guenevere in his arms—which does not speak well for his intelligence.[2] This time Guenevere catches him in the act and banishes him from her sight, whereupon he runs mad. Coming by chance to the Grail castle, he is discovered by Pelles's daughter, is brought into the 'palace adventurous', and is restored to sanity by the Grail.[3] At his own request, he is taken to the Isle of Joy, where there is no winter so severe that Pelles's daughter and her maidens do not dance every day round a pine.[4] After four years Guenevere, repentant, summons him back to court. Galahad is somewhat strangely placed in a nunnery under the care of the abbess, King Pelles's sister, and remains there till the age of fifteen.[5] A hermit announces to Arthur that at Whitsuntide the knight destined to achieve the Grail will come to court, and with this the book ends.

Whatever the merits of the first part of the *Lancelot* as a story of love and friendship, the latter part, in so far as it touches on the Grail theme, offers one of the least satisfactory versions of the subject. Though the plot is worked out with deliberation, it is full of improbabilities. Guenevere plays a dramatic and

---

[1] Sommer, op. cit. v. 139–42, 294–303.   [2] Ibid. 379 f.
[3] Ibid. 399 f.   [4] Ibid. 402 f.   [5] Ibid. 408.

generally sympathetic part, but Lancelot and the mother of his son are presented in an unfavourable light, and King Pelles is nothing short of despicable. If there is morality here it is of the most sophistical sort, and of spirituality there is none.

XII

The *Queste del Saint Graal*: Celtic Story-Patterns in Cistercian Allegory

THE *Queste del Saint Graal*, which follows immediately after the *Lancelot* in the Vulgate cycle, is familiar to many British and American lovers of medieval literature, since (in a form interpolated in certain manuscripts of the Prose *Tristan*) it was translated with considerable omissions and variations by Sir Thomas Malory as Books XIII to XVII of his masterpiece.[1] Both in its original French form and in the English rendering, the *Queste* contains what many critics consider the sublimest passages in all the romances of the Grail.

We meet again some of the chief personages of the *Lancelot* —King Pelles (now a reformed character), Galahad, Lancelot, Bors, Gawain, Arthur, and Guenevere—not to mention lesser figures. There are several brief references to Galahad's mother, the last announcing her death. On the other hand, Bors, who has previously played but a minor part, is advanced to a position second only to Galahad's; and Perceval's sister, who has not figured at all, is judged worthy to accompany for a time the three supreme heroes on their quest. And the very atmosphere changes. The castle of the Grail is no longer the setting for obscurely motivated combats and nightmarish sounds and spectacles, but rather for meaningful sacramental mysteries. The adventures, the visions are interpreted with conscientious precision, morally or typologically or mystically, by hermit or monk or anchoress. At times this tale of knight-errantry rises to a level of solemn beauty comparable to that of the Holy Scriptures. The author has left on his work the stamp of his highly individual genius.

[1] For text, commentaries, and translations of the *Queste*, see p. 279. For Malory's treatment see Malory, *Works*, ed. Vinaver (Oxford, 1947), iii. 1521-71.

Albert Pauphilet, who wrote a masterly commentary on the *Queste*, has best defined the essential character of the work:[1]

The great originality of our romancer lies in feeling at the same time the really potent charm of the Celtic tales and also the incomplete satisfaction which they afforded to the mind. . . . Everything was in-fused with the tantalizing poetry of chance, incoherence, and dream. But what was the drift of these tales? Why did this happen and not that? . . . The imagination is captivated, but the intelligence is troubled; it longs to bring order to this charming chaos. The author of the *Queste* was far from suspecting that it had not always been a wild phantas-magoria, and that these strange narratives were in the main the distorted expression of ancient pagan beliefs. But he had the rare perspicacity to realize that in the state in which the Frenchmen of his time found them, Celtic marvels, in spite of their incomparable fascination, were only empty frames. What he introduced into them was naturally his Chris-tian conception of the universe and of Man.

Pauphilet demonstrated, in fact, that the concept of Man's duty and destiny envisaged by the author was that specifically taught by the great monastic order of Cîteaux. This order, founded in 1098, represented a protest against the intricate and dazzling solemnities and the crowded life of the Benedictines. The typical Benedictine house had become a highly organized community, occupied during many hours of the day and night in glorifying God with elaborate rituals in churches adorned with splendid wall-paintings and marvellous sculp-tures, and in praying for the souls of wealthy benefactors. Endowed with vast possessions, the monks were distracted from spiritual contemplation by worldly duties, by the man-agement of estates, the raising of funds, and the entertain-ment of patrons. The Cistercian order was the most successful of several efforts to return to the ideals and practices of St. Benedict. The rule enjoined poverty, a strict discipline, and a simpler ritual. Above all, there was a new concentration on the purification of the individual soul. St. Bernard, founder of the daughter monastery of Clairvaux, became through his preaching and writing one of the most powerful influences on

---

[1] *Études sur la 'Queste del Saint Graal'*, pp. 192 f.

the thought and religious life of his time. Though called upon
to deal with the urgent practical issues of his day, and though
fierce in his denunciation of the enemies of the Church, without and within, he held up as the monastic ideal an inner life
of loving communion with God, culminating in the mystic
vision.

Spreading from its centre in Burgundy, the Cistercian order
by 1152 counted three hundred and thirty abbeys scattered
over Western Christendom. The ruins of many still stand, as
at Tintern and Fountains, in something like their original
majesty, and it is an austere majesty. Even the casual tourist
will note the comparative severity of the architecture and the
absence of sculptures such as adorn the twelfth-century work
at Glastonbury and Malmesbury.

A somewhat similar difference may be observed between
Perlesvaus and the *Queste del Saint Graal*. Though the former
is not concerned with the monastic life at all, and with the
eremitic life only in a superficial way, it adopts, as we have
seen, a point of view which was typical of decadent Bene-
dictinism—a preoccupation with relics, miracles, and mass
conversion by the sword. Perceval, in spite of his messianic
role, is guilty of manslaughter and even of cruelty. On the
other hand, the author of the *Queste*, employing the same
kind of narrative material, composed an affecting and profound allegory of the monastic life. Its hero pursues much of
his quest alone; his foes are those which war against the soul.
The fantastic experiences of the knights are reasonably interpreted as the trials and glories, the punishments and the
rewards, which await the seeker after the ultimate beatitude,
union with the Godhead. Readers who do not share these
aspirations may yet feel the author's deep sincerity and elevation of mind, just as those who do not belong to John Bunyan's
conventicle may admire the same qualities in *The Pilgrim's
Progress*—which, indeed, like the *Queste*, was an allegory
fashioned, at least partly, out of the materials of medieval
romance.

Pauphilet showed in his admirable study how intimate was

the relation between the abbey of Cîteaux and the romance.[1] It appears in the very first sentence.[2] 'At the vigil of Pentecost, when the companions of the Table Round were come to Camelot and had heard the service, and the tables were about to be set at the hour of none [about three o'clock], then there entered the hall on horseback a very fair damsel.' At Cîteaux, also, it was the custom on the vigil of Pentecost to celebrate the office before none. The Cistercian habit was white, and Galahad's first adventure took place at a 'white abbey'.[3] Bors, after undergoing trials and temptations, was refreshed and instructed at an abbey of white monks.[4] Lancelot was similarly entertained at a white abbey.[5] and the Maimed King at the castle of Corbenic, when he had been healed, retired to a religious house of white monks.[6]

The account of Lancelot's repentance and confession at the end of Malory's thirteenth Book, follows point by point the first five stages requisite for a complete purification from sin, as set forth in a sermon by Nicholas, a monk of Clairvaux.[7] First, realization of sin; second, repentance; third, sorrow of heart; fourth, confession of mouth; fifth, penance through fasts and vigils; sixth, reformation of life; seventh, perseverance in good works.

Let us now recall the awesome scenes which deal with the coming of Galahad from the nunnery, where he had been placed by his grandfather, to Camelot, his testing, the appearance of the Grail, and the departure of the knights on their high quest; and let us have recourse to Malory's incomparable rendering.[8] The day is Whit Sunday, the anniversary of the descent of the Holy Ghost; the time is undern, or midmorning.

---

[1] Pauphilet, *Études*, pp. 53–83.   [2] Ibid., p. 75.   [3] Ibid., p. 54.
[4] Ibid., p. 55. Sommer, *Vulgate Version*, vi. 130. Ed. Pauphilet, p. 182.
[5] Pauphilet, *Études*, p. 55. Sommer, vi. 184. Ed. Pauphilet, p. 261. Malory, Book xvii, ch. 17.
[6] Pauphilet, *Études*, p. 55. Sommer, vi. 191. Ed. Pauphilet, p. 272. Malory, Book xvii, ch. 21.
[7] Pauphilet, *Études*, pp. 77–80. Sommer, vi. 45–51. Ed. Pauphilet, pp. 63–71.
[8] Book xiii, chs. 2–8. Sommer, vi. 5–17. Ed. Pauphilet, pp. 4–21.

So when the King and all the knights were come from service, the barons espied in the sieges of the Round Table, all about, written with golden letters: 'Here ought to sit he,' and 'He ought to sit here.' And thus they went so long till they came to the Siege Perilous, where they found letters newly written of gold, which said: 'Four hundred winters and four and fifty accomplished after the passion of our Lord Jesu Christ ought this siege to be fulfilled.'

Then all they said: 'This is a marvellous thing and an adventurous.' 'In the name of God,' said Sir Lancelot; and then accounted the term of the writing from the birth of our Lord unto that day.

'It seemeth me,' said Sir Lancelot, 'this siege ought to be fulfilled this same day, for this is the feast of Pentecost after the four hundred and four and fifty year; and if it would please all parties, I would none of these letters were seen this day, till he be come that ought to achieve this adventure.' Then made they to ordain a cloth of silk, for to cover these letters in the Siege Perilous.

Then the King bade haste unto dinner. 'Sir,' said Sir Kay, the steward, 'if ye go now to your meat ye shall break your old custom of your court, for ye have not used on this day to sit at your meat or that ye have seen some adventure.'

'Ye say sooth,' said the King, 'but I had so great joy of Sir Lancelot and of his cousins, which be come to the court whole and sound, so that I bethought me not of mine old custom.'

So, as they stood speaking, in came a squire and said unto the King: 'Sire, I bring unto you marvellous tidings.' 'What be they?' said the King.

'Sire, there is here beneath at the river a great stone, which I saw float above the water, and therein I saw sticking a sword.' The King said, 'I will see that marvel.'

So all the knights went with him, and when they came unto the river, they found there a stone floating, as it were of red marble, and therein stuck a fair rich sword, and in the pommel thereof were precious stones, wrought with subtle letters of gold. Then the barons read the letters which said in this wise: 'Never shall man take me hence, but only he by whose side I ought to hang, and he shall be the best knight of the world.'

When the King had seen the letters, he said unto Sir Lancelot:

'Fair sir, this sword ought to be yours, for I am sure ye be the best knight of the world.'

Then Sir Lancelot answered full soberly: 'Certes, sire, it is not my sword; also, sire, wit ye well I have no hardiness to set my hand thereto, for it longed not to hang by my side. Also, who that essayeth to take the sword and faileth of it, he shall receive a wound by that sword that he shall not be whole long after. And I will that ye wit that this same day shall the adventures of the Sankgreal, that is called the holy vessel, begin.'

'Now, fair nephew,' said the King unto Sir Gawain, 'essay ye, for my love.'

'Sire,' he said, 'save your good grace I shall not do that.'

'Sir,' said the King, 'essay to take the sword and at my commandment.'

'Sire,' said Gawain, 'your commandment I will obey.' And therewith he took up the sword by the handles, but he might not stir it.

'I thank you,' said the King to Sir Gawain.

'My lord Sir Gawain,' said Sir Lancelot, 'now wit ye well this sword shall touch you so sore that ye shall will ye had never set your hand thereto for the best castle of this realm.'

'Sir,' he said, 'I might not withsay mine uncle's will and commandment.' But when the King heard this, he repented it much and said unto Sir Percival that he should essay, for his love.

And he said, 'Gladly, for to bear Sir Gawain fellowship.' And therewith he set his hand on the sword and drew it strongly, but he might not move it.

Then were there more that durst be so hardy to set their hands thereto.

'Now may ye go to your dinner,' said Sir Kay unto the King, 'for a marvellous adventure have ye seen.'

So the King and all went unto the court, and every knight knew his own place and set him therein, and young men that were knights served them. So when they were served and all sieges fulfilled save only the Siege Perilous, anon there befell a marvellous adventure that all the doors and windows shut by themself. Not for then the hall was not greatly darked; and therewith they abashed both one and other. Then King Arthur spoke first and said, 'By God, fair *fellows and lords, we have seen this day marvels, but or night I suppose we shall see greater marvels.'*

In the meanwhile came in a good old man and an ancient, clothed all in white, and there was no knight knew from whence he came. And with him he brought a young knight, both on foot, in red arms, without sword or shield, save a scabbard hanging by his side. And these words he said, 'Peace be with you, fair lords.'

Then the old man said unto Arthur, 'Sire, I bring here a young knight, the which is of king's lineage and of the kindred of Joseph of Arimathea, whereby the marvels of this court and of strange realms shall be accomplished.

The King was right glad of his words and said unto the good man, 'Sir, ye be right welcome, and the young knight with you.'

Then the old man made the young knight to unarm him, and he was in a coat of red cendal, and bare a mantle upon his shoulder that was furred with ermine, and put that upon him. And the old knight said unto the young knight, 'Sir, follow me.' And anon he led him unto the Siege Perilous, where beside sat Sir Lancelot; and the good man lifted up the cloth and found there letters that said thus: 'This is the siege of Galahad. . . .'

'Sir,' said the old knight, 'wit ye well that place is yours.' And then he set him down surely in that siege.

And then he said to the old man, 'Sir, ye may now go your way, for well have ye done that ye were commanded to do; and recommend me unto my grandsire, King Pelles, and unto my lord Pechere [Fisherman], and say them on my behalf, I shall come and see them as soon as ever I may.' So the good man departed; and there met him twenty noble squires, and so took their horses and went their way.

Then all the knights of the Table Round marvelled greatly of Sir Galahad, that he durst sit there in that Siege Perilous, and was so tender of age; and wist not from whence he came but all only by God. All they said, 'This is he by whom the Sankgreal shall be achieved, for there sat never none there but he, but he were mischieved.' Then Sir Lancelot beheld his son and had great joy of him.

★   ★   ★   ★   ★

Then came King Arthur unto Galahad and said, 'Sir, ye be welcome, for ye shall move many knights to the quest of the Sankgreal, and ye shall achieve that never knights might bring to an end.'

Then the King took him by the hand, and went down from the palace to show Galahad the adventures of the stone. The Queen heard thereof, and came after with many ladies and showed them the stone, where it hoved on the water.

'Sir,' said the King unto Sir Galahad, 'here is a great marvel as ever I saw, and right good knights have essayed and failed.'

'Sir,' said Sir Galahad, 'that is no marvel, for this adventure is not theirs but mine; and for the surety of this sword I brought none with me, for here by my side hangeth the scabbard.'

And anon he laid his hand on the sword, and lightly drew it out of the stone, and put it in the sheath, and said unto the King, 'Now it goeth better than it did aforehand.'

★　　★　　★　　★　　★

Therewith the King and all espied where came riding down the river a lady on a white palfrey toward them. Then she saluted the King and the Queen, and asked if that Sir Lancelot was there. And then he answered himself, 'I am here, fair lady.'

Then she said, all with weeping, 'How your great doing is changed since this day in the morn!'

'Damsel, why say ye so?' said Lancelot.

'I say you sooth,' said the damsel, 'for ye were this day the best knight of the world, but who should say so now, he should be a liar, for there is now one better than ye, and well it is proved by the adventures of the sword, whereto ye durst not set to your hand; and that is the change and leaving of your name. Wherefore I make unto you a remembrance that ye shall not ween from henceforth that ye be not the best knight of the world.'

'As touching unto that,' said Lancelot, 'I know well I was never best.'

'Yes,' said the damsel, 'that were ye and are yet, of any sinful man of the world. And, Sir King, Nacien the hermit sendeth thee word that thee shall befall the greatest worship that ever befell king in Britain; and I say you wherefore, for this day the Sankgreal appeared

in thy house and fed thee and all thy fellowship of the Round Table.'
So she departed and went the same way that she came.

'Now,' said the King, 'I am sure at this quest of the Sankgreal
shall all ye of the Table Round depart, and never shall I see you
again whole together; therefore I will see you all whole together in
the meadow of Camelot to joust and to tourney, that after your death
men may speak of it that such good knights were wholly together
such a day.'

As unto that counsel and at the King's request they accorded all,
and took on their harness that longed unto jousting. But all this
moving of the King was for this intent, for to see Galahad proved,
for the King deemed he should not lightly come again unto the court
after his departing. So were they assembled in the meadow, both
more and less. Then Sir Galahad, by the prayer of the King and the
Queen, did upon him a noble jesseraunce, and also he did on his helm,
but shield would he take none for no prayer of the King. And then
Sir Gawain and other knights prayed him to take a spear. Right so
he did, and the Queen was in a tower with all her ladies, for to behold that tournament. Then Sir Galahad dressed him in midst of
the meadow and began to break spears marvellously that all men had
wonder of him, for he there surmounted all other knights, for within
a while he had defouled many good knights of the Table Round, save
twain, that was Sir Lancelot and Sir Percival.

*   *   *   *   *

And then the King and all estates went home unto Camelot, and
so went to evensong to the great minster, and so after upon that to
supper, and every knight sat in his own place as they were toforehand.
Then anon they heard cracking and crying of thunder, that them
thought the place should all to-drive. In the midst of this blast entered a sunbeam more clearer by seven times than ever they saw day,
and all they were alighted of the grace of the Holy Ghost. Then
began every knight to behold other, and either saw other, by their
seeming, fairer than ever they saw afore. Not for then there was no
knight might speak one word a great while, and so they looked every
man on other as they had been dumb.

Then there entered into the hall the Holy Grail, covered with white samite, but there was none might see it nor who bare it. And there was all the hall fulfilled with good odours, and every knight had such meats and drinks as he best loved in this world. And when the Holy Grail had been borne through the hall, then the holy vessel departed suddenly, that they wist not where it became. Then had they all breath to speak. And then the King yielded thankings to God, of his good grace that he had sent them.

'Certes,' said the King, 'we ought to thank our Lord Jesu greatly for that he hath showed us this day at the reverence of this high feast of Pentecost.'

'Now,' said Sir Gawain, 'we have been served this day of what meats and drinks we thought on; but one thing beguiled us, we might not see the Holy Grail, it was so preciously covered. Wherefore I will make here avow that tomorn, without longer abiding, I shall labour in the quest of the Sankgreal, that I shall hold me out a twelvemonth and a day, or more if need be, and never shall I return again unto the court till I have seen it more openly than it hath been seen here; and if I may not speed, I shall return again as he that may not be against the will of our Lord Jesu Christ.'

When they of the Table Round heard Sir Gawain say so, they arose up the most part and made such avows as Sir Gawain had made. Anon as King Arthur heard this, he was greatly displeased, for he wist well they might not againsay their avows.

* \ * \ * \ * \ *

And therewith the tears filled in his eyes. And then he said, 'Gawain, Gawain, ye have set me in great sorrow, for I have great doubt that my true fellowship shall never meet here more again.'

'Ah,' said Sir Lancelot, 'comfort yourself; for it shall be unto us a great honour and much more than if we died in any other places, for of death we be siker.'

'Ah, Lancelot,' said the King, 'the great love that I have had unto you all the days of my life maketh me to say such doleful words; for never Christian king had never so many worthy men at his table as I have had this day at the Round Table, and that is my great sorrow.'

When the Queen, ladies, and gentlewomen wist these tidings, they had such sorrow and heaviness that there might no tongue tell it, for those knights had held them in honour and charity. But above all other Queen Guenevere made great sorrow. 'I marvel,' said she, 'my lord would suffer them to depart from him.'

Then was all the court troubled for the love of the departition of those knights. And many of those ladies that loved knights would have gone with their lovers, and so had they done, had not an old knight come among them in religious clothing; and then he spake all on high and said, 'Fair lords, which have sworn in the quest of the Sankgreal, thus sendeth you Nacien the hermit word that none in this quest lead lady nor gentlewoman with him, for it is not to do in so high a service as they labour in; for I warn you plain, he that is not clean of his sins, he shall not see the mysteries of our Lord Jesu Christ.' And for this cause they left these ladies and gentlewomen.

★　　★　　★　　★　　★

And then they went to rest them. And in the honour of the highness of Galahad he was led into King Arthur's chamber, and there rested in his own bed.

Malory omitted a passage which tells how, when on the next morning all the knights were armed and had heard mass, they assembled in the hall and made a more solemn vow than the first, on holy relics. Thus we are told how Galahad kneeled before the relics and swore that he would continue the quest for a year and a day, and more if need were. Lancelot followed and then Gawain, Percival, Bors, Lionel, and the rest of the fellowship of the Round Table to the number of one hundred and fifty.[1]

There is nothing more sublime and affecting in the literature of the Grail than the passages which have just been quoted. To be sure, a commonsensical reader might inquire why Lancelot and Bors, who had visited the castle of King Pelles more than once and had already seen the Grail openly,

---

[1] Sommer, op. cit. vi. 18 f. Ed. Pauphilet, pp. 22 f. Malory, Book xvii, ch. 4.

should have found it incumbent on them to return and why they should have had difficulty in finding their way; and above all why Galahad, who two days before setting out had sent a message to King Pelles and the Fisher King,[1] fully confident of its prompt delivery, should find the journey to the same destination a long and arduous task. It is sufficient to reply that, in passing from the *Lancelot* to the *Queste*, we have entered a world where the rules of common sense do not apply. To behold the Grail openly is not to see a sacred vessel in an earthly castle, but the Beatific Vision, vouchsafed by God's grace only to those who have fitted themselves by discipline and contemplation for the ineffable experience.

Let us see whether we can distinguish the materials which went to the fashioning of this majestic overture to the quest of the Grail, for only so can we pretend to understand the French author's art. He had, of course, precedents in Chrétien's *Perceval* for Arthur's custom of awaiting an adventure before beginning a banquet,[2] and for the assembly of knights who swore to undertake a quest. It is possible that the concept of the Grail, gliding through the air and feeding the assembled knights, was borrowed from the First Continuation, but there is no verbal similarity. The withdrawal of the sword from the block of marble was surely influenced by a similar incident in Robert de Boron's *Merlin*, where Arthur proves his right to the kingship by drawing the sword from the stone; and the changes wrought to adapt the incident to the testing of Galahad display a rare feeling for atmosphere and purpose. To quote Professor Carman:[3]

The *Merlin* presents a quarrelsome mob, each man jostling his fellow to have the first chance, restrained only by the efforts of a church dignitary. In the *Queste*, we see the three best knights of Arthur's court reluctant to undertake the test, one, the greatest, refusing in all humility, another putting his hand to the hilt only at the repeatedly expressed wish of his king and family chief, the third undertaking the adventure

---

[1] Sommer, vi. 8. Ed. Pauphilet, p. 8.
[2] On this motif see *Zeitschrift für französische Sprache und Literatur*, xlv[1] (1917), pp. 102 ff.   [3] *PMLA*, liii (1938), p. 595.

out of courtesy to him who had already failed, as well as from obedience to the king. . . . In this change, which is all to the advantage of the *Queste*, its author has been guided by one of the ends that inspires his whole romance. Here begins the humiliation of the Arthurian world before austere Christianity. Here the Good Knight, inspired by Grace, first vanquishes the adherents of the courtly ideal.

Opinions will differ as to the extent to which the opening scenes of the *Queste* depend on Chrétien, his continuators, and Robert de Boron, but even if one grants a large measure of borrowing from these authors, there remains the framework —consisting of the arrival of a destined hero at a royal court, the testing of his powers, the enrolment of warriors in the enterprise of which he is to be the leader—which in this combination is not to be matched in any other Arthurian romance. Readers familiar with Irish literature, however, will recall a similar sequence of events in the famous Irish saga, the *Second Battle of Moytura*, dated before 908, namely, the coming of the youthful Lug to the court of the god Nuada, here euhemerized as King of Ireland and predecessor of Lug in the kingship. Let me quote from Miss Maud Joynt's retelling, which, by eliminating accretions, forms a coherent story.[1]

Nuada prepared a great feast at Tara, and summoned to it all the nobles to take counsel together. When all were assembled in the hall, the doorkeeper at the gate saw a company approaching, at their head a youthful warrior of handsome form and equipped like a king. . . . Then Nuada bade him be admitted. And Lug entered the hall and took his place in the midst of the Tuathan chiefs, in the seat of the Sage, which was set apart for the wisest. . . . Then the champion Ogma, wishful to try the stranger's strength, lifted up a huge stone which lay on the floor of the hall and was beyond the power of ordinary man to move, and he hurled it through the roof-window out over the ramparts of the fort. But Lug went out and flung it back to the spot where it had lain. . . . When Nuada and the Tuathan chiefs beheld Lug's powers and saw that he was in truth the *Samildanach* (master of many arts), they felt they had at last found the hero who could lead their hosts and free them from bondage; and Nuada gave up his place to Lug for the space of the war, so that henceforth Lug sat in the king's seat. The next day Lug called

[1] M. Joynt, *Golden Legends of the Gael* (Dublin, n.d.), pp. 14–17. For a complete translation into German by Lehmacher see *Anthropos*, xxvi (1931), pp. 435–59.

together the great warriors and wise men of the Tuatha, . . . and he asked of each man what he could do. First spoke the druids Mathgen and Figol. . .

'I will make rivets for the spears and hilts for the swords and bosses for the shields,' said Credne.

'And I,' said Luchta the wright, 'will fashion shields and spear-staves out of wood.'

The roll-call of the divine craftsmen and warriors follows, like that of the knights of the Round Table. If one recalls a gloss in the manuscript of this saga, which asserts that Lug had a red colour on him from sunset to morning,[1] and if one realizes that the seat of Nuada, which Lug occupied, was doubtless a couch rather than a throne,[2] the parallel between the arrival of Lug and the arrival of Galahad hardly needs demonstration. Though the two stories have followed divergent paths for centuries, they present ten common features: the assembled court, the empty seat awaiting a worthy occupant, the coming of a handsome youth with a red colour on him, his taking the seat, the demonstration of his superior strength which involves a block of stone, the recognition by the members of the court that this is the destined hero, the king's relinquishing his couch to the newcomer, the assembly on the morrow, the demand that each should participate in the enterprise, the list of those who did so. In spite of all the vicissitudes and confusions of oral transmission through widely differing channels, the basic design of the arrival of Galahad and the commencement of the quest can be plainly discerned in the *Second Battle of Moytura*. In fact, this confrontation of the Irish and the Arthurian narratives affords one of the strongest proofs of the Celtic origin of the Grail legends.

It was a happy accident which furnished the author of the *Queste* with a traditional story about a youthful warrior, whose arrival was awaited and whose destiny it was to deliver his people, but it was the author's own sagacity which recognized here the theme of the Messiah, so appropriate to his purpose

[1] *Revue Celtique*, xii (1891), p. 127.
[2] *Studies in Honor of A. M. Elliott* (Baltimore, 1911), i. 34 f.

of depicting the ideal Christian life under the guise of chivalric adventure.[1] A brief passage in the French text, which Malory omitted, makes the messianic role of Galahad quite clear.[2] The venerable man in white who brought the youth to Camelot, addressing Arthur, said: 'I bring thee the desired knight (*le chevalier desiré*), who is descended from the high lineage of King David.' Arthur replied, 'Sir, ye are welcome if this word be true, and welcome is the knight. For this is he whom we expect to accomplish the adventures of the Holy Grail; never was such joy made of man as we shall make of him.' This leitmotif of the messianic hope and the messianic mission is sounded again and again throughout the book.

Indeed, the very name Galahad was chosen to carry out this concept. Its biblical origin has long been known, since it occurs in the Vulgate Old Testament, the standard text of the Middle Ages, in the form Galaad. Sometimes it refers to a place, sometimes to a person. It remained for Pauphilet to discover its astonishing fitness for the messianic hero of the *Queste*.[3] He showed that, according to Genesis xxxi. 47–52, Galaad meant 'heap of testimony', and that Isidore of Seville, Walafrid, Strabo, and the Venerable Bede construed this etymology as a reference to Christ. He clinched the matter by quoting from a Cistercian work, the *Sermons on the Canticles* of Gilbert of Holland—the very same work which prompted the identification of the Bald Damsel with the Old Law by the author of *Perlesvaus*. In the twenty-third sermon we read:[4] 'Who is this heap of testimony but Christ, on whom all the testimonies of the prophets are piled, to whom the prophets, John [the Baptist], the Heavenly Father, and His own works bear witness?'

Nothing better illustrates the ingenuity of the author of the *Queste* than the selection of this name. It is probable that among the lost romances which he knew was one in which Gawain was the hero of a Grail quest, as he is in some measure in the First Continuation of the *Conte del Graal* and in

---

[1] Pauphilet, *Études*, pp. 142–4.   [2] Sommer, vi. 7. Ed. Pauphilet, p. 7.
[3] *Études*, pp. 135–8.   [4] *Patrologia Latina*, clxxxiv, col. 119.

Heinrich von dem Türlin's *Crone*. It is also probable that in this lost romance Gawain's name took some such form as Galaain, and that Galaain was depicted as a paragon of chivalric virtues, even as Gawain was in the early stages of Arthurian fiction, according to William of Malmesbury and Wace.[1] Furthermore, the supposition that Galahad has taken the place which Gawain held in an earlier romance fits in with the evidence presented in the last chapter that Lancelot's begetting Galahad on King Pelles's daughter was a remote cognate of King Lot's begetting Gawain on Morcades. The author of the *Queste*, however, differentiated this ideal knight—named, perhaps, Galaain—from Gawain, whose reputation had lost by this time its pristine lustre; and he went so far as to blacken Gawain's character in order to use him as a foil to the perfections of Galahad.[2] The happy discovery that the biblical name Galaad was construed as a reference to the Messiah led him naturally to rechristen his hero, whose role in romance as a long-awaited healer and deliverer adumbrated that of Christ.

In a number of episodes and in divers ways this concept of Galahad is carried out. For him alone was destined the shield with the red cross. He delivered the Castle of Maidens from seven evil knights, signifying at the same time Christ's descent into hell to release the souls of the righteous, and the liberation of pure souls from the seven deadly sins.[3] Here one may discern in the background the ancient Irish theme of a visit to the land of women (represented in the *Voyage of Bran Son of Febal*) and the equally ancient theme of the rescue of a faery queen from her foes (represented in the *Wasting Sickness of Cuchulainn*).[4] The deliverance of the Castle of Maidens, then, is a traditional pattern in Arthurian romance; in *Perlesvaus* it is represented by the rescue of the Queen of Maidens from the King of Castle Mortal.[5] The version incorporated in the

[1] Loomis, *Arthurian Tradition*, pp. 146 f.
[2] Pauphilet, *Études*, pp. 126 f.
[3] Sommer, vi. 40. Ed. Pauphilet, p. 54.
[4] Dillon, *Ancient Irish Literature*, pp. 106, 119, 122, 128.
[5] *Perlesvaus*, ed. Nitze, i. 176–80; ii. 295–7.

Queste situates the Castle of Maidens on the Severn, seemingly because the Welsh identified the castle by a curious mistake with Gloucester (Caer Loyw), which lies on that river.[1]

Nowhere is the messianic character of Galahad more clearly and exquisitely treated than in the brief account of his visit to King Mordrain, which occurs late in the romance.[2] It forms the pendant to an earlier unsuccessful visit by Perceval,[3] who finds at a monastery the blind king, sorely wounded in battle four hundred years before and awaiting a descendant to heal him. He had tasted no food save that which the priest shows in the sacrament, 'that is the Body (*cors*) of Jesu Christ'. When at last Galahad arrived, Mordrain received his sight and exclaimed: '"Galahad, the servant of Jesu Christ, whose coming I have abidden so long, now embrace me and let me rest on thy breast, so that I may rest between thine arms. . . ." When Galahad heard his words, then he embraced him and all his body. Then said he: "Fair Lord Jesu Christ, now I have my will. Now I require Thee, in this point that I am in, Thou come and visit me." And anon Our Lord heard his prayer; therewith departed the soul from the body.'

The pattern of the Maimed King awaiting his healer and deliverer is obvious, and approximates the form found in the *Didot Perceval*, where the Fisher King, Bron, who had lain in languishment for two generations awaiting his grandson, was healed by Perceval on his second visit, and died within three days.[4] It is unnecessary to point out here, as well as in the story of Mordrain's healing, vestiges of the Welsh tradition of Brân the Blessed. With great taste and feeling the author of the *Queste* has worked over the traditional pattern with intent to suggest St. Luke's story of Simeon, who had been assured by the Holy Ghost that he should not see death before he had seen the Lord's Christ, and who, taking up the infant Saviour in his arms, uttered the sublime words of the *Nunc dimittis*: 'Lord, now lettest Thou Thy servant depart in peace, . . . for mine

[1] Loomis, *Arthurian Tradition*, pp. 451–7.
[2] Sommer, vi. 184 f. Ed. Pauphilet, pp. 262 f.
[3] Sommer, vi. 59–63. Ed. Pauphilet, pp. 81–7.
[4] *Didot Perceval*, ed. W. Roach (Philadelphia, 1941), pp. 239–42.

eyes have seen Thy salvation.'[1] It is probable that Mordrain's blindness and the restoration of his vision, for which there is no parallel in traditions of the Maimed King, were suggested by the words of Simeon: 'Mine eyes have seen Thy salvation.'

Let us turn our attention next to the author's conception of the Grail. We know that he derived from more or less remote Celtic sources the concept of the vessel as a large, food-providing dish, such as the *Dysgl* of Rhydderch, and the miraculous power of service without a visible bearer, such as that possessed by the drinking horn in the *Adventure of Art Son of Conn*. Already the Grail had been identified with the dish from which the Saviour ate the Passover lamb at the Last Supper, and an elaborate legend had been created to account for its transmission to Britain and its preservation in the castle of King Pelles. But it was not enough for our author that the vessel was one of the holiest of relics; it must have symbolic meaning, and that meaning he made quite plain. Harking back to the description of the supper in Arthur's hall, when the Grail appeared, we note that the date was the four hundred and fifty-fourth anniversary of the descent of the Holy Ghost on the expectant disciples, assembled at Jerusalem.[2] All the knights assembled in Arthur's hall were 'alighted of the grace of the Holy Ghost'. To be sure, the rushing wind and the tongues of fire described in the Book of Acts, are replaced by a crash of thunder and a dazzling beam of light; nevertheless, the resemblance to the first Pentecost is sufficiently clear not only to suggest the essential nature of the Grail but also to suffuse with an odour of sanctity the uncanny manifestations ultimately derived from pagan myth.

In a long discourse of the hermit Nascien, which Malory abridged too much to serve our purpose, the symbolism of the Grail becomes explicit. Referring to a spring from which Lancelot had tried to drink, in vain because of his sin, Nascien

[1] Luke ii. 25–30.
[2] Malory, Book xiii, chs. 2, 7. Sommer, vi. 5, 13. Ed. Pauphilet, pp. 4, 15.

declared:[1] ' "The fountain is of such a kind that one cannot exhaust it, for never will one be able to take enough of it away. It is the Holy Grail, it is the grace of the Holy Spirit. The fountain is the sweet rain, the sweet word of the gospel, in which the heart of the truly repentant sinner finds such great sweetness that the more he tastes it, so much the more does he desire it. This is the grace of the Holy Grail." '

Now in the terminology of the medieval Church 'grace' is the unmerited favour or love of God bestowed on human beings. For a fuller comprehension of the Grail as a symbol of grace let me quote Gilson's footnote in *Les Idées et les Lettres*:[2]

In order to follow the guiding thought of the *Queste*, the simplest way is to start from St. Augustine's conception of grace, which inspired St. Bernard and the Cistercians. First, there is the definition of God Himself, namely, that He is love: 'Deus charitas est' (I John, iv. 16). On the other hand, the grace which is in us is in its essence nothing else than the same love which is God, but shared by fallen man in the form of a free gift. It is then love, or charity, like God Himself—and it is for this reason that the *Queste* does not recognize any attribute of the Grail which does not also belong to God—but it is not God, for God is love in its very essence, whereas grace is that which God has freely given us of His love in order to recall us to Himself: 'Charitas ex Deo est' (I John, iv. 17). God and grace may then bear the same name, *charitas*, though an infinite difference separates them, since grace is a created gift, while God is its creator.

If one may sum up the essential doctrine of the *Queste*, it is this. The Grail is a symbol of grace, and grace is God's love for man. One of the supreme manifestations of that love was the descent of the Holy Ghost in the form of fire; thus the entrance of the Grail in the hall at Camelot was preceded by a dazzling ray, and all were at once illumined of the Holy Ghost. Through grace all man's spiritual desires may be satisfied; thus the Grail dispensed to every knight such meats and drinks as he best loved in the world. God's love begets a response in the hearts of men and draws them to Him; thus the knights of the Round Table were moved to seek the Grail.

[1] Sommer, vi. 114 Ed. Pauphilet, pp. 158 f.
[2] É. Gilson, *Les Idées et les Lettres* (Paris, 1932), p. 63, n. 1.

But only by full purgation and strict self-denial can one succeed in this quest; hence the emphasis on confession, abstinence, and celibacy as the conditions on which the vision of the Grail depends. The rewards of those who fulfil these conditions are states of rapture in which God's love is made more clearly manifest, particularly in the sacraments; thus to the three elect who reach the castle of the Grail, Christ Himself is made visible, first entering the consecrated Host, and then, as the officiant, administering it to them from the Grail. For Galahad alone is reserved in the land of Sarras the highest of earthly joys, an ecstasy which permits him to look within the holy vessel and see openly what tongue cannot describe nor heart conceive, the marvel of marvels. This is the Christian mystic's supreme desire and reward, a foretaste of the Beatific Vision.

To some modern readers, even those of the Christian faith, the ascetic ideal of life embodied in Galahad is distasteful, even repellent. Bruce, though he could on one page praise the *Queste* as expressing 'the mystical spirit of the Middle Ages with a power that is rarely equalled elsewhere', could two pages later write: 'The air of the enchanted forests of Arthurian romance thus becomes heavy with symbolism. A religious fanatic has entered and put them under the spell which was already binding and cramping the minds of the Middle Ages in every other line of effort.'[1]

But though one may not be drawn to Galahad as a type, it is not necessary to make him out a prig or a bloodless, impossible figure of perfection. There is in him humility, tolerance, and warmth. His human side is most clearly revealed in his relations with his father, the sinner Lancelot. He is never self-righteous or sanctimonious. So, one night, when he entered the ship in which Lancelot had been voyaging alone, sustained only by the grace of the Holy Ghost, he asked his father, ' "What is your name? for much my heart giveth unto you." "Truly," said he, "my name is Lancelot du Lake." "Sir," said he, "then be ye welcome, for ye were the

---

[1] Bruce, *Evolution*, i. 423, 425.

beginning of me in this world." "Ah," said he, "are ye Galahad?" "Yea, forsooth," said he; and so he kneeled down and asked him his blessing, and after took off his helm and kissed him. . . . There is no tongue can tell the joy that they made either of other, and many a friendly word spoken between, as kin would.'[1]

After they had sailed together for half a year and shared many perilous adventures, a white knight summoned Galahad to leave his father and ride away in the quest of the Grail. Then Galahad went to his father 'and kissed him sweetly, and said, "Fair sweet father, I wot not when I shall see you more till I see the body of Jesu Christ." . . . "Now, son Galahad," said Lancelot, "since we shall depart, and never see other, I pray to the High Father to conserve me and you both." "Sir," said Galahad, "no prayer availeth so much as yours." '[2] When at last Galahad was about to die in the land of Sarras, he said to Sir Bors, ' "Fair lord, salute me to my lord, Sir Lancelot, my father, and as soon as ye see him, bid him remember of this unstable world." '[3] There is simplicity and poignancy about this brief account of the companionship of father and son which recalls such great stories as that of David and Absalom or Jacob and Joseph.

Let us resume consideration of the originally pagan Celtic themes which have been transmogrified and sanctified by the author of the *Queste*. The most bizarre and the most elaborate example is the adventure of King Solomon's ship, treated at length by Pauphilet.[4] The author must have been acquainted with a description similar to that in the Breton lai of *Guigemar*, composed by Marie de France before 1189.[5] The hero of the lai, though sorely wounded, rode to a harbour and beheld

[1] Malory, Book xvii, ch. 13. The corresponding passage in the *Queste* (Sommer, vi. 177; Ed. Pauphilet, p. 250) does not mention Galahad's kneeling and asking his father's blessing.

[2] Malory, Book xvii, ch. 14. Sommer, vi. 178. Ed. Pauphilet, p. 252.

[3] Malory, Book xvii, ch. 22. Sommer, vi. 197. Ed. Pauphilet, p. 278.

[4] *Études*, pp. 144–56.

[5] Ibid., p. 156, n. 1. *Guigemar*, vss. 145–87.

there a ship with a sail of silk. He went aboard but could find not a soul within. In the midst there was a bed, of which the legs and the sides were made, in the fashion of Solomon, of cypress and ivory all inlaid with gold, and the quilt and the pillow were of the costliest fabrics. Guigemar lay down on the bed, only to discover presently that the vessel had carried him out to sea. There can be little doubt that the description, in the *Queste* has been influenced by verses in the Canticles, chapter iii, describing the litter (*ferculum*) constructed by Solomon,[1] but there can be little doubt also that the magic ship which bore Guigemar away to unknown shores was not of biblical origin but of Celtic and had its counterpart in the coracle of Manannan, the Irish sea-god, which bore the three sons of Turenn over the sea, without the aid of oar or sail, on their several quests.[2]

It was, perhaps, the description in *Guigemar*, especially the reference to Solomon, which fired the imagination of the author of the Grail romance. In any case, he drew on apocryphal legends of the Tree of Life, on the symbolic interpretation of the Canticles, on St. Paul's definition of the sword of the Spirit, and on the concept of the Virgin as the agent by which the Old Law of the Jews was replaced by the New Law of Christ, and he constructed about the image of the mysterious vessel and the magnificent bed of Breton tradition an elaborate symbology of the Christian faith. Some of the meanings are expounded by the text itself, but it remained for Pauphilet to set forth in his brilliant analysis the why and the wherefore of each detail. The quotations which follow are from Malory's translation, to which the reader is referred for a condensed version of the adventure of Solomon's ship.

First, there is the vessel itself, with the inscription: 'Thou man, which shall enter into this ship, beware thou be in steadfast belief, for I am Faith.'[3] Now the Church Fathers and commentators on the Bible, including St. Augustine and

[1] Abercrombie in *Mod. Lang. Rev.* xxx. 353.
[2] Loomis, *Wales*, pp. 30 f. P. W. Joyce, *Old Celtic Romances* (Dublin, 1920), pp. 62–64.
[3] Malory, Book xvii, ch. 2. Sommer, vi. 144. Ed. Pauphilet, p. 201.

Rabanus Maurus, repeat the statement: 'Ecclesia est navis.'[1] The ship, then, was the Church, which none may enter without faith. Why are we told that it was built by Solomon? Because Solomon was the builder of the Temple at Jerusalem, the Church of God under the Old Law.

What of the bed? The same Cistercian abbot, Gilbert of Holland, who interpreted the name Galahad as a reference to Christ, equated in his second sermon the bed of Solomon with the cross of Christ.[2] 'Dulcis lectulus illud crucis tuae lignum', 'A sweet bed is the wood of Thy cross.' This equation being accepted, it followed that Galahad, the Christ-knight, was destined to lie upon the bed, and so he does later on the voyage to Sarras.[3] Now there were two famous legends concerning the cross. The first asserted that the tree of Man's salvation was descended from the tree of Man's fall, the tree of the knowledge of good and evil. This belief, of course, formed a part of that elaborate system of prefigurations by which the events of the Old Testament foreshadowed those of the New. The second legend, which a rationalistic historian might suspect was invented to account for the variety of woods which, distributed throughout Europe, were adored as pieces of the 'true cross', asserted that three (or four) different trees were used for the making of the cross. One may find a form of this legend near the beginning of *Mandeville's Travels*.[4] The author of the *Queste* seems to have invented himself a highly poetic synthesis of these two legends.[5] Eve, after the expulsion from Paradise, planted a branch of the fatal tree, which grew and flourished but remained completely white so long as Eve was a virgin, and white were all the offshoots taken from it. But when at God's command Adam knew Eve carnally, the white tree became green and put forth leaves, flowers, and fruit, in token of the fructifying act, and green too were the trees

[1] Pauphilet, *Études*, p. 150, n. 1.

[2] Ibid., p. 151. Migne, *Patrologia Latina*, clxxxiv, col. 21.

[3] Sommer, vi. 193. Ed. Pauphilet, p. 275.

[4] *The Voiage and Travayle of Syr John Maundeville, Knight*, Everyman's Lib., pp. 18–21. See Esther C. Quinn, *The Quest of Seth for the Oil of Life* (Chicago, 1962).

[5] Pauphilet, *Études*, pp. 145–50. Sommer, vi. 151–61. Ed. Pauphilet, pp. 210–25.

which sprang from it. Finally, the colour of the tree turned from green to red when Cain shed the blood of Abel, and henceforth it bore no more fruit. So when Solomon had the bed made which symbolized the cross, he bade a carpenter cut three pieces of wood or spindles, one from the white tree and one each from its green and red descendants, and had them fitted into the frame of the bed. Thus Eve, who was the cause of Man's downfall, was an instrument in his salvation by planting the tree which was destined to bear the Saviour of mankind.

The sword which lay at the foot of the bed and which was destined for Galahad affords another extraordinary example of the author's practice of blending romantic motifs from the Matter of Britain with biblical themes and mystical interpretations.[1] He identifies the weapon with the sword of Strange Hangings, which the Loathly Damsel in Chrétien's *Conte del Graal* proclaimed as the reward of him who would deliver the damsel of Montesclaire.[2] This sword may well have been the subject of traditional story, for there are numerous references to it scattered through the romances; but it is doubtful whether the author who inserted in the First Continuation of the *Conte del Graal* an account of Gawain's adventure at Montesclaire and his winning the sword (which turned out to be that of Judas Maccabeus) was indebted to tradition or to his own imagination.[3] Certain it is that his story bears no resemblance to the early history of the weapon which Perceval's sister related in the *Queste*,[4] and which is a fantastic *mélange* of the motifs discussed earlier in connexion with Gawain's visit to the Grail castle—fragile brands, which require to be reunited, lances discharged by invisible foes, a dolorous stroke which destroys the fertility of a land. It is odd that the author does not realize how inconsistent is this early history of the sword with the symbolic meaning which he ascribed to it.

[1] Pauphilet, *Études*, p. 152.
[2] *Percevalroman*, ed. Hilka, vs. 4712; pp. 716–18.
[3] *Continuations of the Old French 'Perceval'*, ed. W. Roach, ii (Philadelphia, 1950), pp. 131–8.
[4] Sommer, vi. 146–50. Ed. Pauphilet, pp. 204–10.

Making use of these borrowings from the Matter of Britain, he proceeded to add to the exotic associations of the sword by describing the hilt as made in part from a serpent of Caledonia called Papalustes, and in part from a small fish found in the Euphrates called Ortenax—creatures reminiscent of the bestiaries but not to be found there. The symbolic meaning of the sword was inescapable. Had not St. Paul declared, in the Epistle to the Ephesians, vi. 17: 'Take the helmet of salvation, and the sword of the Spirit, which is the word of God'? And the word of God, needless to say, is the Holy Scripture. Now it happens that in chapter iii, verse 8 of the Canticles, next to that which mentions the bed of Solomon, we read: 'Uniuscujusque ensis super femur suum.' The comment of Abbot Gilbert in his sixteenth sermon contains these sentences:[1] 'Let the sword of the Spirit be versatile in thy hand that it may serve in every need that arises. . . . Let the sword of the word be at thy side, not out of sight. Gird it upon thy thigh that thou mayst be strong and prompt both to encourage with wholesome doctrine and to refute those who speak against thee.'

Thus the symbolism of the sword was fixed by St. Paul, and the obligation of the Christian to hang it by his side was proclaimed by Abbot Gilbert. But what of the 'strange hangings', traditional in Arthurian romance?[2] Unless I am mistaken, no description of them has survived, except the one given by the author of the *Queste*, and this he seems to have invented to harmonize with the symbolic interpretation of the sword.[3] When the ship containing the bed and the sword was ready to sail, Solomon's wife, personifying the Old Law of the Jews, attached to the scabbard a girdle of hemp. When the King protested, she replied that she had nothing worthy to sustain so high a sword, but that in due time a maid would provide

---

[1] Migne, *Patrologia Latina*, clxxxiv, col. 84.

[2] On the meaning of the word *renges* see M. D. Legge in *Romania*, lxxvii (1956), pp. 88–90. On references to this sword see R. Heinzel in *Denkschriften der Wiener Akademie*, phil.-hist. Kl., xl (1891), p. 24, n. 3.

[3] Pauphilet, *Études*, pp. 152 f. Sommer, vi. 147, 161–3. Ed. Pauphilet, pp. 205, 223–8.

a better girdle. This prophecy was fulfilled when Perceval's virgin sister, typifying the New Law of Christ, produced from a casket a girdle made of silk, gold thread, and her own hair, attached it to the scabbard in place of the old girdle, and hung the weapon at Galahad's side. Thus, through the instrumentality of the Virgin Mary, the Old Testament was superseded by the New, and the prophecies of the Old Law were fulfilled in Christ.

To quote Pauphilet:[1] 'The myth of the ship is like a synthesis of the means adopted by the author of the *Queste* to make what we have called a romantic transcription of his religious theme; the intervention of the Deity, scenes of allegory, mystic symbols, and saints' legends have been assembled and blended with reminiscences of Celtic themes.'

The climax of the *Queste* as a work of art comes with the experiences of the three chosen knights, Perceval, Bors, and Galahad, at the castle of Corbenic or, as Malory calls it, Carbonek—a name about which more will be said in Chapter XIV. On their arrival they were welcomed with great joy by King Pelles, his saintly niece, and his son Eliazar. This youth put the new arrivals to the familiar test of the broken sword, and, as in two earlier sword tests, Galahad succeeded where the others failed, and rejoined the pieces so that it seemed as if the blade had never been broken. Nine other knights opportunely joined the company, thus making the desired number of twelve, and announced that they had come to partake of the Holy Feast. Four damsels carried into the hall a bed on which lay a crowned man, and then retired. This royal invalid, who was surely the Maimed King, mentioned in the *Lancelot* as the father of Pelles, welcomed Galahad as the long-awaited knight who would allay his pain—an obvious repetition of the Mordrain theme. At the command of a mysterious voice, King Pelles, together with his son and daughter, left the hall. Here let me quote from Malory's condensed but fine version:[2]

And therewithal beseemed them that there came an old man and

---

[1] Pauphilet, *Études*, p. 155.   [2] Book xvii, chs. 20, 21.

four angels from heaven, clothed in likeness of a bishop, and had a cross in his hand; and these four angels bare him in a chair, and set him down before the table of silver whereupon the Sankgreal was; and it seemed that he had in middes of his forehead letters the which said: 'See ye here Joseph(es) [son of Joseph of Arimathea], *the first bishop of Christendom, the same which Our Lord sacred in the city of Sarras in the spiritual palace.' Then the knights marvelled, for that bishop was dead more than three hundred year tofore.*

'O knights,' said he, 'marvel not, for I was sometime an earthly man.'

With that they heard the chamber door open, and there they saw angels; and two bare candles of wax, and the third a towel, and the fourth a spear which bled marvellously, that the drops fell within a box which he held with his other hand. And they set the candles upon the table, and the third the towel upon the vessel, and the fourth the holy spear even upright upon the vessel. And then the bishop made semblant as though he would have gone to the sacring of the mass. And then he took the obley which was made in likeness of bread. And at the lifting up there came a figure in likeness of a child, and the visage was as red and as bright as any fire, and smote himself into the bread so that they all saw it that the bread was formed of a fleshly man; and then he put it into the holy vessel again, and then he did that longed to a priest to do to a mass. And then he went to Galahad and kissed him and bade him go and kiss his fellows; and so he did anon.

'Now,' said he, 'servants of Jesu Christ, ye shall be fed afore this table with sweet meats that never knights tasted.'

And when he had said, he vanished away. And they set them at the table in great dread, and made their prayers. Then looked they and saw a man come out of the holy vessel, that had all the signs of the passion of Jesu Christ, bleeding all openly, and said:

'My knights and my servants and my true children, which be come out of deadly life into spiritual life, I will now no longer hide me from you, but ye shall see now a part of my secrets and of my hidden things; now hold and receive the high meat which ye have so much desired.'

Then took He himself the holy vessel and came to Galahad; and he kneeled down and there he received his Saviour, and after him so received all his fellows; and they thought it so sweet that it was marvellous to tell. Then said He to Galahad: 'Son, wotest thou what I hold betwixt my hands?'

'Nay,' said he, 'but if ye will tell me.'

'This is,' said He, 'the holy dish wherein I ate the lamb on Sher-Thursday. And now hast thou seen that thou most desired to see, but yet hast thou not seen it so openly as thou shalt see it in the city of Sarras in the spiritual palace. Therefore thou must go hence and bear with thee this holy vessel; for this night it shall depart from the realm of Logres, that it shall never be seen more here. And wotest thou wherefore? For He is not served nor worshipped to his right by them of this land, for they be turned to evil living; therefore I shall disherit them of the honour which I have done them. And therefore go ye three tomorrow unto the sea, where ye shall find your ship ready, and with you take the sword with the strange girdles, and no more with you but Sir Percival and Bors. Also I will that ye take with you of the blood of this spear for to anoint the Maimed King, both his legs and all his body, for he shall have his health.'

'Sir,' said Galahad, 'why shall not these other fellows go with us?'

'For this cause; for right as I departed my apostles, one here and another there, so I will that ye depart; and two of you shall die in my service, but one of you shall come again and tell tidings.'

Then gave He them His blessing and vanished away. And Galahad went anon to the spear which lay upon the table, and touched the blood with his fingers, and came after to the Maimed King and anointed his legs. And therewith he clothed him anon, and start upon his feet out of his bed as an whole man, and thanked our Lord that He had healed him. And that was not to the world ward, for anon he yielded him to a place of religion of white monks, and was a full holy man.

It is hardly necessary to identify once more in this majestic version of the visit to the Grail castle the elements which originated in Celtic paganism. The very setting in a castle, rather than a minster or chapel, betrays the ultimate origin of

the theme in an Irish *echtra*. The sword-mending test, as shown
in Chapter VIII, may be remotely related to the mending of
the sword of Cailte in the *Colloquy of the Old Men*. King Pelles
is descended from the Welsh King Beli; and the Maimed
King, whose legs required the healing ministrations of Galahad, is descended from Beli's kinsman Brân, wounded in the
foot or thigh. The sacramental wafer, owing to mistranslation,
has taken the place of Brân's horn of plenty, and the Grail
itself represents the Welsh *Dysgl* or platter of plenty. The
bleeding spear derives from the fiery weapon of the god Lug.
But several of the conventional features have disappeared;
angels have replaced the Grail Bearer for obvious reasons, and
there is no question test nor any reference to the Waste Land.
The venerable figure of Bishop Josephes has been brought in
from some version of the early history of the Grail.[1]

The author's main purpose in recasting this traditional
material was to illustrate certain doctrines or concepts attached
to the sacrament of the mass, and these have been identified
and illuminatingly set forth by Pauphilet.[2] They are three in
number: (1) the divine liturgy; (2) the apostolic communion;
(3) transubstantiation visualized, the motif previously illustrated in *Perlesvaus*.

The divine liturgy, meaning the participation of the celestial
hosts in the terrestrial office of the mass, was a natural development of Christian thought and one which found early expression. Surely even the heavenly ones would wish to participate
at times in so high a sacrament, and the verse of the Psalmist,
'Thou art a priest for ever after the order of Melchizedek,'
suggested that in this celestial liturgy Christ is the officiant as
well as the victim. To the eyes of faith this invisible solemnity
might become visible, and as far back as the fifth century the
patriarch John was reported to have seen, as he performed the
holy sacrifice, angels descending from heaven in splendid
vestments and remaining motionless until the consummation

---

[1] The *Estoire del Saint Graal*, in which Josephes is most prominent, must be
ruled out if, as scholars agree, it was composed after the *Queste*. J. D. Bruce,
Evolution of Arthurian Romance, i. 374–9.

[2] Pauphilet, *Études*, pp. 94–102.

of the mystery. Presumably it is this well-established belief in the presence of angelic visitants at the celebration of the Eucharist and in the assumption of the priestly office by Christ Himself which has led to the introduction of these two features into the high mass at Corbenic.

The second eucharistic theme which the author of the *Queste* blended with the first is the apostolic communion, a re-enactment of the Last Supper. Taking the very dish which He had used on that memorable evening before the Crucifixion, the Lord administered the bread which He had broken to the kneeling twelve. Judged by rigid standards of structural harmony, the idea of the apostolic communion is not happy, for it has forced the author to bring in suddenly and without preparation nine knights to join the three elect. Who are they, and what have they done to deserve this supreme privilege? But where so much is mystery, one mystery the more should not be disturbing.

The third eucharistic theme is one which we have met already in *Perlesvaus*—transubstantiation made visible. There is no need to recall the fact that at the time when these romances were composed the doctrine of the Real Presence of Christ's body in the consecrated Host did not lack for ocular demonstration, if the reports of visionaries are to be believed. And in 1215, at the Fourth Lateran Council it was proclaimed an article of faith.

The daring with which the author of the *Queste* combined these disparate materials, drawn in part from the marvels of Arthurian fiction and in part from the mysteries of the Christian faith, is matched only by the lofty and tender feeling with which he endowed this climactic scene.

I regret to say that the remainder of the *Queste* is something of an anti-climax, both as narrative art and as meaningful allegory. Once more the three heroes embark on the seas, this time for the land of Sarras—that is, the Holy Land, then occupied by *Sarrasins* (Saracens, Moslems). On the voyage a symbolic Crucifixion takes place when Galahad lies down on the bed of Solomon, but it is related in an extremely casual fashion.[1] At the gates of Sarras a cripple is miraculously cured, in obvious imitation of Peter's curing the lame man at the gate of the Temple at Jerusalem, and the three heroes of the quest are promptly imprisoned as were the apostles, according to the Book of Acts.[2] The coronation of Galahad after their release has, of course, no biblical counterpart, but seems rather to represent an intrusion of secular history of the author's own era—the crowning of several Christian kings at Jerusalem between 1100 and 1187, before the city fell to Saladin. The description of the mass celebrated by the *revenant* Joseph of Arimathea in the palace of Sarras and Galahad's mystic vision, though doubtless intended as the culmination of the work, suffers from the perfunctory repetition of several features of the mass at Corbenic.[3] Even the ascent of Galahad's soul to the skies, attended by a multitude of angels, is not an inspired passage. Altogether, the experiences of the three chosen knights in the land of Sarras, if one is expecting significant allegory or symbolism or an elevation of tone comparable to the scene at Corbenic, are disappointing.

[1] See above, p. 187, n. 3.   [2] iii. 1–10; v. 17–19.

[3] See, however, Gilson, op. cit., p. 87, n. 1: 'Le seul auteur qui ait vu et dit que la fin de la *Queste* est une extase de Galaad est, à notre connaissance du moins, Mme Myrrha Lot-Borodine . . . "Voilà pourquoi, ayant goûté une première fois aux délices de l'extase, Galaad qui se révèle en ce moment comme le plus pur mystique, ne veut pas survivre à l'extase qui l'attend plus complète encore, il le sait, là-bas . . .".'

XIII

Parzival, the Spiritual Biography of a Knight

IN several ways the *Queste del Saint Graal* presents an antithesis to the German masterpiece, the *Parzival* of Wolfram von Eschenbach:[1] the one composed in lucid French prose, the other in German rimed couplets, tending at times to eccentricity and obscurity of expression; the one consistently serious, the other shot through with glints of ironic humour and streaks of whimsy; the one confined in its geographical interest, except at the close, to Arthur's Britain, the other spreading over nearly every Christian land and extending eastwards to Bagdad and the land of Prester John; the one extolling a life of celibacy and mystic contemplation, the other setting forth a more secular but no less Christian ideal which combined trust in God with chivalric obligations and the strong ties of marriage and family.

Both authors realized the necessity of remodelling their material and displayed great originality and sense of design, rejecting and adding in conformity with fixed purposes. The modern reader may admire the flawless Galahad and may enter with sympathy into his ecstasies, but he is likely to prefer a hero like Parzival, who goes through a series of far commoner experiences—makes ludicrous blunders in his youth, learns something of the ways of the world, falls in love and marries, commits through ignorance a grave fault and blames God for the consequences, but later abandons his defiant pose, and returns to domestic felicity. Besides, the *Queste* must always suffer from the preponderance of allegory and sermon

[1] The best accounts in English of Wolfram and the *Parzival* are Otto Springer's chapter in *Arthurian Literature in the Middle Ages*, ed. R. S. Loomis, pp. 218–50 (see also pp. 290–4); M. F. Richey, *Studies of Wolfram von Eschenbach* (Edinburgh, 1957); and J. D. Bruce, *Evolution of Arthurian Romance*, i. 313–41. The best complete translation is by H. M. Mustard and C. E. Passage (New York, 1961).

in its make-up, whereas *Parzival* has the roundedness and solidity of the epic or the novel.

The poem was composed between 1200 and 1210 and was therefore roughly contemporary with Robert de Boron's *Joseph* and a decade or two earlier than *Perlesvaus* and the Prose *Lancelot*. The poet was a Bavarian knight, well known in his day for his lyrics and his redaction of a *chanson de geste* about Guillaume d'Orange, *Wilehalm*. He professed himself unable to read, and his acquaintance with the French language was surely defective, but a man who invented anagrams and quoted Latin with understanding, even if only two words, was certainly no illiterate. He displayed a wider range of miscellaneous information than many literate writers, though of course he does not approach Dante. Among the German poets whose works he knew and from whom he culled proper names were Hartmann von Aue and Ulrich von Zatzikhoven.

The main source for *Parzival* was the *Conte del Graal*, including not only Chrétien's poem but also the First Sequel in the short version, and possibly the so-called *Bliocadran Prologue*, which gives a brief history of Perceval's father and mother and of Perceval's own infancy. But Wolfram concludes his poem with the statement that, Chrétien de Troyes having told the tale amiss, he has chosen to follow Kyot the Provençal. In Book IX he expatiates on the subject. In Toledo, Kyot chanced on a book in heathen characters, written by a Saracen named Flegetanis, who had read about the Grail in the stars! This imperfect record Kyot had supplemented by research in French and Latin tomes and in the chronicles of Ireland, Britain, and Anjou. The composite work, we are asked to believe, was Wolfram's source.

Acres of printed matter have been filled with discussions of this preposterous claim—a very characteristic example of Wolfram's love of mystification. Only two things are clear: no Provençal influence can be detected in the language or the matter of *Parzival*; it is impossible to prove or disprove that an unknown Frenchman named Guiot wrote a lost work which supplied Wolfram with additional material on the

Grail. But even if Kyot is a phantom, the question of one or more lost French sources, supplementing the *Conte del Graal*, remains.

One of the chief problems of Wolfram scholarship, then, is this: Did Wolfram make use of other traditional materials, whether in oral or written form, concerning Perceval, his ancestry, and the Grail, besides those furnished by the *Conte del Graal*? The answer should not be too hard to come at by the application of common sense. If Wolfram, when he deviates from the *Conte del Graal* as he knew it, agrees again and again on significant points with other versions of the Grail legend, then he must have been acquainted either with these works, or their sources, or their congeners. In some cases chance may account for the agreement, but in others, where details of a very specific kind are involved, chance is ruled out. I propose to deal with this question by pointing out at once two instances of such precise agreement, and reserving further instances till they turn up in the discussion of other matters.

1. Wolfram tells of two brothers, hostile to Parzival's mother, who have seized his patrimony and killed one of his knights.[1] There is no specific statement of this kind in the *Conte del Graal*, but in *Perlesvaus* the Lord of the Fens and Cahot the Red made war on Perceval's mother, seized his patrimony, and killed one of her knights.[2]

2. According to Wolfram, a river called Sabins flows within view of the Castle of Ladies.[3] Chrétien does not name the river, but calls the castle Roche de Sanguin.[4] The *Queste del Saint Graal* places the castle of the captive maidens on the river Saverne,[5] the Severn, of which the medieval latinized form was Sabrina. There is strong support for the view that this localization of the Castle of Maidens on the Severn was traditional.[6]

---

[1] *Parzival*, 128, 3–128, 12; 140, 26–141, 10.

[2] *Perlesvaus*, ed. Nitze, i, ll. 1015–20, 1065–78, 3201–9, 5295–303.

[3] *Parzival*, 604, 1.

[4] *Percevalroman*, ed. A. Hilka, vs. 8817. This is the reading of four MSS., and is supported by the explanation that the name was due to the green, sanguine, and scarlet cloths dyed there.   [5] *Queste*, ed. Pauphilet, pp. 47–50.

[6] Loomis, *Arthurian Tradition*, pp. 451–7.

Thus it is clear that Wolfram must have derived two specific features of his romance from some other source than the *Conte del Graal*. Since he could not have taken them from *Perlesvaus* or the *Queste*, he must have been acquainted with at least one lost traditional source. And in due course we shall discover other evidence of the same kind.

The first two books of *Parzival*, which cover the history of Gahmuret, the hero's father, are involved in the Kyot problem, since it is still debated whether they betray the influence of any other Perceval story besides Chrétien's:[1] but the problem is too remote from the central theme of the Grail to delay us here. The early adventures of Parzival himself correspond in a general way to the outline provided by Chrétien, and though deviations occur, they may easily be accounted for as signs of Wolfram's independence of mind and imagination. Taking up the story with Parzival's arrival in the hall of the Fisher King, we may see that imagination at work.[2]

A hundred candelabra, filled with many candles, hung above the members of the household, and small candles were set around the walls. Parzival beheld a hundred couches, prepared by the servants, and a hundred quilts spread on them. Each couch furnished seats for four; between them there was space and a round rug lay in front. The son of King Frimutel (Fil lu Roy Frimutel) *could well afford such luxury. Another thing, which did not seem too costly, was not forgotten: three square fireplaces built of marble and piled with wood, of which the name was 'lignum aloe'. Neither before nor now has so great a blaze been seen here at Wildenberg. They were worth a great price.*

The lord of the castle had been laid by his command on a folding bed beside the middle fireplace. He and Joy had parted company, and his life was naught but dying.

Into the hall came radiant Parzival and was well received by him who had sent him there [the Fisher King], *and who bade him no longer stand at the door but to come nearer and sit down. 'Come*

[1] *Arthurian Literature in the Middle Ages*, ed. Loomis, p. 225, n. 3; p. 291. Newstead in *Romanic Review*, xxxvi (1945), pp. 3–7.   [2] *Parzival*, 229, 24–240, 30.

hither to me! If I let you sit farther away, I would be treating you as a stranger.' So spoke the tortured host.

Because of his malady he had ordered the great fire and clad himself in warm garments, made of wide and long sable skins, both inside and outside, and he wore over them a mantle. Even the poorest of the furs was worthy of praise, and was black and gray. Likewise he had on his head a rich cap of most precious sable, and around it a band of Arabian stuff, with a knob of glowing ruby in the middle.

There sat many a goodly knight, and there, before them, a dolorous thing was brought in. A squire rushed in through the door, holding a lance—it was a custom which ever wakened grief. From the point blood flowed, ran down the shaft to the hand, and trickled into the sleeve. Weeping and shrieking arose throughout the wide hall. The people of thirty lands could not shed more tears. The squire bore the lance in his hands around the four walls, and back to the door, and then sprang out. Stilled was the people's outcry, which had been called forth by the anguish of which the lance borne by the squire reminded them.

If it will not weary you, I will now begin to tell how the knights were served in courtly fashion. At the end of the hall a steel door opened, and in came two highborn girls—hear how they were arrayed —who could well reward love if any man did them service; they were pure maidens. Two chaplets of flowers were the only covering of their locks. Each bore in her hand a golden candlestick. Their hair was long and curled and yellow. They carried shining lights. We must not forget the dress of the maidens as they entered. The Countess of Tenabroc (Edinburgh) wore a gown of brown wool, and her companion also. The gowns were clasped close at the waist with girdles. Next came a duchess and a companion, bearing ivory trestles; their red mouths were aglow. All four bowed, and two at once set the trestles before the host. This done to perfection, the four made a group, all fair to look on and all dressed alike.

Behold, without further tarrying eight other ladies entered, four bearing large candles, four carrying without difficulty a slab of precious stone, through which by day the sun shone. It was a red jacinth by name, and was long and broad. To make it light in weight, he who designed it for a table had cut it quite thin. From this the host *was wont to eat in lordly fashion. These eight went straight to the host and bowed their heads, and four laid the table on the ivory trestles, white as snow, which had already been set up. This done, they withdrew with grace and joined the other four. These eight wore gowns greener than grass, samite of Azagouc, which were long and wide. Rich girdles, narrow and long, confined them round the waist. Each of these eight noble ladies wore a garland of flowers about her hair. The daughters of Count Iwan of Nonel and Count Jernis of Ril, who had been chosen and had travelled many a mile to serve here, now approached, splendidly garbed. Each of the two carried on a napkin, a knife, sharp as a fishbone, a wonder to behold. The knives were of silver, hard and bright, and such craft had been bestowed on them that they were sharp enough to cut steel. The bearers of the silver were preceded by four pure maidens whose duty was to carry lights. These six came forward; now hear what each of them did.*

They bowed. Then the two who carried the silver knives laid them on the beautiful table and then joined the first twelve. If I have counted aright, there should now be eighteen women standing in a group. And look, now six more were seen approaching, wearing costly robes made half of gold brocade, and half of silk from Nineveh. They and the six who went before wore particoloured gowns, bought at a great price.

After them came the Queen; her countenance shone so that it seemed to all that the sun was rising. The lady was clad in silk of Arabia, and she bore, resting on a green silk cloth, the perfection of the Earthly Paradise (der wunsch von pardise), *both roots and branches. It was a thing men call the Grail, which surpassed every earthly ideal. Repanse de Joie was the name of her to whom the Grail granted the office of bearer, for it was of such a nature that only she who guarded her chastity and shunned deceit had the right to tend it.*

There passed now in front of the Grail lights which gave no hint of poverty, six tall shapely vessels of clear glass, in which balsam flamed. As these came from the door in fair array, the Queen and all the maidens who bore the vessels of balsam bowed. The pure Queen then set the Grail down before the lord of the castle. The story says that Parzival fixed his eyes and thoughts on her who had brought the Grail and who had previously sent him the mantle he wore. Then these seven ladies withdrew with dignity to join the first eighteen, and she who was of the highest degree took her place in the midst, with twelve on each side, as I was told. She stood resplendent, the maiden with her crown.

Then to all the knights seated throughout the hall chamberlains brought water in golden basins to wash their hands, one to every four, and fair pages served them with white towels. Everywhere were signs of opulence. A hundred tables were brought in through the door, and were set down, one for every four noble knights, and white cloths were spread on them. The host himself, void of joy, was the first to wash, and Parzival with him. Then the son of an earl on bended knee handed them a fine silk towel. To every table four squires were assigned to tend the wants of those who sat at it, two to kneel and carve, and two to serve diligently drink and food.

Listen and hear of further splendours. Four wagons were rolled in, laden with many a precious vessel of gold for the use of the seated knights, and were stationed one at each of the four walls. Four knights put the vessels on the tables, and each was followed by a scribe whose duty was to see that the vessels were all accounted for after the repast.

Harken to another strange thing. At the command a hundred squires came before the Grail and ceremoniously took bread on white napkins, and then distributed themselves at the tables. I have been told, and I tell you on your oath (if I deceive you, then you as well as I will be liars), that whatever one held his hand out for lay ready in front of the Grail—hot food, cold food, fresh dishes, second helpings, meat of tame and wild animals. Many a man will say that such a thing has never been seen, but they do wrong to doubt. For the Grail was the fruition of joy, such abundance of earthly sweetness that it nearly equalled what we are told of heaven. In little golden vessels each man received whatever sauces each dish required, whether salty, peppery, or sour. Both modest and immoderate appetites were satisfied. Everything was set before them with great ceremony. If a man held out his cup, whatever drink he could name—mulberry juice, wine, red sinopel—he found in it through the magic of the

Grail. *Thus the noble assemblage enjoyed the hospitality of the Grail.*

Well did Parzival observe the abundance and the great wonders, but courtesy made him loath to inquire about them. He thought: 'Gurnemanz counselled me, in all sincerity and good will, not to ask many questions. Perhaps my stay here will extend as long as my stay with him. Then without asking I shall learn the ways of this company.'

As he was pondering, a squire approached, carrying a sword. The scabbard was worth a thousand marks, the hilt was a ruby, and the blade seemed to be a worker of marvels. The host gave it to his guest, saying: 'Sir, I bore it in perils in many lands before God smote my body. Now may it serve as recompense to you if your reception here has fallen short. Take it wherever you go, and if ever you put it to the test, it will protect you against your adversaries.'

Alas that Parzival did not then put the question! I grieve for him still. When he grasped the weapon, it should have prompted him to ask. I sorrow too for his gracious host, suffering an affliction which a question would have relieved.

Now all had been amply fed, and the attendants took up and bore away the gear. First the wagons were loaded. Then each lady did her part, and those who had come first were now the last. They escorted their mistress back to the Grail, and she, the Queen, and all the damsels made seemly obeisance to the lord of the castle. Then they carried all that they had ceremoniously brought with them out through the door.

Parzival gazed after them, and, before the door was closed, he glimpsed lying on a couch in the chamber beyond, the fairest old man he had ever seen. I dare say, without exaggeration, his hair was greyer than the mist. Who he was, you will learn later, and I will also tell about the host, his castle, and his land in due time in orderly fashion, without dispute and without delay.

The rest of Parzival's visit to the Grail castle is easily explained as an elaboration of Chrétien's narrative and needs no comment. And indeed a comparison of the whole adventure with the translation of the French text in Chapter IV shows that there is a close relation. Most of Wolfram's divergences fall into neat categories. First, we note a tendency to stress the luxury and magnificence of the Fisher King's household. There are three great fires in the hall instead of one. There are twenty-five women in the Grail procession instead of two, and the bearer of the talisman is a crowned queen. Secondly, great emphasis is laid on the proprieties: the word *zuht*, meaning 'breeding, discipline, manners,' occurs repeatedly. Thirdly, names, either coined by Wolfram or picked at random from various sources, are assigned to persons whom Chrétien left anonymous. Fourthly, there is an evident desire to render the events, however spectacular and marvellous, more reasonable. The gift of the sword to Parzival, instead of being a meaningless or even absurd irrelevance as in the French poem, is postponed and linked up with Parzival's failure to ask the question. The repeated passing of the Grail procession with every course served in the hall, which is so difficult to reconcile with Chrétien's later description of the Grail Bearer's errand, has been expunged.

Wolfram knew not only Chrétien's poem but also the short version of the First Sequel, translated in Chapter VI, and it seems clear that he took over from this source certain details which he conflated with his main source, Chrétien. These borrowings from Gawain's visit to the Grail castle are: the ruby worn by the Fisher King; the spreading of the tablecloths; the washing of hands, first by the Fisher King, then by Parzival; the provision by the Grail, first of bread, then of food and drink. From this same source Wolfram may have taken the hint for postponing the presentation of the sword till after the repast. Thus Wolfram's narrative of the visit to the Grail castle seems clearly explicable as an adaptation to the poet's taste and intelligence of the elements supplied either by Chrétien or the first continuator.

There is one noteworthy feature, however, which is not to be found in these two sources but which is represented in *Peredur* and *Sone de Nansai*. In the Welsh tale, it will be remembered, when Peredur was being entertained by the second of his two uncles, two youths entered bearing a large spear, streaming with blood.[1] 'When all the company saw this, they began wailing and lamenting, so that it was not easy for anyone to endure it.' Likewise, in *Sone*, when the abbot who ruled over the monastery in the castle of Galoche exhibited the holy spear-head, 'he and the monks wept and seemed to dissolve in tears.'[2] This outcry, provoked by the appearance of the lance, seems, therefore, to be a matter of tradition, and since Wolfram could not have read *Peredur* or *Sone*, he probably derived it from some lost account of Perceval's visit to the Grail castle.

To be sure, the first continuator mentions repeatedly the lamentation of the folk about the mysterious corpse on the bier, but he links this manifestation of grief in no way with the spear, which is fixed upright in the hall. The correspondence between Wolfram on the one hand and *Peredur* and *Sone* on the other is far closer on this point than any correspondence between Wolfram and the First Sequel. Accordingly, unless it is due to pure chance, we have in this outburst of woe a third traditional element, not derived from the *Conte del Graal*, to add to those already discovered—the two invaders of Parzival's patrimony and the name of the river, Sabins.

Parzival's meeting with his female cousin is modelled on Chrétien's version, and does not need to be rehearsed. It is characteristic of Wolfram's whimsical coinage of proper names that he calls the lady Sigune, obviously an anagram formed from the French common noun *cusine*. She is described as perched on a linden-tree—a saintly dryad, clasping the embalmed body of her lover. This curious situation of the mourning maiden is surely due to a defective manuscript, which read *sor*, 'on', instead of *soz*, 'beneath'. One of the significant differences between Wolfram and Chrétien is the suppression of the unrealistic attribution of Perceval's silence to his sin in abandoning his mother; instead Wolfram has substituted as the cause of the youth's fateful silence the wholly realistic and meaningful fault of callousness to suffering.[3] Sigune exclaims: 'Dishonoured and accursed man! You bear a wolf's venomous

---

[1] See above, p. 90.   [2] See above, p. 138.   [3] 255, 13–255, 19.

tooth since a canker has rooted itself vigorously in your heart. You should have taken pity on your host, on whom God has brought so strange a calamity, and you should have inquired about his woe.' Here then at last, through Wolfram's boldness and intelligence, the motif of the question test has assumed a poignant meaning.

Sigune alludes to what may well be a traditional folk-tale motif attached to the Grail castle: if anyone beholds it, it must be without deliberate intent.[1] There is no such statement in Chrétien or in the First Sequel, though the notion might be suggested by either one. Similar statements recur in other Grail romances. In *Perlesvaus* a hermit, when asked by what way one may go to the hostel of the Fisher King, informs Gawain that 'no one can show you the way unless the will of God leads you there'.[2] In the Prose *Tristan* (Bib. Nat., fr. 101, fol. 392*v*) we read: 'If anyone asks me why errant knights did not go straight to Corbenic when they knew that the Holy Grail was there, I would answer him as the ancient history testifies. The castle of Corbenic surely does not move, but Tanaburs, an enchanter who lived before Uther Pendragon, and who was the wisest man in necromancy except Merlin only, so bewitched the castle that no stranger knight who sought it would find it unless chance led him.' Whether these various assertions that the Grail castle was not to be reached except by the will of God or by chance had a common origin in a folk-tale motif is a matter on which opinions may differ. It is possible that they represent rational inferences arrived at separately on the basis of the *Conte del Graal*. They cannot, therefore, be claimed with certainty as of traditional origin.

The arrival at Arthur's court of the Loathly Damsel, whom Wolfram calls Kundrie, differs not greatly from the incident as told by Chrétien, except that she is described in even more fantastic terms.[3] She was an accomplished linguist, speaking Latin and French as well as the tongues of heathendom, and was versed in dialectic, geometry, and astronomy. Her hideous

---

[1] 250, 26–30.
[2] *Perlesvaus*, ed. Nitze, i, ll. 947–9.   [3] 312, 6–314, 10.

animal features were accentuated by her fashionable and costly attire. She wore a mantle of cloth of Ghent, cut in the French fashion; a new London hat trimmed with peacock feathers hung at her back; her whip was of silk with a ruby handle. Yet such were her features that seldom was there jousting in her honour!

Kundrie denounced the hero more violently than did her counterpart in Chrétien's poem, and, like Sigune, she made it clear that his grievous fault lay in his callousness to suffering.[1] 'Tell me, Sir Parzival, why, when the unhappy Fisherman sat beside you, bereft of joy and comfort, did you not deliver him from sorrow?'

The effect on Parzival of this public humiliation before the court of Arthur was twofold. He acknowledged to a lady who tried to cheer him that he had failed in compassion: that is, the fruit or the manifestation of 'charity' or love of one's neighbour, enjoined by Christ in the second great commandment. ' "Ah, help-forsaken Anfortas, what help didst thou get from me?" '[2] But he feels that his punishment has been excessive, questions the justice of God, and rebels against Him in a very modern way. As the Welshman prepares to leave the court in disgrace, he says to Gawain:[3] ' "What is God? Were He almighty, He would not have put us both to open shame. I have served Him faithfully because I hoped for His grace. Now I will renounce His service! If He hates me, I will endure it." '

Whether justified or not, this reaction to calamity is one which many have experienced since Homo Sapiens first began to ponder his fate, and it is not uncommon today. The Book of Parzival thus begins to take on something of the dignity and depth of the Book of Job. Wolfram has endowed the ancient and tangled tale with ageless relevance and meaning.[4]

But Professor W. T. H. Jackson has demonstrated that the poet, being a man of his age, treated Parzival's psychology in accordance with prevailing ideas about the virtues and vices

[1] 315, 26–315, 30.   [2] 330, 29 f.   [3] 332, 1–332, 8.
[4] Mary E. Thomas, *Medieval Skepticism and Chaucer* (New York, 1950), pp. 28 f.

as illustrated, for instance, in *The Fruits of the Flesh and the Spirit* of Hugh of St. Victor.[1] Wolfram was far from being an adept in the subtleties of the schoolmen (though some scholars would like to have us think so), but he could not help absorbing what was taught from the pulpit and imaged in the arts.

Parzival in his outburst had committed the blackest of sins, pride and anger, and these in turn involved him in others. Pride led him to vainglory, boasting of his prowess in arms, and to disobedience, refusal to submit to God's will. Anger led him to blasphemy, to foolhardiness, and finally to gloom and despair. Parzival has reached this stage when we meet him again in Book IX. Like Chrétien's hero, he has ridden at adventure for several years, has unhorsed many adversaries, and at last on Good Friday meets a group of penitents. To the old knight who asked why he was fully armed on this holy day, he replied that he paid no heed to weeks and days, and that, though he had once served and trusted God, God's help had failed him.[2] And he thought: 'I am at strife with Him whom they love. He has been chary of His help to me, and has not preserved me from misery.' But as he parted from the penitents, he said to himself: 'What if God's help can end my sorrow? If He ever rewarded the service of a knight, if today is His day for helping, let Him help, if help He can!'

In this chastened mood, Parzival came to the dwelling of his uncle, the hermit Trevrizent. At this point Wolfram inserts the long passage about Flegetanis and Kyot which has been summarized at the beginning of this chapter.[3] In the course of it we learn that the Grail had been left on earth by the neutral angels when, after the downfall of Lucifer, they returned to the region above the stars. (Though many scholars have assumed that the Grail was brought down from heaven, Wolfram does not say so.) Since that time it has been in the keeping of chaste Christians.

Welcomed by the hermit and putting off his armour, Parzival confesses to a hatred of God, as the father of his sorrows,

---

[1] *Germanic Review*, xxxiii (1958), pp. 118–24.
[2] 447, 19–447, 30. [3] 453, 1–456, 4.

and maintains that it is to God's shame that, having the power to help, He denies His help to Parzival. Thereupon Trevrizent assures the doubter of God's love, made manifest through the Incarnation, and convinces him of his folly. When asked concerning the nature of the Grail, he begins a long and amazing discourse.[1]

'*I know well that many knights abide with the Grail at Munsalvaesche* [the Grail Castle]. *Often they ride out seeking adventure. These same Templeisen, whether they meet with defeat or victory, make atonement for their sins. There a noble fellowship dwells, and I will tell you how they are sustained. They live by virtue of a stone most pure. If you do not know its name, now learn: it is called* lapis exilis (small, or paltry, stone).[2] *By the power of the stone the phoenix is burned to ashes, but the ashes speedily restore it to life. The phoenix thus moults and thereupon gives out a bright light so that it is as beautiful as before. Never is a man so ill but that, if he sees the Grail on any day, he is immune from death during the week that follows. Besides, his looks never change; he retains the same appearance as on the day he saw the stone. Whether it be maid or man, even if he beholds the stone two hundred years he keeps the appearance of his prime, except that his hair turns grey. Such virtue the stone gives to men that flesh and bones grow young at once. The stone is also called the Grail.*

'*Today there comes to it a messenger on which its highest power depends. This is Good Friday, when a dove is expected surely to descend from heaven and bring a little white mass-wafer and lay it on the stone. The dove itself is gleaming white and returns to heaven. Always on Good Friday, as I have said, it brings to the stone that from which it obtains the power to provide whatever good thing grows on earth of food and drink, as it were the perfection of Paradise* (als wunsch von pardis). *The stone also supplies them with every kind of game under the sky, whether it flies or runs or swims. Thus the virtue of the Grail sustains the knightly brotherhood.*

[1] 468, 23–471, 29.
[2] Only one inferior MS. gives the reading *lapis* (469, 7); most of the others read *lapsit*. One cannot be certain, therefore, as to what the poet actually wrote, but since he identified the Grail with a stone and knew the *Iter Alexandri ad Paradisum* (see below), he probably wrote *lapis*.

'Hear next how those who are chosen for the service of the Grail
are revealed. Around the end of the stone an inscription in letters tells
the name and lineage of those, be they maids or boys, who are called
to make the journey to the Grail. No one needs to erase the inscription, for as soon as it has been read it vanishes. All who now form
the great company came as children, and happy the mother who bore
a child destined to that service. Parents, whether poor or rich, rejoice
alike if their child is summoned to join that band. From many countries these children are gathered. From sin they are preserved, and
they receive their reward in heaven, for when they die here they are
awarded their supreme recompense there.

'The noble and worthy angels who took neither side when Lucifer
warred with the Trinity were sent down to earth as custodians of
this stone, which is forever pure. I know not whether God forgave
them or destroyed them; if His justice so ordained, He recalled them
to Himself. Since that time, those whom He has called and to whom
He sent His angel guard the stone. Sir, such is the nature of the
Grail.'

When Parzival asserts on the strength of his deeds of prowess, God ought to elect him to that company, Trevrizent
rebukes him with the words: 'There in that fellowship you
must with humble heart guard against pride. Your youth may
easily lead you to violate the law of modesty. Pride is always
doomed to fall.'

As we look back over what Wolfram says of the Grail, it is
easy to see that it owes little to Chrétien but the attendance of
maidens and youths upon an object sanctified by the eucharistic wafer, and owes little to the first continuator but the notion
that the object was a miraculous provider of food and drink.
It is a legitimate conclusion that Trevrizent's exposition of the
mysterious stone, its history and properties was in large measure original with the German poet. This need not mean,
however, that it was as purely fanciful as his account of Kyot's
book, which was the alleged source of all his information. In
fact, it is possible to detect with more or less certainty both

[1] 472, 13-472, 17.

traditional elements and literary materials which went into the make-up of his elaborate description of the Grail.

One cannot but notice the marked concurrence of *Parzival* with *Perlesvaus* in ascribing to the talisman the power of averting the signs of age. The hermit, in the latter romance, who looked only forty years old when he was over seventy, said that all who served the Grail were youthful in seeming; and Gawain found in the Grail castle twelve grey-haired knights who, though they were over a hundred years of age, seemed to be only forty. Most striking is the statement concerning the two elders whom Perceval met on the island where the Grail was finally destined to repair. Their beards were white as snow, and they had known Joseph of Arimathea before the Crucifixion, but yet they seemed young of visage. Compare this with Trevrizent's declaration that whoever beholds the stone two hundred years retains the appearance of his prime, except that his hair turns grey. This miraculous immunity from physical decay, it was demonstrated in Chapter IX, was ascribed to the followers of Brân the Blessed as they spent eighty years on the island of Grassholm, and has been carried down into the Arthurian romances and applied to those who formed the household of the Fisher King. Naturally, the Grail was taken to be the cause of the miracle. We now have four traditional elements in Wolfram's *Parzival* which cannot be found in Chrétien or the First Sequel.

Still a fifth traditional feature, not supplied by Chrétien or the first continuator, is the association of the Grail with the Earthly Paradise. This linking was not of Celtic provenance, though in the *Voyage of St. Brendan* there was a similar fusion of the Celtic Elysium with the Garden of Eden. Wolfram twice referred to the Grail itself as the 'wunsch von pardise'— a phrase not easily translated but presumably suggested by the paradisal plenty of food and drink supplied by the talisman. But this idea was not the German poet's invention. *Perlesvaus*, we have seen, described the castle of the Fisher King as encircled by one of the rivers of Paradise and assigned to it the name of Edein. We read in Gerbert's continuation of the *Conte del Graal*[1] that hardly had Perceval left the site of the same castle when, riding along a river bank, he came to an enclosure walled with red and white marble and heard music of harps and organs within. He was refused entrance, however, and was told by a white-haired man that the enclosure was the Earthly Paradise. According to the *Didot Perceval*[2] the hero beheld two children playing in the branches of a beautiful tree, who told him that they came from Paradise and gave him directions in his quest of the Grail; and shortly after he did indeed reach the dwelling of the Fisher King. In the *Jüngere Titurel* (c. 1270) it is stated that the Grail knights 'had Earthly Paradise from the Grail'. Gert van der Schuren in his *Chronicle of Cleves* (1478) remarked that the Knight of the Swan came from the Earthly Paradise, which some folk call the Grail.[3] Thus we may feel assured that there was a persistent tradition which identified the Grail castle with the Terrestrial Paradise or placed it in the vicinity thereof. This tradition Wolfram must have known, and also the tradition that those who dwelt in the castle and were fed by the Grail were exempt from the ravages of age.

What more natural than that a poet so curious about Oriental wonders should have turned to some version of the journey of Alexander the Great to the Earthly Paradise? Ehrismann, Ranke, and Krogmann have proved that he must have known this popular legend,[4] but in what form is not clear. In Lamprecht's *Alexanderlied*, vs. 7107, he could have read that the stone sent to Alexander from the gate of the Earthly Paradise gives 'den alden di jugint', 'gives youth to the old'. While this text would account for the identification of the Grail with a rejuvenating talisman, the *Iter Alexandri ad Paradisum* suggests why Wolfram asserted that it was called *lapis exilis*.[5] This

---

[1] Ed. Mary Williams (Paris, 1922), i, vss. 138–285.

[2] Ed. W. Roach (Philadelphia, 1941), p. 203. See on this episode ibid., pp. 73–76, and E. S. Greenfield in *Traditio*, x (1954), pp. 323–71.

[3] Blöte in *Zeitschr. f. deutsches Altertum*, xlii. 4. See P. S. Barto, *Tannhäuser and the Mountain of Venus* (New York, 1916), pp. 9–11.

[4] *Zeitschr. f. deutsches Altertum*, lxv (1928), p. 63. *Trivium* (Zürich), iv (1946), pp. 24–26. *Zeitschr. f. deutsches Altertum*, lxxxv (1954), pp. 35–38.

[5] *La Prise de Defur and Le Voyage d'Alexandre au Paradis Terrestre*, ed. Peckham

Latin text informs us that the stone sent to the conqueror from Paradise was of great brilliance and rare colour, but was like in form and size to a human eye. Alexander consulted his wise men in vain, but an ancient Jew told him that the stone, when placed in scales, would outweigh any quantity of gold; but, when it was covered with a little dirt, a feather would tip the scales against it. It was like the human eye because human cupidity for earth's treasures is insatiable; but when the eye is closed with dust, all lust for power and riches departs. 'This stone [*lapis*] prefigures thee, master of the world, warns thee, and rebukes thee; this small [*exilis*] substance restrains thee from the cravings of basest ambition.' Alexander took the lesson to heart and abandoned his scheme of world conquest.

The tale of Alexander and the stone from Paradise is therefore a parable. Derived originally from Jewish sources, it attained considerable celebrity in the West through its Latin, French, and German forms. It seems clear that in it Wolfram found an answer to what must have puzzled him, the meaning of the word *graal*, which even Frenchmen frequently misunderstood. Neither in the description of the feast at Munsalvaesche nor elsewhere did the German poet give a hint that the talisman was a vessel. Ignorant of the true meaning of *graal* but impressed by its paradisal associations and by the youth-preserving virtue traditionally ascribed to the object, he assumed that the Grail and the stone of the Alexander legend were one and the same thing.

Wolfram took full advantage of this discovery. If the *lapis exilis* was conceived as a rebuke to Alexander's pride and as a symbol of man's insignificance, it fitted neatly into the ethical framework of his poem. As already observed, Parzival in questioning the justice of God had committed the sin of pride, and needed to be taught the lesson of humility. Accordingly, we find that Trevrizent in his discourse to Parzival twice admonished him to avoid pride and practise humility.[1] And

and La Du (Princeton, 1935), pp. xxxii–lii. On the legend see Lascelles in *Medium Ævum*, v (1936), pp. 36–45; H. R. Patch, *The Other World* (Cambridge, Mass., 1950), pp. 157 f.   [1] 472, 13 f., 473, 4. Compare 798, 30.

through the practice of this virtue the youth attained that sympathy with other human beings which on his first visit to Munsalvaesche he had lacked. Thus the two virtues of humility and compassion, once he had learned them, qualified Parzival to reign over the holy kingdom of the Grail.

Though Wolfram indubitably took over this concept of the Grail from some form of the *Iter ad Paradisum*, he seems to have magnified the size of the talisman, for he tells us that it received on its end the names of those elected to its guardianship. He evidently thought of the guardians as forming an order like that of the Knights Templars, dedicated to the defence of the Holy Sepulchre at Jerusalem.[1] The Grail knights, like the Templars, were vowed to celibacy, while the Grail Kings, like the Kings of Jerusalem, were not. It is this analogy which the poet had in mind when he applied to the guardians of the holy stone the name Templeisen.

His originality and genius also appear in his statement that the stone owed its powers to a mass-wafer deposited on it every Good Friday by a dove descending from heaven. This, we may well believe, is a deliberate alteration of Chrétien's concept of the Grail as a receptacle for the Host—a concept first set forth by the hermit on Good Friday. It also embodies a eucharistic doctrine which can be traced back to the fourth century, namely that it is the Third Member of the Trinity who descends on the bread and wine at the celebration of the mass and changes them into the body and blood of the Second Member.[2] Shortly after Wolfram's time Jacques de Vitry reported that an anchoress received the Host every Friday from a dove, needless to say, the Holy Spirit made visible.[3] It should be observed that by this change Wolfram avoided Chrétien's blunder of assigning the administration of the sacrament to a woman.

Less understandable is Wolfram's assertion that before the Grail stone came into the custody of the Templeisen it was in

---

[1] Singer in *Sitzungsberichte d. Wiener Akad.*, Phil.-hist. Kl. clxxx. 4 (1916), pp. 93ff.

[2] Vacant and Mangenot, *Dict. de Théologie Catholique*, v, cols. 1143, 1171.

[3] *Percevalroman*, ed. Hilka, p. 742.

the charge of angels who had been neutral in the war between God and Lucifer. What seems to be the same notion is found in Gerbert's continuation of the *Conte del Graal*, for there we find that the Queen of the Castle of Maidens and her cousin, Perceval's mother, brought the Grail to Britain.[1] But angels took it away by the command of the Most High because the land was being ravaged by evil men. In time, however, the vessel was entrusted to the keeping of the Fisher King. Now, since Wolfram could not have read Gerbert, nor Gerbert Wolfram, the notion that the Grail was in the custody of angels before it came into the possession of the Fisher King must have been derived by both authors from a common tradition. This constitutes the sixth tradition known to Wolfram but not known to Chrétien or his first continuator, and it may well have been Celtic. Hertz adduced the testimony of the folklorist Sébillot that the old folk near Mené in Brittany believed the neutral angels to have been sent down to earth for a time and to have assumed the form of fairies.[2] If this belief was current in the Middle Ages, then the Bretons would have equated Morgain la Fée and her attendant damsels with the neutral angels, and, as was shown in Chapter XI, one branch of Grail tradition assigned to Morgain the role of Grail Bearer.

From the subject of the Grail Trevrizent's discourse turned to the history of his brother Anfortas, the Maimed King, and opened with the sentence: 'The grief which was the reward of his pride ought evermore to waken pity in you and in me, poor though I be.'[2] Thus the leitmotifs of Wolfram's poem are again sounded—compassion and humility. Anfortas's pride expressed itself in his battle-cry 'Amor'—love not of God but of a mistress, in whose service he performed feats of arms. At last a heathen, born in the land where the Tigris flows from the Earthly Paradise, met him in combat and

[1] Gerbert de Montreuil, *Continuation de Perceval*, ed. Mary Williams (Paris, 1922), vss. 3180–93.

[2] Wolfram, *Parzival*, trans. Hertz, 5th ed. (1911), p. 524. Sébillot, *Traditions de la Haute-Bretagne* (Paris, 1882), i. 74 f.

[3] 472, 21–472, 26.

wounded him in the genitals with a poisoned spear.[1] Brought back to the Grail community, Anfortas had ever since suffered extreme agony, only partially relieved by thrusting the spear into the wound; but he was kept alive by the vitalizing vision of the Grail. His people searched the remotest lands to find a remedy, but none was of any avail, not even herbs washed down by the four rivers of Paradise.[2] At last, in response to the prayers of the Grail company, a prediction appeared on the stone that a knight would come, and, if he asked the right question, without prompting, Anfortas's torment would cease and the querist would become King in his stead.

The two references to the Earthly Paradise betray again the fascination which the subject exerted on Wolfram's mind; in fact, the second reference confirms the hypothesis—if any confirmation be needed—that he had read some version of the *Iter Alexandri ad Paradisum*, for in it he would have found mention of the leaves washed down from the 'paradisus voluptatis'.

After a noon-meal of roots and herbs, Parzival confesses to his uncle that it was he who had failed to ask the healing question at Munsalvaesche and begs forgiveness.[3] Trevrizent then tells more of Anfortas's wound, of the spear, of the guardian knights, and of the maidens who serve the Grail. He tells also of his own wide travels as a knight errant, before adopting the eremitic life. Fifteen days Parzival spent in penance with Trevrizent, and before he left inquired concerning the old man whom he had spied after the banquet at Munsalvaesche, stretched on a couch before the Grail. ' "That," said the hermit, "was thy mother's grandsire. He was the first chosen to guard the Grail. Now, crippled by a disease called gout, he lies helpless, yet remains fair as of old because he has seen the Grail so often that he cannot die." ' The property of the Grail to preserve the aged from physical decay, which we found also in *Perlesvaus*, is once more stressed.

Assured by the hermit of absolution, Parzival rides forth, and not till Book XIV does he reappear to engage incognito

---

[1] 479, 3–479, 17.   [2] 481, 8–481, 27.   [3] 488, 3–488, 20.

in combat with Gawain. Then Gawain's identity is revealed by the cries of spectators, Parzival throws away his sword, and the two friends repair to the camp of Arthur. Parzival is there received back with honour into the fellowship of the Round Table. After various complications the feud between Gawain and Gramoflanz (Chrétien's Guiromelans) is ended with the marriage of the latter to Gawain's sister. Other weddings take place at the same time, but Parzival sadly thinks of his own wife, whom he has not seen for five years, and slips away. Wolfram based his account of these events on the First Continuation, but the introduction of Parzival seems to be of his own contriving, as does the remainder of the poem.

In Book XV Parzival meets by chance his half-brother, the piebald Feirefis (French *vair fils?*), who had come from the East to seek news of his father. Feirefis proves himself a match for Parzival in prowess and magnanimity; recognition follows, and the two are welcomed by Arthur. A feast, held to celebrate the induction of Feirefis into the fellowship of the Round Table, is interrupted by the arrival of Kundrie, as hideous as ever, who in tears implores Parzival's forgiveness and announces joyous news. An inscription has appeared on the Grail: Parzival is to be King of the Grail realm. His wife, who has borne him twins, shall be Queen. It only remains to ask the question and bring the woes of Anfortas to an end. In Book XVI we read:[1]

Thus Parzival and Feirefis rode up to Munsalvaesche with tears of joy. They found there countless people, many a handsome old knight, noble youth, and servant. The sorrowful company might well rejoice at their arrival. Feirefis and Parzival both were warmly welcomed at the steps before the palace. They entered the hall, where lay, as before, a hundred wide round rugs, and on each was spread a cushion, filled with down, and a long quilt of samite. Since the two were men of experience they easily found seats there while their armour was removed. A chamberlain approached, bringing rich robes,

[1] 793, 28–796, 21.

alike for both. All the knights present then sat down. Many a dish of gold and not of glass was brought. Feirefis and Parzival drank and then approached Anfortas, the tortured man. You know already that he had to recline and could not sit up; you know, too, how sumptuous his couch was. He received the two with joy, and yet with woe. He said to Parzival:

'I have waited in pain on the chance that you would bring me happiness once more. You left me aforetime in such a pass that if you are now capable of ruth you will show tokens of grief. If you have achieved fame, implore these folk, knights or maidens, to give me death and let me end my agony. If your name is Parzival, keep me from the sight of the Grail for seven nights and eight days. Then would my torment end. No further counsel may I give you. Blest shall you be if you are acclaimed my deliverer. Your companion is a stranger here. I am sorry to keep him standing. Why do you not let him go to his room?'

Weeping sorely, Parzival spoke: 'Tell me, where in this place the Grail is found? If God's goodness prevails in me, it will be manifest to this company.' Then, turning toward the Grail, he fell thrice on his knees in prayer in honour of the Trinity, and strove that the cruel suffering of the wretched man might be relieved. He arose and said: 'Mine uncle, what is thine affliction?' And he who through St. Silvester restored a bull from death to life and who bade Lazarus arise, made Anfortas whole and sound. His colour came back to his skin, as it were what the French call flori. *By contrast even Parzival's beauty was only a puff of wind. Not Absalom, David's son, nor Vergulaht of Ascalon, nor all who were born of fair ancestors, nor Gahmuret when he appeared resplendent at Kanvoleis could compare in beauty with Anfortas when he had been healed. Manifold are the powers of God. Then no other choice was possible save him whom the writing on the Grail had designated as lord, and there Parzival was declared King and lord.*

As a climax to the mysterious quest of the Grail the scene is entirely appropriate and intellectually satisfying. The old and meaningless motif of the question test has been made to point a moral, not unlike that of the parable of the Good Samaritan

—the virtue of compassion. But as artistry the scene falls short of its possibilities of grandeur and suspense. The treatment is too concise, and Parzival has previously been advised too often and too explicitly what the nature of his question must be. The element of surprise is absent, and the merit of asking the question is diminished by the coaching the hero has received.

The main story ends shortly after with the joyful reunion of Parzival and his wife, each hastening to meet the other; with their sharing the nuptial couch; and with their ceremonial reception at the Grail castle, where the holy talisman ministers as before to the whole company and where the anguish of Anfortas no longer pervades the hall with its ironic gloom. Wolfram's preoccupation with family history, however, exemplified by the elaborate ancestry he invented for Parzival, led him to add two sequels. Feirefis, smitten with a sudden love for Repanse de Joie, the Grail Bearer, accepts the condition of baptism, weds her, takes her back to India, where she bears a son destined to become Prester John, the imaginary Christian king of the East who had been made famous in the West by a forged letter about 1165. Another legendary figure, the Knight of the Swan, best known to modern readers through Wagner's opera *Lohengrin*, Wolfram identified as Parzival's son Loherangrin and gave a brief sketch of his marriage to the Duchess of Brabant and his departure when she broke the taboo he had imposed.

We have seen with what an independent spirit Wolfram transformed the materials supplied him by the *Conte del Graal* as he knew it, what other traditional elements he added from French sources now lost, and what religious and moral significance he infused into the legend of the Grail, and there is no need to recapitulate. But one should not fail to observe as well certain characteristics of the poet's mind which appear throughout his work and perhaps most fully in the last books, which were of his own invention.

There is a singular breadth of sympathy displayed in the treatment of the heathen. Feirefis, son of a Moorish queen and himself a pagan, who worships Jupiter and Juno, is as gallant and magnanimous a knight as any Christian, is at once welcomed into the order of the Round Table, and after conversion has no difficulty in winning the supremely beautiful Repanse de Joie for his bride. Respectful, even admiring, is the poet's attitude toward the black Moorish queen Belacane and the Indian queen Secundille. There is a striking contrast in this respect between Wolfram and the author of *Perlesvaus*, who conceives of the worshippers of a copper bull as deserving no better fate than to be crushed to death by the mallets of automata.[1] Even greater is the contrast with the authors of the *chansons de geste*, who regard the paynim with scarcely mitigated hatred and scorn. Does Wolfram's attitude in part reflect a widespread change brought about by a century of contact with the Moslems in the Near East and Sicily and by the noble and chivalric conduct of Saladin?

In fact, though Wolfram is devoutly religious and his outlook is essentially Christian, including submission to God's will, the virtue of meekness, the value of abstinence, the sanctity of marriage, and the sinfulness of amatory adventures, he is what would be called today a 'broad churchman'. It was Flegetanis, the worshipper of a calf, who read in the stars somewhat concerning the Grail.[2] If this means anything, it means that even idolators might be granted limited knowledge of celestial things. The talisman itself is tended solely by women; no priest ministers to it, and no clouds of incense envelop it. Parzival's confessor, Trevrizent, is a layman, and thus, according to strict doctrine, powerless to prescribe penance or offer absolution. God's forgiveness is therefore not dispensed through a priestly intermediary. Celibacy is ordained for the Grail knights, but marriage for their king, evidently an estate at least equal in rank. Wolfram's religion is thus strangely tinged with unorthodoxy, if orthodoxy is identified with the creed of *Perlesvaus* and the *Queste del Saint Graal*, with a strict sacramental system, with intolerance of other religions, and with the exaltation of virginity. Remark-

[1] *Perlesvaus*, ed. Nitze, i, ll. 5952-9.   [2] 453, 23-454, 30.

able, too, is the absence of any trace of the cult of the Virgin, though, of course, she is mentioned. There is not much to distinguish Wolfram's faith from that of a liberal Protestant.[1]

His attitude toward women avoids the two extremities of medieval male feeling and theorizing about the fairer sex. On the one hand, there was the extreme misogynist view that woman, though created by God, had become the Devil's most valuable ally. She was not only inferior to man, she was naturally vicious. The Wife of Bath expressed, in the Prologue to her Tale, the opinion that it was an impossibility for any cleric to speak good of wives, except those in the lives of holy saints. On the other hand, there were the troubadours of Provence and other lyricists who celebrated their mistresses, often the wives of other men, as beings so far superior that life offered no greater joy or higher privilege than to adore and obey them. Wolfram, a married man, a composer of lyrics, held a position far removed from that of the misogynists, yet also removed from the sublimated adultery of the troubadours. At one point, to be sure, he adopted one tenet of courtly love doctrine. When Parzival was engaged in a desperate fight, incognito, with Feirefis and was getting the worst of it because of the magic gems in his opponent's mantle, his wife Condwiramurs, though separated from him by four kingdoms, heard his battle-cry 'Belrapeir', the name of her castle, and mysteriously sent him the physical strength he needed.[2] This is the sort of magic which, according to the troubadours, emanated from a dazzlingly beautiful mistress to her paramour. But for the most part Wolfram deals with his ladies in a much more realistic fashion, and he has given us a series of admiring and admirable portraits of maidens, wives, and widows. The title which Chaucer gave to his quizzical biographies of Cupid's saints, *The Legend of Good Women*, might be applied more fittingly to the largely or entirely original stories of Belakane, Herzeloide, Condwiramurs, Sigune, Obilot, and Kundrie. Even the capricious, mocking Orgeluse,

[1] On Wolfram's religion see C. F. Bayerschmidt in *Germanic Review*, xxix (1954), pp. 214–23.   [2] 744, 2–744, 6.

in whose service Anfortas transgressed the laws of the Grail community and suffered his grievous wound, was motivated by devotion to her murdered lover, and at last, a reformed character, was wedded to Gawain.

In short, there breathes throughout the poem a spirit bold, realistic, generous, tender, and magnanimous. For most moderns who can either read the original German or can find a satisfactory translation (no easy task in English), *Parzival* is the most satisfying medieval treatment of the legend of the Grail.

XIV

Joseph of Arimathea, an Evangelist by Error

IN the preceding chapters we have seen the Grail in many settings, performing varied functions, conceived in strangely different ways. It was borne repeatedly through the hall of the Fisher King by a stately maiden; it glided through the same hall or into Arthur's palace without visible bearer; it contained a single consecrated wafer; it dispensed viands and beverages to a large company of knights; it was the receptacle of a severed head, swimming in blood; it was a wide and slightly deep platter of gold, encrusted with jewels; it was the dish of the Last Supper; it was made of no recognizable material; it was a chalice, filled with the Saviour's blood; it appeared under five different forms.

In spite of this extraordinary diversity, it has been possible to explain most of these developments as the ramifications of a pagan legend concerning a large dish of plenty which provided the sea-god Brân son of Llŷr, his household, and his mortal guests with an abundance of whatever food each one desired. Several of the persons connected in one way or another with the vessel, as well as Brân himself, were identifiable with characters of Celtic mythology; Brân was the prototype of the Fisher King; Ériu and Modron bequeathed their attributes to the Grail Bearer; Beli became King Pelles. The Waste Land motif can be discerned in the *Adventure of Art Son of Conn* and in the *mabinogi* of *Manawydan*.

But we have also met with references to personages who do not belong in this category and yet are intimately associated with the Grail: Joseph of Arimathea, who received the vessel from Pilate as a reward for his services, and his son Josephes, the first bishop of Christendom, who, though dead for four hundred years, mysteriously appeared in the castle of King

Pelles and celebrated the mass of the Grail. Neither of these figures was mentioned in Chrétien's poem nor in the original form of the First Continuation; but an interpolator of the First Continuation and the author of *Perlesvaus* knew an account of the coming of Joseph of Arimathea and Nicodemus to Britain. Both Joseph and his son Josephes were introduced in the *Queste del Saint Graal* and *Sone de Nansai*, and Joseph's story forms the bulk of the poem by Robert de Boron entitled *Joseph d'Arimathie*. A greatly extended version in prose, *L'Estoire del Saint Graal*, constitutes the first member of the Vulgate cycle, and brings the history of the vessel down to the time of Merlin.

There was, however, a legend of Joseph of Arimathea centuries before he was associated in any way with the Grail. It started with the historic fact, vouched for by the four gospels, namely, that after Christ died on the cross, a rich disciple of Arimathea named Joseph begged the holy body from Pilate, wrapped it in a linen cloth, and placed it in a new tomb. St. John's gospel adds that Nicodemus brought spices for the burial, and that is all we learn from the Scriptures.

But in the large body of New Testament apocrypha which grew up one of the most widely known was the *Evangelium Nicodemi*. Here we read that during the trial of Christ before Pilate, Nicodemus, a ruler of the Jews, testified in His favour, infuriating the accusers. After Joseph had deposited the body of the Crucified in the sepulchre, the Jews imprisoned him, but when on Easter Day the door was opened, he was not to be found. Search was made at Nicodemus's advice, and Joseph was discovered at his home in Arimathea. Brought to Jerusalem he testified that at midnight of the Sabbath day, the prison in which he was confined rose into the air, and fell to the earth. The risen Christ appeared to him, lifted him up, and brought him to his house.

It is this apocryphal text, not earlier than the fourth century, which lies at the base of the Interpolation in the First Continuation of Chrétien's *Perceval* noted in Chapter VI and preserved in two manuscripts. It may be translated as follows:[1]

It is true that Joseph caused it [the Grail] to be made—that Joseph of Arimathea who so loved the Lord all his life, as it seemed, that on the day when He received death on the cross to save sinners, Joseph (who did much worthy of praise) came with the Grail which he had caused to be made to Mount Calvary, where God was crucified. He was sorely grieved at heart but he dared not appear so openly. He placed it at once below His feet, which were wet with blood which flowed down each foot, and collected as much as he was able in this Grail of fine gold. A very precious treasure was it, and right well he had it guarded, as you will hear me tell. Then he locked it up and put it in safe-keeping. Neither hairy man nor bald knew of this, but he alone.

After that he did not wait long before he asked Pilate for the precious body of Jesus Christ as a reward for his services, and he sought for no other pay. Pilate granted it readily. Joseph, the noble knight, right sweetly took the holy body, brought it down from the holy cross, wrapped it in the cloth which he had bought, and then laid it in the sepulchre. . . .

I will bring you back to the subject of the Grail and you will hear what happened to Joseph, who held it very dear. He has locked the Grail in a precious carved wardrobe, and there were two large, rich candles burning before it continuously. There he went every day, on rising, to pray, in fidelity and in honour of the true blood of Our Lord; until his custom was observed and perceived by his people. Out of envy they reported it to the evil Jews, and the latter sought him and caused him to be imprisoned (he had done no greater crime than you have heard) in a very high tower, with high walls around it.

But he was not there long. He prayed his Lord sweetly that He would free him from the tower and guard the Grail so well that no Jew would gain possession of it, and that in time of need, if it pleased Him, He would return it by His mercy. The true God accepted the

---

[1] *Continuation of the Old French 'Perceval'*, ed. W. Roach, iii (Philadelphia, 1952), pp. 480–8.

C 877   Q

prayer of the noble man, for, in a word, the tower rose so high that Joseph issued forth without difficulty or labour, and also from the walls around it. He took charge and custody of the Grail as was reasonable and right. But rumour, which is swifter than the wind, swiftly brought the news to the Jews, who were by no means delighted but rather were deeply dejected. Among themselves they held a council in order to banish Joseph and expel him from the land, and they informed him at once that he must depart because of his crime, he and all his friends, and also Nicodemus, who was a marvellously wise man, and a sister of his. Nicodemus had carved and fashioned a head in the likeness of the Lord on the day that he had seen Him on the cross. But of this I am sure, that the Lord God set His hand to the shaping of it, as they say; for no man ever saw one like it nor could it be made by human hands. Most of you who have been at Lucca know it and have seen it.

When Nicodemus knew that he must depart and leave the land, he took the head secretly, without the knowledge of anyone, and carried it without delay to Jaffa, put it in the sea and commended it to the Lord God, in whose likeness he had shaped it. Then he returned to Joseph, to whom the Lord had appeared and told him not to be dismayed; let him go confidently, for he would have lands to the extent of his desire, where he could protect himself and his company. Let him wander securely without fear.

Joseph and his company prepared their fleet and entered without delay, and did not end their voyage till they reached the land which God had promised to Joseph. The name of the country was the White Isle; well I know that thus it was called. One part belongs to England, which is enclosed and locked by the sea. There they made port and went ashore, built lodges there and whatever else they needed. Two whole years they were there before anyone made war on them or seized a foot of land. But in the third year the people of the country gathered together and made war and often wrought harm. Often they fought and either won or lost. When Joseph was defeated and there was a famine, he prayed God, his Creator, that He would lend him, by His favour, that Grail of which I tell you and in which he had collected the blood. Then he caused a horn to be blown and all went to wash their hands, and seated themselves ceremoniously at the tables. The Grail came at once and served the wine to all and other dishes in great plenty. Thus Joseph preserved the land against his enemies as long as he had life and health.

At the end of his life he prayed God sweetly that He would consent that Joseph's lineage would be rendered illustrious by the Grail. And thus it befell; it is the pure truth. For after his death no man in the world of any age had possession of it unless he was of Joseph's lineage. In truth the Rich Fisher descended from him, and all his heirs and, they say, Guellans Guenelaus and his son Perceval.

This is the shortest and simplest account of Joseph's connexion with the Grail and his voyage to Britain, and though the date when it was incorporated in the First Sequel to *Perceval* may have been well into the thirteenth century, it must represent an early stage in the development of the Joseph–Grail tradition. Why? Because it could not have been derived from any of the more famous versions of the tradition. There is no trace of any of the apocrypha except the *Evangelium Nicodemi*, whereas the other versions show a dependence also on the *Vindicta Salvatoris*. There is no mention of the missionary activities of Joseph, so emphasized in the other versions. His son Josephes is not mentioned either. These differences exclude the possibility that the Interpolation was derived from one or more of these other texts, and therefore, it could be earlier than any of them. In fact, it seems to represent the first step in bridging the gap between the apocryphal history of Joseph of Arimathea and the British tradition of the miraculous vessel of plenty. An interesting accretion is the legend of the *Volto Santo*, supposedly carved by Nicodemus and still to be seen at Lucca in Tuscany.

One of the most important and most puzzling texts about Joseph is the poem written by Robert de Boron, a Burgundian from near the modern Swiss border.[1] Boron, which may have been his birthplace or his property, is a village near

---

[1] On Robert's *Joseph* see Le Gentil in *Arthurian Literature*, ed. Loomis, pp. 251–62. The best edition is that of W. A. Nitze under the title of *Roman de l'Estoire dou Graal* (Paris, 1927), translation in M. Schlauch, *Medieval Narrative* (New York, 1928), pp. 179–95.

Montbéliard, and he tells us that he wrote under the patronage of a certain lord known to history, Gautier de Montbéliard, who departed for Italy in 1199, took part in the
Fourth Crusade, and never returned.[1] Whether the poet was
a layman or a cleric is hard to decide, since the unique manuscript inconsistently refers to him as *Messires* and *Maistres*.
But if a layman, he displayed an unusually pious bent and
a not-too-common preoccupation with dogma, biblical and
apocryphal history, and religious symbolism, though it is
possible that some of this knowledge merely reflected his
source. He fancied himself, it would seem, on his gift of
riming, for he wrote a *Merlin* as sequel to the *Joseph*, and possibly added a Perceval quest in which two figures prominent
in the latter part of the *Joseph*, Bron and Alein, are represented
as surviving into King Arthur's time. Such poetic talents as
Robert possessed did not include clarity, and the confusions
and self-contradictions of his poem have exasperated and
baffled scholars ever since it was first published in 1841.

He gave two inconsistent statements as to the originality of
his material. He proclaimed in vss. 929–36 that he would not
have dared to tell his story if he had not had 'le grant livre' in
which great 'clers' had written the histories and the great
secrets which one calls the Grail. At the end of the poem he
referred to Bron, the good Fisher, as one about whom many
words were spoken, and he promised to continue the narrative
of Bron's son Alein and of Petrus, Moyses, and the Rich
Fisher, if he could find them in a book, 'se en livre les puis
trouver'. Taken together these passages imply that Robert
had depended for the matter of his work on a 'grant livre',
that this had come to an end, and that he had to obtain a
continuation before he could follow the fortunes of the characters mentioned. But it is in the latter of the two passages that
we find Robert asserting that never had the great history of the
Grail been told before he related it for Gautier de Montbéliard.
What is this but a denial of the existence of the 'grant livre'?

Most scholars have been inclined to accept Robert's claim

[1] Nitze's introduction, p. xi. Bruce, *Evolution*, i. 221.

to originality, in the sense that he was the first to combine the already existing apocryphal legends of Joseph of Arimathea, St. Veronica, and the destruction of Jerusalem with selected elements from the literary tradition of the Grail. They have therefore been obliged to take Robert's appeal to the authority of the great book about the secrets of the Grail either as a falsehood or else as a highly inaccurate reference to some Latin work on the symbolism of the mass or even to one of the New Testament apocrypha. Even this interpretation of the reference to the great book does not do away with the implication that Robert could not continue his poem till he could lay hands on a sequel to that book. For the answer to the problem of his originality we must pursue our inquiry farther, and give our attention to the story which he told and its glaring inconsistencies.

After an outline of the doctrine of the Fall and the Redemption, we are introduced to a mercenary officer of Pilate's, at first anonymous; but suddenly Joseph of Arimathea takes his place and we are left to infer that the two are identical.[1] Joseph secretly loved Jesus, and after the Crucifixion he asked Pilate, as compensation for his services, for the body (*cors*) of the Crucified, and Pilate gave assent.[2] But the guards refused to let Joseph take down the body, and he appealed again to Pilate. This time Pilate not only assigned Nicodemus to accompany Joseph but also, in a casual way, gave the latter the vessel which Christ, on the night of His betrayal, had used to make His sacrament.[3] Accompanied by Nicodemus, Joseph was able to depose the body (*cors*) of the Redeemer from the cross, and he collected the blood, which still flowed from the wounds, in the vessel which Pilate had given him, and placed the body in the tomb. When on the third day, the Jews discovered that the body was missing, they accused Joseph of stealing it and threw him into a dungeon. The Crucified appeared to the prisoner in a blaze of light, presented him with the same vessel in which he had collected the holy blood,

[1] Vss. 199–316. [2] Vss. 439–72. [3] Vss. 395–438, 507–18.

and told him that he was to have the guardianship of the vessel and would have only three successors, in token of the Trinity. Christ also instructed Joseph in the symbolism of the mass, and informed him that the vessel containing the divine blood was to be called 'calice'.[1] Then the visitant departed.

So far, of course, the *Joseph* agrees with the Interpolation and presumably had a common twelfth-century French source, which in turn drew on the *Evangelium Nicodemi*. But at this point the *Evangelium* is abandoned, other apocrypha are laid under contribution, with the result that Joseph's deliverance from prison was postponed till after the fall of Jerusalem in A.D. 70. According to the *Vindicta Salvatoris*, Vespasian, son of the Roman emperor, was converted as a result of the miraculous cure effected by the sight of Veronica's veil, on which was imprinted the face of Christ. He promptly set out to avenge the death of Jesus, assembled the Jews, and, learning from their own lips their responsibility for the Crucifixion, caused a number of them to be executed. One, however, tried to save his life by revealing where Joseph was incarcerated. Vespasian had himself lowered into the dungeon and found him still alive. When Joseph expounded the doctrines of the Fall and the Redemption, Vespasian was convinced and delivered the prisoner. Thus the *Evangelium Nicodemi* and the *Vindicta Salvatoris* have been drawn on successively to form a background for the legend of Joseph of Arimathea.

At vs. 2307 two kinsfolk of Joseph, hitherto unmentioned and quite unknown to the apocrypha, make their entrance: Joseph's sister Enygeus and her husband, who is oddly called Hebron 13 times and Bron 23 times. Since the form Bron has a heavy majority, and is that employed in the *Estoire del Saint Graal* and the *Didot Perceval*, which are related to the *Joseph*, it will be used in the rest of this synopsis. Bron, Enygeus, and a company of Jews, who had been won over to the Christian faith, joined Joseph and went into exile. A long

[1] Vss. 851–909.

time passed, and, their crops having failed, they were threatened with starvation. Some, surely, had sinned, but who were the culprits? Joseph knelt before his vessel, and in answer to his prayer the voice of the Holy Spirit announced that certain members of his company were guilty of lust, and commanded him to search for a table in memory of that used at the Last Supper, to dispatch Bron to catch a fish, and to place it on the table together with the Grail.[1] Joseph must then take the seat corresponding to that of Christ, with Bron on his right, and thereupon a space will open between them to signify the seat of Judas. This will never be filled till Enygeus shall have a child. When the table is ready, Joseph is to summon his company and invite them, if they have kept the commandments, to take their seats.

The divine instructions were obeyed. When summoned to the table, only a part of the company were able to take their seats and they were filled with sweetness and the satisfaction of their desires. The lustful ones, left standing, felt nothing, and, shamefaced, departed.[2] Thus was the discriminating power of the vessel tested, and because it delights (*agree*) all who behold it, it was given the name *graal*. (An absurd etymology!) Moyses, one of those who failed to pass the test, stayed behind and begged to be admitted to the table, and was allowed to do so on condition that he was free of sin. But when he sat in the empty seat corresponding to that of Judas, the earth swallowed him up. We are told that only the *grandson* of Bron and Enygeus will be worthy to occupy it.[3] (Note the discrepancy between this statement and the earlier prediction that Enygeus's child is the appointed occupant.)

Years slipped by, in which Enygeus bore twelve sons to Bron. When they were grown up, their parents were naturally worried about their future, and consulted Joseph. In answer to his prayer, an angel directed that the twelve sons be summoned and given their choice between the wedded and the single state. Eleven of them chose marriage, but one, who is at first anonymous, vowed celibacy.[4] When Joseph

[1] Vss. 2487–512.   [2] Vss. 2555–86.   [3] Vss. 2788–96.   [4] Vss. 2937–62.

prayed again before his vessel a voice announced that this same celibate nephew would have a male heir! (Note this second inconsistency.) He is to have the rule over his eleven brothers and their wives, and to proceed with them to the extreme Occident, and there exalt the name of Christ. The angel also foretold that on the morrow a great light would descend on the assembly and bring a letter. This is to be read to one named Petrus, and he is then to go wherever he wishes, carrying the letter with him, and to await the coming of the son of Alein.[1] (Who Alein was the author does not inform us, but leaves us to infer from later references that he was Joseph's celibate nephew.) Petrus, the angel added, shall not die till someone shall read the letter to him. (This seems to be inconsistent with the angel's command to Joseph to cause the letter to be read to Petrus on its arrival.)

The next day, as predicted, a great light shone, bringing a letter, which Joseph then handed to Petrus. Petrus, when asked, declared his intention to go to the vales of Avaron, a savage land in the Occident.[2] Bron assembled his sons and daughters and instructed them to obey their brother Alein; whereupon they departed under Alein's leadership to strange lands. Our Lord then bade Joseph give over the vessel to the guardianship of Bron and to teach him the secrets of the Grail. Bron is to be called the Rich Fisher and to proceed with his people to the Occident and there await the coming of his grandson, to whom he shall transfer the custody of the vessel. Obeying the divine command, Joseph delivered the Grail to Bron, and taught him the secret word which Christ had spoken to Joseph in the dungeon.[3] After three days Bron and his company set forth on their mysterious journey, leaving Joseph behind. In conclusion the author alludes to the many tales told of the good Fisher and announces his intention to relate what happened to Alein, Petrus, Moyses, and the Rich Fisher, if he can find it in a book, 'se en livre les puis trouver'.

What, then, is one to make of this strange poem? Can one

[1] Vss. 3119–28.   [2] Vss. 3219–22.   [3] Vss. 3407–20.

figure out its relation to earlier Grail traditions? An hypothesis favoured by some learned inquirers, namely, that Robert derived all such information as he had about the Grail from Chrétien de Troyes, seems on reflection to be rather naïve. Why, if this were so, did Robert convert the large platter containing the sacred Host into a chalice filled with blood? Why did he convert the maimed Fisher King, contemporary of Arthur, into the able-bodied Rich Fisher, a contemporary of Joseph of Arimathea? Whence did he get the name Bron? Surely Robert de Boron must have derived his notions of the Grail and its keepers from a source very different from Chrétien.

A consideration of the astonishing peculiarities of the *Joseph* leads to the conclusion that the author must have been following, at least for the latter part of his work, something which he called 'le grant livre'. How else can one understand why Robert twice committed the error of introducing an important figure anonymously and then abruptly referring to him by name, as if the reader had already been informed of it? Presumably in the 'livre' the identification by name was clearly made, but Robert absent-mindedly omitted the identifying phrase or sentence.

The gross inconsistencies, noted above, may also be accounted for by a similar carelessness. To be sure, even the greatest of modern realistic novelists may be caught by an attentive reader in anachronisms and other slips, but in none so crass, I venture to assert, as Robert's references to the son of Alein—Alein who declared that he would rather be flayed alive than marry! If some critics are right in holding that Robert had a creative mind and devised his own plots, he must have been drunk or subject to fits of dementia when he forecast an important role for the son of a virgin!

On the other hand, a scrutiny of the first passage predicting that Bron's grandson would occupy the empty seat at the Grail table (vss. 2788–96) suggests a simple explanation of the blunder. The voice of God announced to Joseph of Arimathea: ' "I tell thee for thy comfort that this place shall not be

filled before the third man will come who will descend from
thy lineage and will issue from thy family. Hebron is destined
to beget him, and Enygeus, thy sister, to bear him: and he who
will issue from his son shall fill this very place." ' Observe the
specific statement that the seat is reserved for Hebron's son,
immediately contradicted by the statement that it was destined for his son's son. Is it not fairly obvious that Robert
de Boron, having read something like the first statement,
referring to Bron's son, came upon an additional statement
referring to 'his son', namely Bron's, and, mistaking the
reference of the possessive pronoun, created a grandson for
Bron? It is easy to understand how a man whose head was
not screwed on too tight could have committed the blunder,
but not so easy to understand why he failed to correct it
when he discovered that he had credited the celibate Alein with
male issue. Apparently, he must have accepted it as another
miracle, and in vss. 3361–74 he even repeated the reference to
Bron's grandson and interpreted the three successive keepers
of the Grail—Bron, his son, and his grandson—as signifying
the blessed Trinity!

There is reason to believe, moreover, that Robert was right
when he first assigned the vacant seat to Bron's son Alein; in
other words, that in the particular branch of Christian Grail
tradition whence Robert drew his material the occupant was
a virgin like Alein and bore a name which might easily under-
go metamorphosis into Alein. We saw in Chapter XII that it
was the virgin knight Galahad who according to the *Queste
del Saint Graal* was the awaited occupant of the Siege Perilous,
and that his name was probably an ingenious substitution for
some such form as Galaain. Now Bruce and other scholars
have pointed out that proper names in manuscript transmission sometimes lost the initial letter. Thus we find the
name of Morgain la Fée corrupted into such forms as Orgu-
ein and Argant.[1] Therefore, there is nothing to surprise us
in the assumption that the name Galaain became Alaain
through a scribal error, and was naturally replaced by the

[1] Bruce in *Mod. Lang. Notes*, xxvi (1911), pp. 65 ff. Loomis, *Wales*, pp. 106 f.

familiar Breton name Alain or Alein. It may be said that all this is mere conjecture. Nevertheless, the hypothesis does account for the chief absurdity in the *Joseph* in a way which is reconcilable with Robert's sanity and which accords with the role of Alein as a Grail hero. The only serious objection is that neither Galahad nor Gawain corresponds to Alain as a son of Bron, but in view of the confusion which prevails in regard to the identity and the progeny of the keepers of the Grail, the objection is not fatal.

That Robert was working, conscientiously but blunderingly, from an earlier treatment of the Grail, is corroborated by a comparison with the *Estoire del Saint Graal.*[1] This long prose romance, which forms the first member of the Vulgate cycle, and which adds to the story of Joseph, bringing him to Britain as an evangelist, and carries the history of the vessel and its successive keepers almost down to Arthur's time, has often been thought to be an elaboration of Robert's poem, since it was composed later and the manuscripts attribute it to Robert de Boron. That in its present state the *Estoire* has undergone some influence from Robert's *Joseph* it would be foolish to deny; but it would be equally foolish to assume that the resemblance between the two works could be explained only by that influence. For there are striking divergences which force one to assume also a common source for the *Joseph* and the *Estoire*. Not only is the latter free from the muddle about the offspring of Bron, but it is also right on two significant points where Robert went astray. It never uses the form Hebron instead of Bron, as Robert frequently did; and it is quite clear that the Grail was a dish (*escuele*),[2] not a chalice as Robert mistakenly thought. To be sure, mere common sense would have led the author of the *Estoire* to eliminate such a palpable absurdity as Alein's begetting a son, but common sense alone would not account for the elimination of the form Hebron and the correction of Robert's mistake about the meaning of the word *graal*. A different explanation must

[1] H. O. Sommer, *Vulgate Version of the Arthurian Romances*, i. 13.

be sought and what better one is there than a source which did not contain the errors committed by Robert de Boron?

Moreover, the *Estoire* gives a version of the establishment of the Grail table, the fate of Moyses, the marriage of Bron's eleven sons, and Alein's choice of celibacy which differs in several respects from Robert's version, and in one respect at least seems to stick closer to tradition.[1] This whole sequence of events has been transferred from the Holy Land to Britain, and Josephes, the son of Joseph of Arimathea, already mentioned, takes the place of his father as leader of the Grail company. When he and Bron sat down at the Grail table, there was a space between them, corresponding to that of Jesus (not Judas) at the Last Supper. Josephes refused to let anyone occupy it, but when some of the company protested, he allowed Mois (that is Moyses), who had been proved a worshipful man (*preudomme*) of very good life to essay the adventure. As soon as he did so, flaming hands descended from heaven, cast fire on him so that he began to burn, and finally carried him away. (In Robert's poem, let us remember, Moyses was swallowed up by the earth.) After the rest of the company had eaten at the Grail table, Bron desired Josephes to send for Bron's twelve sons and ask them whether they wished to marry or not. All but one chose the wedded state, but Alain vowed to remain a virgin and serve the Grail, and Josephes promised him the lordship of the holy vessel after his own death.

At a casual glance it might seem quite unnecessary to postulate any other source for this narrative than Robert's *Joseph*; but there is one difference between the two which strongly suggests, even if it does not prove, that the *Estoire* remained more faithful to tradition than the *Joseph*, namely, the fiery fate of Mois. We have preserved in the Prose *Lancelot* a longish, originally independent episode which is easily identifiable as a secular counterpart to the pious story just summarized from the *Estoire*.[2] Bors arrived before the castle of

---

[1] Compare Sommer, op. cit. i. 246–9 with Robert de Boron, vss. 2466–3000.   [2] Sommer, iv. 264–70.

La Marche (the Border), where King Brangorre was holding a great tournament. (The castle is the very same as Dinas Brân near the border of Wales, mentioned in Chapters IX and XI, which according to *Fouke Fitz Warin* was called 'la Vele Marche', 'the Old Border'. King Brangorre is another of the numerous hypostases of the Welsh Brân son of Llŷr.)[1] The King's daughter fell in love with Bors at first sight, and when he had distinguished himself in combat, she and her damsels picked him out as the best knight and chose twelve other knights as the next best. King Brangorre had two pavilions pitched in the meadows, one for himself (the Welsh Brân banqueted under tents), and one for Bors and the twelve knights. A table was set up in both. The King's daughter clad Bors in red samite, and when he sat in the golden chair, he blushed all red with modesty. King Brangorre bade him choose the fairest damsel as wife for himself, and twelve other damsels for the champions, but he pleaded that he could not then take a wife, but selected brides for his twelve companions. King Brangorre's daughter, deeply aggrieved that Bors had not chosen her, nevertheless contrived by means of a magic ring to bring about their union, and thus Helain le Blanc was conceived in spite of the fact that Bors had intended to be a virgin all his life.

It requires no great perspicacity to detect four correspondences between this chivalric narrative and the pious tale in the *Estoire*.

Prose *Lancelot*	*Estoire*
1. A table was set up by Brangorre's command, at which Bors sat with twelve lesser knights.	1. A table was set up for Bron and Josephes on the model of that at which Christ sat with the twelve disciples.
2. Bors, a valiant knight, occupied the chief seat and blushed red.	2. Mois, a worshipful man, occupied Christ's seat, and was set aflame.
3. The twelve knights were assigned wives.	3. The eleven sons of Bron chose to wed.

[1] Loomis, *Wales*, p. 48. H. Newstead, *Bran the Blessed*, pp. 51–54.

4. Bors refused to wed, for he had vowed to remain a virgin.

4. The twelfth son refused to wed and vowed to remain celibate.

One can hardly avoid drawing five significant conclusions from a comparison of these stories. First, in spite of the differences, the stories must be somehow related. Secondly, the evidence of the name Brangorre and his castle of La Marche proves that the story in the Prose *Lancelot*, which contains them, could not have been derived from the story in the *Estoire del Saint Graal*, from which they are absent. Thirdly, since the converse relationship is equally impossible, there must have been a common remote source. Fourthly, that source would seem to have contained a curious statement that the occupant of the seat of honour at the table turned red—a statement which was interpreted by one author to mean that Bors blushed, and by the other to mean that Mois was consumed with fire. Fifthly, the fact that Robert de Boron assigned Moyses a quite different fate, being swallowed by the earth, indicates that the *Joseph* was not the immediate source of the *Estoire*.

There are several converging lines of evidence, therefore, which tend to prove that the *Estoire* was not derived directly from Robert's poem, as is often supposed, but from a common immediate source, presumably from the 'grant livre', whose authority Robert himself invoked. Robert, in spite of his bungling and changes, probably followed the book with some fidelity till it broke off with the departure of the various members of Joseph's company to the Occident. The author of the *Estoire*, on the other hand, though retaining features of the original discarded by Robert, took a more independent course, and, realizing that four centuries at least separated the period of Joseph of Arimathea from that of Arthur, filled in the interval with a miscellaneous assortment of battles, miracles, crimes, punishments, and conversions.[1]

The answer to two of the questions posed near the beginning

---

[1] For a summary of the *Estoire del Saint Graal* see Bruce, ii. 308–12; for sources of the *Estoire* see ibid. i. 386–90.

of this chapter seems to be definitive. Robert de Boron was telling the truth when he referred to a book about the secrets of the Grail as the source of his information. This book was also the source of much of the *Estoire*. Not Robert but the author of the 'grant livre' was the bold and clever man who linked certain authentic, originally Celtic traditions of the Grail with the early Christian legend of Joseph of Arimathea.

In the light of previous discussions we can discern what some of the authentic traditions embodied in the book were. The Grail itself, envisaged as a dish endowed with miraculous properties of satisfying every taste and discriminating between the worthy and the unworthy, is a Welsh heritage. So, too, is the figure of Bron, custodian of the Grail and the subject of many tales. His title, the Rich Fisher, is most plausibly to be explained as a relic of the fact that the Welsh Brân was originally a sea-god. Its very obscurity necessitated the invention of a new tale to account for it—the tale of Bron's catching a fish and Joseph's placing it on the Grail table. The table, modelled after that at which Our Lord sat with His twelve apostles, seems to reflect the same tradition as that represented in *Sone de Nansai* by the Fisher King's foundation of a community consisting of an abbot and twelve monks. The ultimate source of the tradition was the pagan Celtic custom of a chief's banqueting with his twelve chosen warriors about him.

The motif of the vacant seat awaiting a worthy occupant occurs not only in the Grail romances as we know, but also in *Lanzelet* and *Wigalois*,[1] and can be traced back to the Irish saga, *The Second Battle of Moytura*, which relates how the youthful Lug took the Seat of the Sage.[2] In the French version which came down to the authors of the 'grant livre' and of the *Queste del Saint Graal* the successful occupant of the seat probably bore some such name as Galaain, and for this Alain and Galaad were substituted. What tradition, if any, lay

---

[1] See Ulrich von Zatzikhoven, *Lanzelet*, trans. K. G. T. Webster (New York, 1951), pp. 96, 209 f.   [2] See above, pp. 177 f.

behind Mois's ill-advised attempt and his fiery end, and what suggested applying to him the totally inappropriate name of the Jewish law-giver, is hard to discover.

Even when these many problems of origin have been solved, one cannot but wonder what were the causes of this elaborate sanctification of the heathenish legends, why the vessel of plenty was identified with the dish of the Last Supper, and why Joseph of Arimathea was chosen as its first custodian.

Two factors were, in my opinion, primarily responsible. First, the miraculous virtues attached to the vessel resembled those ascribed to Christian relics closely enough to convey the implication that it must be an object of peculiar sanctity; and the word *dyscyl*, correctly translated as *graal*, pointed to the most sacred dish of all, the *escuele* of the Last Supper. Secondly, the old sea-god Brân son of Llŷr was invested, already in the Welsh stage, with an aura of holiness, for he enjoyed the epithet *bendigeid*, 'blessed'.[1] Thus a process was started which naturally led to the belief that the miraculous vessel found its way into the possession of a holy man named Bron. The journey of Brân's followers to an island off the west coast of Wales, as related in *Branwen*, was reshaped as the journey of Bron and his followers to the western isle of Britain. Thus the appearance of the vessel of the Last Supper in Arthur's land was accounted for.

But if the author of the 'grant livre' was led to believe that the Grail was the dish from which the Saviour ate the lamb on the eve of His betrayal and that it was transported to Britain by a holy man named Bron, he was faced by a problem. How did this Bron, unmentioned in the New Testament or the apocrypha, gain possession of the precious relic? He must have obtained it from someone mentioned in one or the other of these sources as concerned in the events leading up to or following the Crucifixion. One of the Apostles actually present at the Last Supper might have been considered likely

---

[1] On this epithet see R. Bromwich in *Arthurian Literature*, ed. Loomis, p. 51.

to preserve the dish as a memento. However, the choice fell upon Joseph of Arimathea.

Was this merely a plausible guess, or was there a reason? Over and over again in the preceding pages we have observed that tradition supplied a reason for what might too easily be considered a pure flight of fancy. We have seen that Brân's horn of plenty, appearing in French as a *cors* with miraculous powers of supplying food and drink, was misunderstood and taken to be a body. Thus in Chrétien it is represented by the Corpus Christi, the mass-wafer, so unsuitably placed in the Grail; in *Sone de Nansai* it is represented by the body of the Fisher King, who is so oddly identified with Joseph of Arimathea. In our study of *Sone* we discovered, moreover, that the account of the Fisher King's career preserved elements of the Welsh tradition of Brân to be found in no other Grail romance. Now though the magic horn of Brân, translated as the *cors* of the Fisher King, could be taken, and was taken, to refer to the corpse of the Fisher King, it could also be interpreted as the body in the possession or keeping of the Fisher King. What if the body was the most sacred of all bodies, that of the crucified Christ? Then it was a reasonable inference that the Fisher King was Joseph of Arimathea, who according to Scripture begged for the body of Christ, took it down from the cross, and kept it in his sepulchre until the third day. This may seem rather a strained explanation, but what other is there for the fantastic equation of the Fisher King with Joseph of Arimathea? The author of the 'grant livre', however, unable to reconcile what he knew of the two persons, differentiated them, but, believing that there was some connexion, made the Rich Fisher, Bron, the brother-in-law of Joseph and his successor as custodian, not of the physical body of Christ, for that was unthinkable after the Resurrection, but of the sacred dish which tradition associated with the sacred *cors*.

If this hypothesis, even though it accounts for certain strange facts, involves too many suppositions to be readily acceptable, there is still further evidence that a tradition concerning the miraculous horn of Brân came down to the

French romancers in association with the tradition of the sacred dish known as the Grail. In both the *Estoire* and the *Queste del Saint Graal* the name of the castle which was built to house the Grail is given as Corbenic. There, as we saw in Chapter XII, Bishop Josephes, the son of Joseph of Arimathea celebrated the sacrament, using the Grail as a ciborium from which he extracted the Host. Bruce maintained that Corbenic was a slight variation on Corbéni,[1] the name of a town near Laon, where there was once a palace and a Benedictine establishment. But it has not been explained why so ardent a Cistercian as the author of the *Queste*, or anyone else, should have adopted the name of a Benedictine house for a castle in which the sublimest of mysteries were enacted.

Now the Dutch *Lancelot* was translated in part from a manuscript of the French Prose *Lancelot* in which the castle was repeatedly referred to as Cambenoyc, Cambenoyt, or Cabenoyt.[2] Manessier's continuation of the *Perceval* gives Corlenot.[3] Obviously, the form Corbenic cannot be regarded as necessarily the original and authoritative one, and it is a fair guess that the source of all the forms was Corbenoit, a compound made up of the objective case of *cors* and *benoiz*, meaning 'blessed horn'. This guess is substantiated by two facts. The *Estoire* makes the absurd statement that Corbenic meant in the Chaldean language 'saintisme vaissel', 'most holy vessel'.[4] Though the author doubtless was thinking of the holy dish, the Grail, he probably based the statement on the correct interpretation of 'cor benoit' as 'blessed vessel', referring to the horn, which he found in his source. The second corroborative fact is the mention by the first continuator of the *Conte del Graal* of a magic drinking-horn (*cors*) which, according to three manuscripts, was called either Beneoiz or Beneïz, that is 'Blessed'.[5] Here, then, is a 'cors beneoiz'

[1] Bruce, *Evolution*, i. 394. J. N. Carman, *Relationship of the 'Perlesvaus' and the 'Queste del Saint Graal'*, *Bulletin of the Univ. of Kansas*, xxxvii (1936), p. 287.

[2] J. L. Weston, *Legend of Sir Lancelot* (London, 1901), p. 159.

[3] C. Potvin, *Perceval le Gallois* (Mons, 1866–71), vi. 150, n. 2.

[4] Sommer, op. cit. i. 288.

[5] Loomis, *Arthurian Tradition*, p. 173, n. 33. W. Roach, *Continuations of the Old French 'Perceval'*, ii (Philadelphia, 1950), vs. 12315.

(objective case *cor beneoit*), and this vessel tests the chastity of the ladies of Arthur's court as Joseph's vessel discriminated, though in a different way, between the chaste and lustful members of his company. To quote Schofield, 'The Holy Grail . . . was a criterion of chastity not unlike the horn of Caradoc. In one case the conception has been exalted into an inspiring symbol, in the other degraded into a means of ribaldry.'[1]

After considering all these many curious and interlocking facts, can one attribute them solely to fortuitous coincidences? If not, there is no escape from the theory that in early Welsh tradition Brân the Blessed, son of Llŷr, was endowed with the two miraculous vessels listed among the Thirteen Treasures of the Isle of Britain, the *dysgl* (dish) and the *corn* (horn); that these, though not mentioned in *Branwen*, supplied the followers of Brân, when they arrived on the western isle of Grassholm, with unfailing quantities of food and drink; but that, like a third vessel in the same list, the cauldron of Dyrnog, they would not serve the unworthy. We must believe that a whole complex of legends grew up about the dish and the horn in the Welsh stage, in association not only with Brân, but also with his kinsman, King Beli. Already in this early stage we may assume that many disharmonies developed, and a cleavage opened between those tales which retained much of the old heathen beliefs as to the nature of Brân's wound and its effect on the vital forces of Nature, and those other tales in which Brân and Beli acquired an aura of sanctity. This cleavage widened and the confusion increased when the mass of Welsh stories about Brân and Beli, now attached to the Arthurian cycle, reached the French through the Bretons.

Brân's dish of plenty, as it survived in French literature, is not hard to recognize in the *graal* which Bron brought with him to the Occident; but, partly because of the comparative rarity of the word *graal*, the vessel came to be misconceived

---

[1] W. H. Schofield, *English Literature from the Norman Conquest to Chaucer* (New York, 1906), p. 199. See also Cross in *Mod. Phil.* x (1913), p. 292, n. 4.

as a chalice containing the holy blood, or as a receptacle of the eucharistic wafer. This latter misconception was due to the close association of the dish with the blessed horn of Brân, misinterpreted as the Corpus Christi, to which Henry of Lancaster referred as the 'tresbenoit corps en forme de payne', 'the very blessed body in the form of bread'.[1] The Corpus Christi, however, in the historical sense as the body deposed from the Cross and laid in the sepulchre, was in the custody of Joseph of Arimathea, and so we find that the Fisher King, who was traditionally the lord of the *cors benoiz*, was identified by the author of *Sone de Nansai* with Joseph. For what reason? By reason of the fact that both were custodians of the *cors benoiz*.

What theory better accounts on rational grounds for the whole complex of curious facts which bring the Grail into association with Corbenic, and Bron into association with Joseph of Arimathea, than the one sketched above—the coupling of Brân's dish and Brân's horn in Welsh tradition, and the misinterpretation of the latter as the blessed Body of Christ, either in the historic or in the sacramental sense?

Let us give our attention now to other problems presented by the *Estoire del Saint Graal*. We have seen that, like Robert de Boron's *Joseph*, it is based on the 'grant livre' and in some respects adheres more faithfully to its source. It provides a greatly expanded version of the events previous to the passage of the holy vessel to Britain, and an elaborate 'history' of the wars, miracles, visions, and missionary activities which later occurred in Britain and other mysterious regions up to the time of King Pelles and King Ban of Benoic, father of Lancelot. The author, though not to be identified with the author of the *Queste*,[2] was evidently conversant with the plan and the very text of that branch of the cycle, forecast the begetting of Galahad and his achievement of the supreme adventure,[3] and borrowed whole passages such as those

[1] *Livre de Seyntz Medicines*, ed. J. Arnould (Oxford, 1940), p. 11.
[2] Pauphilet in *Romania*, xlv (1918–19), pp. 524–7. A. Nutt, *Studies on the Legend of the Holy Grail*, pp. 108 f. Bruce, *Evolution*, i. 374, n. 1.
[3] Sommer, op. cit. i. 81, 204, 207.

describing Solomon's ship and the fatal wounding of King Lambor or Labran which caused the wasting of the two realms. Though he was patently ignorant of the geography of Britain, he was dominated by the desire to enhance in every way possible the prestige of Joseph, the evangelizer of Britain, and the sanctity of his dish. He claimed an even higher authority for his fantastic work than did the author of *Perlesvaus*, since he professed to have copied it from a book handed to him by no less a personage than the Son of God.[1]

To exalt Joseph of Arimathea, he relegated Bron to a secondary role, not even mentioning him till the band of Christians was about to cross the sea to Britain.[2] Joseph, instead of returning to his birthplace after entrusting the Grail to Bron as in Robert's poem, passed over to Britain and engaged in missionary labours. From the *Queste* or from some common source the author took over the figure of Joseph's son, the first bishop of all Christendom, who was a sort of double of his father.[3] He bore almost the same name—Josephes, assumed the leadership of the Grail company, and shared with his parent in the conversion of the island.

Upon this Josephes the author of the *Estoire* conferred the highest privileges and the highest titles (short of the papacy) within his power. The Lord Himself is represented as anointing and consecrating Josephes in the city of Sarras, and placing a mitre on his head, a crozier in his hand, and a ring on his finger.[4] The Lord Himself gives the new bishop detailed instruction as to the virtues symbolized by the colours of the episcopal vestments, namely, chastity by white, patience by green, justice again by white, and love by vermeil. It is at the Lord's command that Josephes celebrates the first mass for the chosen band, and he is horrified when at the same divine behest he cuts the Child which he finds in his hands into three pieces, and is told to swallow them.[5] Even before these manifestations of the Lord's favour, Josephes is vouchsafed visions

---

[1] Ibid. i. 5, 12.   [2] Ibid. i. 211, n. 5.
[3] On Josephes see Bruce, *Evolution*, i. 379.
[4] Sommer, op. cit. i. 35–39.   [5] Ibid. i. 39 f.

of Christ as He is to appear at the Last Judgment, surrounded by cherubim with flaming swords, and again as the crucified Christ, the blood dripping from His feet into the dish (the Grail) which Joseph had placed there.[1] Incredible though it may seem, the author of the *Estoire* elevated this imaginary character, who is never mentioned in the Scriptures or the apocrypha, to a rank equal to that of the Apostles. Why did he do so with such zest? No one, as far as I know, has given a satisfactory answer.

From the *Queste*, probably, came other characters, some of them bearing names which suggest ultimate Celtic origin. There is Evalach, king of the land of Sarras—that is, the land of the Saracens, imagined as lying contiguous to Egypt. Though there is nothing in Evalach's career corresponding to the little we know of the Welsh Avallach or Aballach, father of Modron, yet the resemblance in names is worth noting. Celidoine, ancestor of Galahad, seems to owe his name, his prophetic powers, and some elements in his story to Merlin, the Caledonian prophet, whom Giraldus Cambrensis called Merlinus Celidonius.[2] From the *Queste* also, it seems, came the wild story of the slaying of King Lambor, or Labran, who of all Christians in the world had the greatest faith.[3] Long before Arthur's time a battle took place in the realm of Logres between this king and a Saracen, Urlain. Fleeing before King Lambor, Urlain found a sword, and turning on his adversary, cleft him and his horse to the ground. There followed such a plague in two realms, including Logres, that never since have the lands yielded their crops to the husbandmen, nor the trees borne fruit, nor have fish been found in the water, save a few. Therefore the land of the two realms was called the Waste Land because it was made waste by this dolorous stroke. This passage affords, of course, another example of the primitive

[1] Sommer, op. cit. i. 32 f.

[2] R. S. Loomis, *Celtic Myth and Arthurian Romance* (New York, 1927), pp. 143 f. Of course, Merlin was not a god. See Jarman in *Arthurian Literature*, ed. Loomis, pp. 20–30.

[3] Compare Sommer, op. cit. i. 290, and vi. 146 f.

belief that the vitality of the ruler affects the vital forces of Nature. It is evidently related to the passage from the First Continuation of the *Conte del Graal*, translated in Chapter VI, where Gawain beholds the corpse of a noble person on a bier in the hall of the Grail castle, and learns from the King, his host, of the great destruction caused by the bleeding spear in the realm of Logres. Unfortunately the King does not disclose the identity of the dead man, but it is perhaps significant that at least three manuscripts of the *Queste* give the name of the pious king whose death brought sterility upon Logres as Labran.

Other elements in the *Estoire* can plausibly be attributed to remote Celtic sources. Laura Hibbard Loomis pointed out that the graves of Canaan and his twelve brothers, marked by a circle of twelve stones with one in the middle, might have been suggested by a prehistoric monument of this type.[1] Pierre, who is of course the Petrus of Robert de Boron, is identified with one of the sons of Bron, and instead of being sent to the vales of Avaron and spreading the faith as in Robert's poem, is most arbitrarily provided with a history modelled on that of Tristan; he suffers from a poisoned wound, has himself set adrift in a boat, is discovered by a princess and by her good offices is cured, slays the King of Ireland, Marahans, in combat, and is offered the hand of the princess by her father. With a curious monotony four different characters are maimed in the thighs—a motif probably traceable back to the wounding of Brân the Blessed in the foot in battle, as related in *Branwen*. An angel punishes Josephes by plunging a lance into his right thigh.[2] A heathen seneschal thrusts a sword through the thighs of Joseph of Arimathea.[3] King Alphasan, builder of the castle of Corbenic, was wounded through the thighs by a lance for daring to spend the night in the holy *palais* where the Grail was kept.[4] Pellehan, the son of King Lambor, was wounded similarly in battle, and was thereafter called the Maimed King.[5]

[1] *Modern Language Review*, xxvi (1931), pp. 413–26.
[2] Sommer, op. cit. i. 77.   [3] Ibid. i. 285.   [4] Ibid. i. 289.   [5] Ibid. i. 290.

Thus the author of the *Estoire del Saint Graal* played his feebly motivated variations on the ancient, heathen theme of the sterilization of the king and the consequent desolation of his realm. Thus he patched together, out of faded scraps of Celtic tradition, reminiscences of the apocrypha, eucharistic visions, explications of Christian dogma, conversion legends, and borrowings from the 'grant livre' and the *Queste*, his prolix early history of the Grail and the evangelization of Britain. The last pages he devoted largely to the succession of kings who were charged with the custody of the Grail from the time of Josephes to that of Merlin. Beginning with Alain, son of Bron, who received the holy dish from Josephes, the line ended with Lambor, Pellehan, and Pelles. As a work of literary art, the *Estoire* ranks low, but as an introduction to the Prose *Lancelot* and the *Queste* it was worked out with considerable ingenuity.

2. *Bishop Josephes gives the Grail, Depicted as a Bowl, to King Alain*
From MS. Bib. Nat. fr. 344, fol. 122. Date c. 1300

XV

Glastonbury, School of Forgery
and Isle of Avalon

WHOEVER, having read Robert de Boron's *Joseph*, which prepares for the evangelization of Britain, and the *Estoire del Saint Graal*, which relates in great detail its fulfilment, realizes that both works were composed by continental Frenchmen, must be astonished at the zeal and the fecundity of imagination displayed in the contrivance of a legend set in a remote period and in a foreign land. What could have moved the authors to glorify a Passion relic which had vanished centuries before? Why did they not exercise their talents on the marvels which attended the extension of the Faith in their homeland? Why did they set up rivals in sanctity and missionary accomplishment to St. Philip, the evangelizer of Gaul, and St. Denis, the patron saint of France? It is an ironic fact that the Joseph of Arimathea legend, which they did so much to publicize, proved very embarrassing to their own compatriots at the Church councils of the fifteenth century, who, when they claimed precedence over the English on the basis of the preaching of Mary Magdalen, Martha, and Lazarus in Provence, were met by the counterclaim of Joseph's prior activities in Britain.[1]

If one seeks a solution to this problem, it is natural to suspect that the original impulse, the nucleus of the whole legendary fabric, came from England, and that the 'grant livre' which was the source of the *Joseph* and the *Estoire* emanated from some English monastery. A clue might be found in Robert de Boron's dispatching Petrus to the 'vales of Avaron', apparently to engage in the conversion of the

[1] See below, p. 264, n. 1.

natives.[1] This was a promising clue, and several distinguished scholars have followed it: Nutt, Baist, Viscardi, and Marx.[2] Was not the fabulous isle of Avalon equated in 1191 with Glastonbury, situated among low-lying marshes?[3] Did not the monks of Glastonbury, who in that year pretended to have discovered the skeletons of Arthur and Guenevere in their cemetery, betray a suspicious tendency to manufacture and propagate tales which would bring renown, as well as revenue in the form of pilgrims' offerings, to their house? Did they not display a bold, creative imagination in claiming that St. David of Wales, St. Patrick of Ireland, and St. Gildas of Brittany had found a last resting-place in their sacred precincts? Did they not cherish a tradition, recorded about the year 1000, that the first preachers of Christ in Britain had found at Glastonbury a church built by no skill of man, and consecrated by Our Lord Himself to the honour of His Virgin Mother? And was not this church the small wattled structure which was standing on the site of the present St. Mary's chapel until 1184, when it was consumed by fire? This, then, would be the earliest Christian sanctuary in Britain. How strong would be the temptation to provide a circumstantial account of the arrival of these first preachers, headed by Joseph of Arimathea! How much prestige it would lend to this mission if Joseph brought with him the wonder-working vessel, celebrated by the *conteurs*, and identified as the dish or the cup of the first sacramental communion!

Then, too, there was clear proof that the abbey must have had an extraordinary interest in relics of the Passion.[4] The sacristy contained what purported to be a part of the table at which the Lord supped with His disciples before His betrayal, and pieces of the following objects: the pillar to which the

---

[1] Vss. 3123, 3221.

[2] A. Nutt, *Legends of the Holy Grail* (London, 1902), pp. 41–44, 66. G. Baist, *Parzival und der Gral* (Freiburg im Breisgau, 1909), p. 39. *Cultura Neolatina*, ii (1942), pp. 87–103. J. Marx, *Légende Arthurienne et le Graal* (Paris, 1952), pp. 304–15.

[3] E. K. Chambers, *Arthur of Britain* (London, 1927), pp. 268–74. J. Armitage Robinson, *Two Glastonbury Legends* (Cambridge, 1926), pp. 8–12. *Perlesvaus*, ed. Nitze, ii. 59–70.

[4] Johannes Glastoniensis, *Chronica*, ed. T. Hearne (Oxford, 1726), i. 23 f.

Lord was bound when He was scourged, the scourge, the garment in which Herod caused Him to be clothed, the sponge from which the Lord drank the wine mingled with myrrh, the other sponge from which He was offered vinegar mixed with gall. Besides there were many pieces of the cross, eight portions of Mount Calvary, some of the earth and a stone where the cross had stood, and some of the hole in which it was fixed, a spike of the crown of thorns, and six fragments of the Holy Sepulchre!

If anything could add lustre to such a collection it would be a vessel which had been sanctified by employment in the first eucharistic rite and by holding the very blood of the Saviour—a vessel, furthermore, whose genuineness was authenticated by a detailed history, which started with the very eve of the Last Supper and continued through the voyage which brought the relic to England—in short, something very like Robert de Boron's source, the 'grant livre'.

But how would such a book come into the possession of the Burgundian poet? Here Francisque Michel and Suchier[1] seemed to supply a neat explanation in the way of certain English documents proving the existence, about the right time, of two Robert de Buruns, one a landowner of Essex, the other of Hertfordshire.[2] Might not one of them have acquired a Glastonbury manuscript in England and sent it to a kinsman of the same name in Burgundy; or might he not be the poet himself, who conceivably might have resided in England before moving to the Continent and attaching himself to Gautier de Montbéliard?

Then, as we already know,[3] there is the plain statement in *Perlesvaus* that the author had translated the book into French from a Latin work in the holy house situated in the isle of Avalon at the head of the Adventurous Marshes; and, of course, this means Glastonbury Abbey. Though few would take this broad claim literally, is it not probable, since the author shows some acquaintance with the topography and

---

[1] F. Michel, *Tristan* (London, 1835–9), I. iii. *Zeitchr. f. Rom. Philologie*, xvi, (1892), p. 274.   [2] See above, Ch. IX.

with the finding of the graves of Arthur and Guenevere, that he took from a Glastonbury source the notion that Joseph of Arimathea and Nicodemus, ancestors of Perceval, were buried in Britain?[1] If so, this source must have been akin to the 'grant livre'.

As if to clinch the matter, the unique manuscript of William of Malmesbury's *De Antiquitate Glastoniensis Ecclesiae* (*Concerning the Antiquity of the Church of Glastonbury*) contains a passage on the conversion of the Britons by a band of twelve missionaries sent by St. Philip, the Apostle, from the land of the Franks, and here we read that Philip, 'as it is said, placed over them his dearest friend, Joseph of Arimathea, who buried the Lord.'[2] We read further that they received from a heathen king an island called Ynyswitrin (meaning Glass Isle), and built there a church of twisted twigs in honour of the holy mother of God. Now, as noted above, a church of wattles was actually standing on the site of what is now St. Mary's chapel until it was destroyed in the conflagration of 1184. Since William collected the materials for his book under the auspices of the abbey about 1125, how can there be any doubt that it was at Glastonbury that the legend of Joseph of Arimathea as the evangelizer of Britain first took form?

It is this array of evidence which has impressed not only credulous enthusiasts but also a few highly respected scholars, and led them to believe that the early history of the Grail originated as a piece of Glastonbury propaganda, deliberately fabricated to enhance the prestige and increase the revenues of the holy house of Avalon, in much the same way as the exhumation of the skeletons of Arthur and Guenevere was planned and carried out for similar ends.

When tested, however, the underpinning of this theory collapses. The long list of Glastonbury relics contains neither dish nor chalice associated in any way with the Last Supper or the Passion. The author of *Perlesvaus*, though professing to

---

[1] *Perlesvaus*, ed. Nitze, ii. 220 f.
[2] Adam of Domerham, *Historia de Rebus Gestis Glastoniensibus*, ed. T. Hearne (Oxford, 1727), ii. 5.

derive his material from the holy house of Avalon, and though obviously acquainted with some account of the coming of Joseph of Arimathea and Nicodemus to Britain, brings neither of them to Glastonbury. The two landowners named Robert de Burun seem to belong to a family settled in England since Domesday Book (1086), for that book mentions two de Buruns, and a member of the family by the name of Robert is known to us from later charters concerned with Derbyshire and Nottinghamshire.[1] But nothing so far discovered connects this family with Somerset or Burgundy. The manuscript of the *De Antiquitate* has been carefully analysed by two scholars, W. W. Newell and J. Armitage Robinson, Dean of Wells,[2] and has been proved a pastiche made up of William of Malmesbury's text and numerous additions. Among these is certainly the passage quoted above, which was written in a hand other than that of the main text, and which Robinson would assign to a date shortly before 1250.[3] Even less authentic is a marginal note referring to Joseph, his son Josephes, and the quest of the Grail, which is plainly based on the Vulgate cycle. No author residing in England, and certainly not William of Malmesbury, ever ascribed to Joseph any share in the evangelization of Britain until we come to these interpolations made about the middle of the thirteenth century.

Another interpolation in the manuscript is an alleged Charter of St. Patrick, which Robinson believes to have been forged about 1220.[4] The date is uncertain, but the document cuts the ground completely out from under the hypothesis of Glastonbury origin of the early history of the Grail. For it was manifestly composed in the interests of the abbey and with official sanction, and it tells a very different story from Robert de Boron's or from the *Estoire del Saint Graal*. In view

---

[1] *Seynt Graal or the Sank Ryal*, ed. F. J. Furnivall, Roxburghe Club, ii, pp. xiii–xix.

[2] *PMLA*, xviii (1903), pp. 459 ff. Robinson, *Somerset Historical Essays*, pp. 1–25. Nitze in *Mod. Phil.* xl (1942), pp. 113–16, and Marx in *Moyen Age*, lix (1953), 83 f., try to reconcile Robert de Boron's connexion with Burgundy and his supposed interest in Glastonbury by the suggestion that the Burgundian poet spent some time in England and returned to his home.

[3] Robinson, *Two Glastonbury Legends*, p. 36.   [4] Ibid., p. 35.

of the fact that the Apostle to Ireland never visited Glastonbury, the document is an amazing example of audacity and
pious fraudulence. Let me translate:[1]

In the name of our Lord Jesus Christ. I, Patrick, humble servant of
God, in the year of His Incarnation 430, being sent by the most holy
Pope Celestine to Ireland, converted by the grace of God the Irish to
the way of truth. Then, when I had established them in the Catholic
faith, I returned to Britain, and then, as I believe, under the guidance of
God, Who is the Life and the Way, I landed on the island of Ynyswy-
tryn. There I found a holy and ancient place, chosen by God and sanctified in honour of Mary the pure Virgin, the Mother of God: and there
I found certain brethren imbued with the rudiments of the Catholic
faith, and of pious conversation, who were successors of the disciples of
St. Phagan and St. Deruvian. . . . And since we were all of one heart and
one mind, we chose to dwell together, and eat and drink in common,
and sleep in the same house. And so they set me, though unwilling, at
their head; for indeed I was not worthy to unloose the latchet of their
shoes. When we were leading the monastic life according to the pattern
of the approved fathers, the brothers showed me writings of St. Phagan
and St. Deruvian, wherein it was contained that twelve disciples of St.
Philip and St. James [the Apostles to Gaul and Spain] had built that old
church in honour of our Patroness aforesaid, instructed thereto by the
blessed archangel Gabriel. And further, that the Lord from heaven had
dedicated that same church in honour of His Mother; and that to those
twelve three pagan kings had granted for their sustenance twelve
portions of land. Moreover in more recent writings I found that St.
Phagan and St. Deruvian had obtained from Pope Eleutherius, who
had sent them, ten years of indulgence. And I, brother Patrick, in my
time obtained twelve years from Pope Celestine of pious memory.

Now after some time had passed I took with me my brother Wellias,
and with great difficulty we climbed up through the dense wood to the
summit of the mount [the Tor] which stands forth in that island. When
we were come there we saw an ancient oratory, well-nigh ruined, yet
fitting for Christian devotion and, as it appeared to me, chosen by God.
When we entered therein we were filled with so sweet an odour that
we believed ourselves to be set in the beauty of Paradise. So then we
went out and went in again, and searched the whole place diligently
and we found a volume in which were written Acts of Apostles, along
with Acts and Deeds of St. Phagan and St. Deruvian. It was in great
part destroyed, but at the end thereof we found a writing which said
that St. Phagan and St. Deruvian by revelation of our Lord Jesus Christ,

[1] Adam of Domerham, *Historia*, ed. T. Hearne, ii. 19–22.

had built that oratory in honour of St. Michael the archangel . . . . That same writing said that the venerable Phagan and Deruvian abode there for nine years, and that they had also obtained indulgence of thirty years for all Christian folk who visit that place with pious intent for the honour of the blessed Michael. Having found therefore this great treasure of divine goodness, I and brother Wellias fasted three months, engaged in prayer and watching, and controlling the demons and beasts that in divers forms appeared. On a certain night, when I had given myself to sleep, the Lord Jesus appeared to me in a vision, saying: 'Patrick, my servant, know that I have chosen this place to the honour of My name, and that here men should honourably invoke the aid of my archangel Michael. And this shall be a sign to thee, and to thy brethren, that they also may believe: thy left arm shall wither, till thou hast told what thou hast seen to thy brethren which are in the cell below, and art come hither again.' So it came to pass. From that day we appointed that two brethren should be there continually, unless the pastors in the future should for just cause determine otherwise.

There follows another paragraph in which the saint writes of the measures he has taken for the preservation of two copies of this charter, and grants a hundred days of pardon to all who will cut down the wood around the Tor and make the chapel easier of approach. Appended to the charter is the following certification of its genuineness:

That these things were truly so, we have proved by the testimony of a very ancient writing, as well as by the narratives of older men. So this saint aforesaid, who is the Apostle of the Irish and the first abbot in the Isle of Avalon, after he had duly instructed these brethren in rule and discipline, and had sufficiently enriched that place with lands and possessions by the gift of kings and princes, when some years were past yielded to nature, and had his rightful burial, by the showing of an angel, and by the flashing from the spot of a great flame in sight of all who were there present, in the Old Church on the right hand of the altar.

The main ingredients which went into this concoction— the ancient church, St. Patrick's sojourn at Glastonbury, his death there, the mission of Pope Eleutherius—were taken over from the genuine *De Antiquitate* of William of Malmesbury, who had previously taken them over from earlier spurious records; while the names of Phagan and Deruvian were probably borrowed from Geoffrey of Monmouth's largely fictitious *Historia*. The most startling feature of the charter is the unprecedented length of the indulgences, to which Robinson called attention:[1] 'Ten years—some said thirty—gained by St. Phagan and St. Deruvian from Pope Eleutherus; twelve more gained by St. Patrick from Pope Celestine: while for those who made the toilsome ascent of the Tor St. Phagan and St. Deruvian had gained thirty more.' These grants meant that a sinner on whom had been imposed a penance of fasting or other severe discipline could, by a pious pilgrimage to the abbey church of St. Mary and the chapel of St. Michael on the Tor, obtain release from the obligation to the extent of forty-two years! When one considers that a pilgrimage to Westminster Abbey in 1208 was efficacious for only one year and forty days, to St. Augustine's, Canterbury, in 1243 for only twenty days, and even to St. Peter's at Rome in 1240 for only three years and three quarantines, the audacity of the Glastonbury claims is staggering. It seems that they were too preposterous to be officially sanctioned, and remained a dead letter.

But that the Charter of St. Patrick contained in the reference to the mission sent by St. Philip and St. James the account of the introduction of Christianity into Britain which was accepted at Glastonbury in the early thirteenth century, there can be little doubt; and no doubt at all that the account differs widely from the story told in Robert's *Joseph* and the *Estoire del Saint Graal*. It knows nothing of Joseph of Arimathea, Bron or Hebron, and Petrus or Pierre; it makes no mention of a holy vessel; it is explicit in attaching the mission to Ynyswytrin and the church of St. Mary. The continental romances, by way of contrast, attribute to Joseph the sending of the mission, emphasize the peculiar sanctity of his vessel, and, except for Robert's perplexing references to the 'vales of Avaron' as the destination of Petrus, suggest no association with Glastonbury. There can be no stronger proof that, when the spurious charter was composed, the legend of

[1] Robinson, *Somerset Historical Essays*, pp. 14–16.

Joseph of Arimathea and the Grail was quite unknown to the brotherhood of Avalon. By the same token, the notion that Robert de Boron or the author of the 'grant livre' worked with the encouragement and connivance of the monastic authorities is refuted by the charter.

Yet the disconcerting references to the 'vales of Avaron' demand some explanation, since most authorities agree that the 'vales' are the low-lying marshlands which surround the monastery and the Tor. Now Robinson made it clear that about 1000 the anonymous biographer of St. Dunstan, abbot of Glastonbury in the middle of the tenth century, asserted that the first preachers of Christ in Britain found at Glastonbury a church built by no skill of man, and consecrated by Our Lord Himself to the honour of His Virgin Mother.[1] William of Malmesbury in the *De Antiquitate* (*c.* 1130) knew this tradition, added that the anonymous evangelists were sent by Pope Eleutherius, but asserted that the church was *restored* by them, whereas it was originally built by actual disciples of Christ. William admitted that this might be true, 'for if the Apostle Philip preached to the Gauls, . . . it may be believed that he cast the seeds of his doctrine across the seas as well'.[2] Therefore, by the year 1130 there was a rumour that certain unnamed missionaries had come to Glastonbury in apostolic times, and this may have spread to France through what we might call the monastic grapevine. Similarly, after the discovery of Arthur's burial place the notion that Glastonbury lay in the vales of Avalon came to be widely accepted, and this, combining with the earlier rumour, might well have led to the report that the anonymous missionaries had voyaged from the Holy Land to the aforesaid vales, just as St. Philip had voyaged to Gaul and St. Thomas to India. Such a report could have been picked up by the continental author of the 'grant livre', accepted as gospel truth', and welcomed as supplying additional detail to the strange story, then current,

---

[1] Robinson, *Two Glastonbury Legends*, p. 35.
[2] Robinson, *Somerset Historical Essays*, p. 9.

about the wanderings of the Rich Fisher and his companions and their arrival in the Occident. This story provided names for some of these holy men—Bron, Alain, and Petrus or Pierre—and, by what seems to us an arbitrary choice, the last name was assigned to the missionary who set out for the vales of Avalon.

This hypothesis would account for the mysterious role which Robert de Boron assigned to Petrus. It would also explain why no character of that name appears in the *Didot Perceval* or *Perlesvaus*, for the role was an invention of the author of the 'grant livre', and only those texts which derived from his book, Robert's *Joseph* and the *Estoire del Saint Graal*, know anything of Petrus or Pierre. Of course, the hypothesis is not founded on direct evidence and never can be, but what other fits the complex of facts? Certainly not the theory of the complicity of the monks of Glastonbury in fabricating Robert's early history of the Grail.

As for the origin of Petrus or Pierre, I have set forth elsewhere my reasons for believing that he, like Bron and Alain, was a figure inherited from Welsh tradition—to be specific, Pryderi, who was one of the followers of Blessed Brân, and partook of the hospitality of the Noble Head in western Wales.[1] But to argue the case here, and to show how Pryderi was replaced by Peredur and Peredur by Petrus, would distract us too far from the main subject of this chapter, the relation of Glastonbury Abbey to the legend of Joseph of Arimathea.

Since we have ascertained that the legend was a continental product and was totally unknown to the monks of the abbey at the time when the Charter of St. Patrick was forged, we may imagine the surprise and bewilderment of these tonsured worthies when, say about 1240, a manuscript of the *Estoire del Saint Graal* came into their hands, and they read an elaborately detailed rival account of the evangelization of Britain,

[1] Loomis, *Arthurian Tradition*, pp. 341–6. *Mod. Lang. Rev.* xxiv (1929), pp. 427–30.

which failed to give credit to St. Philip[1] and St. James, mentioned neither Ynyswytrin nor Avalon, and which silenced all scepticism by the claim to be a faithful transcript of a work written by Christ's own hand and delivered by him to the author! Moreover, it derived some authority from its remarkable familiarity with the origins and early history of a holy vessel called the Grail, which, as everyone knew by this time, thanks to Chrétien and his successors, had manifested its miraculous powers in King Arthur's time.

The situation was embarrassing for the monks of Glastonbury. Should this pious narrative be denounced as a fraud? Or should the long-standing claim of their own house to being the site of the earliest Christian sanctuary in Britain, built by a band of missionaries from Gaul, be abandoned as apocryphal. Or should both be accepted and, if possible, reconciled? It was the third course of action which was adopted, presumably after heated debate, and the first result of which, we know, was the insertion into a copy of William of Malmesbury's book on Glastonbury of a passage about the evangelists sent to Ynyswytrin by St. Philip, which contains the statement that 'over them he [St. Philip] appointed, it is said, his dearest friend, Joseph of Arimathea, who buried the Lord'.[2] Soon after, a scribe made bold to write in the margin: 'That Joseph of Arimathea, the noble counsellor, with his son Josephes and many others, came to Greater Britain (which is now called Anglia) and there ended his life is attested by the book of The Deeds of the Famous King Arthur'—a plain reference to the *Estoire del Saint Graal*.[3] Thus began the process of interweaving the two variant versions, insular and continental, of the first mission to Britain. But many decades were to pass before the officials of the abbey began to take Joseph's coming to the Isle of Avalon seriously.

[1] The *Estoire del Saint Graal* states briefly that St. Philip baptized Joseph of Arimathea at Jerusalem before he and his son Josephes set out on their missionary journey. Sommer, *Vulgate Version of the Arthurian Romances*, i. 19. This is quite a different account from that in the Charter of St. Patrick, which attributed the building of the old church at Glastonbury to twelve disciples of St. Philip and St. James.

[2] Robinson, *Somerset Historical Essays*, p. 6; *Two Glastonbury Legends*, p. 28.

[3] *Two Glastonbury Legends*, pp. 28 f.; *Somerset Historical Essays*, p. 6, n. 3.

Yet gradually the news of this event must have spread, and we have a royal writ of 1345 which tells us that a John Blome of London had petitioned Edward III for license to dig in the monastic precincts, for a divine injunction had been laid on him to search for 'the venerable body of the noble decurion Joseph of Arimathea, which rests in Christ, buried within the bounds of the monastery of Glastonbury, and is to be revealed in these days, to the honour [of God] and the edification of many'.[1] Nothing more is known of this enterprise. Under the year 1367 an East Anglian chronicle records that the bodies of Joseph and his companions had been found.[2] This seems to have been a false rumour. By 1382 official recognition seems to have been given to Joseph as the first to preach Christ at Glastonbury, for in that year Abbot John Chinnock restored the chapel of St. Michael and St. Joseph, and had three sculptures made—of Joseph, Nicodemus, and the Deposition from the Cross.[3] This chapel is not to be identified with the chapel of St. Joseph which was constructed in the crypt of St. Mary's chapel by Abbot Bere a hundred years and more later.

One of the most curious documents concerned with the Joseph legend is a Latin prophecy attributed to an otherwise unknown British seer named Melkin, said to have preceded Merlin. If the following conjectural translation, based on that of Dean Robinson,[4] seems obscure, it is not to be wondered at. When were vaticinations ever noted for clarity?

The Isle of Avalon, claiming with avidity the burial of pagans, adorned more than any others in the world by prophetic stars for the entombment of them all; and in future it shall be adorned by those who praise the Highest. Abbadare, noblest of pagans, mighty in Saphat, with a hundred and four thousand others, fell on sleep. Among them Joseph, of Arimathea by name, found perpetual slumber in marble. And he lies on a two-forked line next the south corner of an oratory built of wattles by the aforesaid thirteen star-betokened dwellers in that place. For Joseph has with him in his sarcophagus two white and silver cruets,

---

[1] *Two Glastonbury Legends*, pp. 63 f.   [2] Ibid., p. 64.
[3] Ibid., pp. 42, 47.   [4] Ibid., pp. 30 f., 60.

3. Joseph of Arimathea Holding Two Cruets
Stained Glass window at Langport Church, near Glastonbury
Date: late fifteenth century

Copyright: Elsie Matley Moore, F.S.A.

filled with the blood and sweat of the prophet Jesus. When his sarcophagus shall be found entire, intact, in time to come, it shall be seen and shall be open to the whole world. Thenceforth neither water nor the dew of heaven shall be wanting to the dwellers in that most noble isle. A long time before the Day of Judgement in [the vale of] Jehoshaphat these things shall be made manifest and declared to living men.

What is to be made of this cryptic effusion, the latinity of which excites as much wonder as the content? First, one gathers that Glastonbury had somehow gained the reputation of being the site of a great pagan, as well as a Christian, burial ground; and that, of the unbaptized, a certain Abbadare of Saphat (otherwise unknown to history or legend) was the most glorious. Secondly, one may infer that a marble coffin of Joseph of Arimathea was supposed to lie in a definite spot near the site of the old wattled church, which he and twelve of his companions had erected. Thirdly, it is prophesied that the coffin is one day to be discovered intact and shall be shown to visitors from all over the world. Fourthly, it is clear that the emphatic claim of the *Estoire del Saint Graal* that Joseph had brought with him the dish of the Last Supper, filled with the blood and water which flowed from the wounds of Christ, has been abandoned. The Grail has disappeared, but in its stead there are two cruets containing the blood and the sweat of the Crucified. Why this substitution was made, one cannot say with assurance, but one may surmise that its purpose was to avoid any possible confusion with the mysterious and not wholly sanctified *graal* which was celebrated in such romances as the First Continuation of Chrétien's *Perceval*. At any rate, the two silver cruets remained the insignia of St. Joseph in the abbey's arms, and may be seen depicted in the portrait of the saint in stained glass at Langport and the portrait on the rood-screen at Plymtree, Devon.[1]

The Prophecy of Melkin was apparently considered authoritative, for when a monk, John of Glastonbury, compiled towards the end of the fourteenth century a miscellany of materials about the house, and brought its history down to

[1] Ibid., pp. 49, 65 f.; plates I, III.

1342, he copied into it the curious document twice. Though the arrangement of his so-called chronicle is haphazard, he performed his task conscientiously and gave us the results of the process of blending the native Glastonbury traditions with the imported matter of the romances. His opening chapter was evidently based on the much interpolated *De Antiquitate* of William of Malmesbury, and tells how in the thirty-first year after the Passion twelve disciples of the Apostle Philip, of whom Joseph was the chief, came into this country, and having obtained from King Arviragus twelve hides of land, built the first Christian church, dedicated by the Lord Himself to His Mother, and there led the life of hermits.[1] In the same chapter John mentions the grave of Joseph near the joining of the original church with a small chapel or chancel to the east, but this is reported simply on the authority of the ancients; evidently no tomb purporting to be that of the founder had yet been 'discovered'.

How important was the place which Joseph, 'the noble decurion', now occupied in the 'history' of Glastonbury may be judged not only by the placing of the twelve disciples of St. Philip, including Joseph, first in a list of saints whose remains were believed to lie in the sacred precincts,[2] but also by a 'treatise' about him which John incorporated in his compilation.[3] This 'treatise', beginning with the entombment of Christ, follows, not the *Estoire del Saint Graal*, but the *Gospel of Nicodemus* up to Joseph's release from prison and his return to Arimathea. But, in resuming the narrative, John again betrays the influence of the *Estoire* and the interpolated *De Antiquitate*, for he tells us that Joseph and his son Josephes were baptized by St. Philip. Then, remembering a Latin text of the Assumption of the Blessed Virgin, supposedly written by Joseph, John briefly states that both Joseph and Philip were present at the passing of Mary. Once more the story combines the strands of the *Estoire* and the expanded *De Antiquitate*, taking over from the former the consecration of Josephes as a bishop in

---

[1] Johannes Glastoniensis, *Chronica*, i. 1 f.
[2] Ibid., p. 17.   [3] Ibid., pp. 48–54.

the city of Sarras (Sarath), and from the latter the mission of
St. Philip to Gaul, and the sending of Joseph and twelve
others to preach in Britain. Then, at last, frankly acknowledg-
ing as his source a book called 'Sanctum Graal', John relates
how one hundred and fifty Christians, who had kept the vow
of chastity, crossed the seas to Britain in one night on the
shirt of Josephes, and how the rest, after repenting of their
guilt, were transported promptly in a ship of Solomon's
building and joined their fellows. Still following the *Estoire*,
the author tells of the vision of Mordrain, his arrival in Britain,
and his release of Joseph from imprisonment. Finally, the
'treatise' returns to the expanded *De Antiquitate* for Joseph's
receiving a grant of the Isle of Glass from King Arviragus, the
building of the old wattled church thirty-one years after the
Passion, and the life of fasting and prayer led by the saintly
twelve until their deaths.

To this ingenious conflation of local tradition, Latin apocrypha, and French romance, John of Glastonbury appended
a transcript of the marginal note in the manuscript of the
expanded *De Antiquitate*, mentioned above, in which there is
reference not only to Joseph and his son, but also to Lancelot,
Gawain, Galahad, and the quest for a vessel called 'Sanctum
Graal'; and for these he invoked, as did his source, the author-
ity of 'the book of the deeds of the famous King Arthur'.[1]
Note that this is the only mention which John makes of the
Grail. This excerpt is followed by the Prophecy of Melkin,
in which, as we have seen, the two silver cruets take the place
of the Grail. Then come eight elegiac verses about Joseph and
Nicodemus; a pedigree of Arthur, traced back to Helaius
(Alain), nephew of Joseph, and derived from the *Estoire del
Saint Graal*; and a similar pedigree, from the same source, of
Loth and his four sons, tracing their descent from Petrus, said
to be a relative of Joseph and King of Orkney.[2] John's 'chronicle' runs on for over a hundred more pages, but, excepting
the Charter of St. Patrick and a repetition of Arthur's pedigree,
there is nothing more which bears on Joseph and his mission.

---

[1] Ibid., p. 55.   [2] Ibid., pp. 56 f.

One can see from the foregoing how seriously at last the romantic legend created by continental authors about the conversion of Britain was taken by the Somerset monks, and how, after being trimmed down, it was grafted on the ancient local tradition. One sees, too, how large Joseph of Arimathea now looms in the fabulous history of Britain, not only as the first evangelist, but also as a collateral ancestor of Arthur. In the fifteenth century the cult of Joseph assumed international importance. At four great Church Councils the English delegation vigorously asserted their right to precedence over the representatives of other nations of Western Christendom on the ground of prior conversion.[1] At Pisa in 1409 they cited Joseph's mission as anticipating the voyage of the Magdalen, St. Martha, and St. Lazarus to Provence. At Constance in 1417, when the French bishops put forward St. Denis as the earliest to preach Christ in the West, the English maintained (contrary to the Glastonbury claim) that Joseph had preached in Britain immediately after the Crucifixion. At Siena in 1424 Richard Fleming, Bishop of Lincoln and founder of Lincoln College, Oxford, opposed the French, Scots, and Spaniards on the same grounds. Finally at Basel in 1434, when the authority of 'very ancient books and archives', particularly those at Glastonbury, was urged in support of Joseph's arrival in Britain in A.D. 63, Alphonso Garcia de Sancta Maria, doctor of laws, challenged their reliability, and called attention to the tradition that Joseph had been released from prison in A.D. 70. Moreover, he argued, it was well known that St. James had founded the Spanish Church during the lifetime of St. Peter. In spite of these damaging arguments, the English people, Catholics and Protestants alike, continued to regard Joseph of Arimathea as the first to introduce Christianity into their island.

By the end of the fifteenth century his popularity had greatly increased. Richard Bere, who became abbot of Glastonbury in 1493, raised the ceiling of the crypt under St. Mary's chapel, which occupied the site of the old church of

[1] J. Ussher, *Britannicarum Ecclesiarum Antiquitates* (London, 1687), pp. 13 f.

wattles, and dedicated the subterranean chapel to St. Joseph. A stone image of the patron was set up, and pilgrims resorted thither in great numbers.[1] A new coat of arms was adopted: on a white field, sprinkled with blood drops, is set a green 'raguly' cross, and beneath the arms of the cross are the two cruets of St. Joseph.[2] Doggerel verses, composed about 1502, were printed in 1520, and recorded the wonders ascribed to the saint.[3] Sick folk flocked to his shrine from Wells, Yeovil, and Ilchester, and were miraculously cured, as frequently happens, whether the shrine be Catholic, Mohammedan, or Buddhist. In this crude poem occurs the first reference to the miraculous property of the thorn-trees of Glastonbury.

> Three hawthorns also, that groweth in Werall,
> Do burge and bear green leaves at Christmas
> As fresh as other in May. . . .

Werall is the hill, now called Weary-all; the freak hawthorns belong to a variety which bears the scientific name *Crataegus oxyacantha praecox* and is by no means limited to the hill. Before the reform of the calendar these trees blossomed at Christmas time, but now early in January. Let us observe that, when these lines were printed, Joseph was not held responsible in any way for the miracle.

The soil of Glastonbury continued to favour the growth of legends long after the downfall of the great monastery in 1539, the judicial murder of the last abbot, and the triumph of Protestantism under Queen Elizabeth I. If anyone is so naïve as to hold that the Middle Ages had a monopoly on wild hypotheses, fantastic blunders, and blind credulity, let him contemplate the extraordinary proliferation of local traditions about Glastonbury and their wide acceptance, even in recent times. They are mainly concerned with the Holy Thorn, the Chalice Well, and St. Joseph's mission.

As we have just seen, there was a popular belief in the early sixteenth century that there was something sacred about a

---

[1] Robinson, *Two Glastonbury Legends*, pp. 47 f.
[2] Ibid., pp. 47, 49.   [3] Ibid., pp. 44 f.

tree which observed the Nativity by faithfully blooming at Christmastide.[1] But this in Elizabeth's reign savoured of superstition, and a Puritan attacked the tree on Weary-all Hill with a hatchet and felled one of the trunks. It was rumoured that the other trunk took revenge, for when he struck it, the steel rebounded and cut his leg, and a chip flew up and marred his eyesight. The original tree, however, seems to have sprung up from the stump again, and did not succumb to Puritan zeal till the Civil War. The first testimony to a link between the Holy Thorn and Joseph comes from 1677, when Dr. Plot wrote: 'Some take it for a miraculous remembrance of the birth of Christ, first planted by Joseph of Arimathea.' Apparently by the early eighteenth century the legend was complete, and an innkeeper launched the story, still familiar to tourists, that Joseph and his companions, landing on the island, ascended Weary-all hill, which took its name from the fact that they were all weary when they reached the top. Here Joseph struck his staff into the ground; whereupon it promptly budded and on Christmas Day burst into flower. The legend being once established, thorn trees descended from the old stock were repeatedly planted on the site, only to succumb one after another to the knives of souvenir hunters. To insure that memory of the miracle should not perish likewise, one John Clark caused a slab of stone to be laid down on the spot, bearing the laconic inscription 'J. A. Anno D. XXXI'. It may still be seen and betrays the fact that Clark mistook the date of Joseph's arrival as 31 years after the Nativity, instead of the Passion, of Christ, thus placing the saint in Britain two years before the Crucifixion!

The legend of the Holy Thorn has appealed to poets. Tennyson, it will be remembered wrote in *The Holy Grail* of 'the good saint, Arimathean Joseph', and his journey to Glastonbury, 'where the winter thorn Blossoms at Christmas,

[1] The traditions of the Glastonbury Thorn may be found in Richard Warner, *History of the Abbey of Glaston and of the Town of Glastonbury* (Bath, 1826), preface, pp. c, cii; appendix, pp. iv, v, xxxvi f.

mindful of the Lord'. And Thomas S. Jones, Jr., the American poet, has fine a sonnet, concluding:[1]

> One ancient miracle enduring still,
> Though earth's old magic seems a myth outworn,
> Has hallowed Avalon's enchanted hill;
> For when men hymn the Son of God reborn,
> Although December woods are bare and chill,
> At wintry Christ-tide flowers the Holy Thorn.

Less poetic is the comparatively recent legend of the Chalice Well, which is filled from a spring and supplies the town with an abundant flow of water. According to local antiquaries and guidebook gossip, the well owes its name to the fact that when Joseph brought the chalice of the Last Supper to Britain, he buried it in the earth above the spring, so that ever since the water leaves a red deposit on the stones.[2] This, of course, cannot be a medieval tradition, since the monastery never accepted the testimony of the French romances that Joseph brought with him either the chalice or the dish of the Last Supper. Nor was it an eighteenth-century tradition, for in 1750 the waters won a brief reputation as a cure for asthma, yet there was no hint that a relic of the Holy Blood was responsible for their therapeutic property.

The Chalice Well legend seems to have been a Victorian invention, since Warner in 1826 did not know it. In the Middle Ages the well was probably known as Chalkwell; the old name is preserved in Chilkwell Street.[3] But, apparently, nothing so prosaic would do for a spring in the Isle of Avalon. The oxide of iron deposited by the water suggested blood; blood suggested the sacramental cup; the cup suggested the vessel of the Last Supper which Joseph had brought to Glastonbury. Thus, we may suppose, sprang the belief that Joseph had buried the chalice in the hillside, and so the name of the well was changed from Chalkwell to Chalice Well. Late as this 'tradition' is in origin, it was taken so seriously by a writer

---

[1] Thomas S. Jones, Jr., *The Shadow of the Perfect Rose* (New York, 1937), p. 92.
[2] *Glastonbury Antiquarian Society, Proceedings for 1886*, pp. 20–36.
[3] M. R. James, *Abbeys* (London, 1925), p. 20.

in the *Publications of the Modern Language Association in America* (1955) as to be offered as proof that the word *graal* meant not a dish but a chalice! No medieval scholar perpetrated a cruder blunder.

Most amazing as an example of modern credulity is the continuing belief among educated people that Joseph's mission to Britain was not fable but fact. Whereas the monastic authorities, though encouraging his cult, never claimed to have found his body and never exhibited his tomb, not many decades ago, if we are to trust a Somerset guidebook, tourists were shown in St. Catherine's chapel in the church of St. John the Baptist at Glastonbury what purported to be the sepulchre of St. Joseph. In the 1920's Mr. Bligh Bond created considerable excitement by publishing a somewhat poetical version of a message obtained through automatic writing and verifying the medieval account of the first Christian mission to Glastonbury.[1] Books have been written explaining away the improbability of Joseph's setting out for so remote a region in the Wild West by the supposition that he was attracted by the tin mines of Cornwall. A clever writer, realizing that Glastonbury is not in Cornwall, and admitting frankly that one 'who feared even to confess Christ openly is the very last Gospel convert we should expect to meet in Somerset', nevertheless went to the greatest pains to persuade us that some other rich proto-Christian Jew might have been attracted to the Mendip Hills by the lead mines, and there combined piety with business by starting a little Christian community on the island among the marshes a few miles away.[2] To make the argument more plausible, he even provided an imaginary scene in which the aforesaid Jew requested a letter of introduction from Vespasian, who had recently been campaigning in the south of England, to the commander of the Second Legion!

The inventors of these amusing speculations may be excused

---

[1] *The Rose Miraculous, The Story of the Sangreal* (Glastonbury, 1924). I can bear personal testimony to the *bona fides* in which these scripts were received, but this is no guarantee of their historical value.

[2] G. Ashe, *King Arthur's Avalon* (London, New York, 1957), pp. 56–60.

for not knowing that Joseph's mission to Britain was an entirely imaginary French fiction, but not for ignoring the fact that the earliest testimony to his coming to Glastonbury is the interpolation in William of Malmesbury's *De Antiquitate Glastoniensis Ecclesiae*, an interpolation which is separated from the alleged event by an interval of 1200 years, more or less. It would seem that even in the twentieth century, even with our nearly universal education, the principles of historical criticism carry little weight when the will to believe is strong. Our generation can ill afford to smile superciliously at the mistakes and the credulity of our medieval ancestors.

It would be a stupid and almost an impious thing to leave the subject of Glastonbury on a note of disenchantment and supercilious contempt. Even if the abbey sheltered for some centuries what Ferdinand Lot called 'une officine des faux', 'a laboratory of forgeries',[1] even if it fostered in later centuries a cult of St. Joseph based on error and pure fantasy, even if in modern times legends and theories equally preposterous have found ready acceptance with sentimental pilgrims, that is not the whole story. It is possible, though not probable, that the old church of wattles was one of the earliest Christian shrines in Britain. The Chapel of St. Mary, which stands on the same site, though partly in ruins, is a precious example of Norman architecture and sculpture, and the walls of the great church rise aloft in mournful majesty. The painted chests which Edward I caused to be opened at Eastertide, 1278,[2] did not contain the genuine remains of Arthur and Guenevere, but the romantic imagination may properly dwell on the solemn scene in the candle-lit dusk of the church when the white bones were exposed to the awed gaze of Edward and his queen, and one cannot but regret the destruction of the marble monument which the King erected to house them. The landscape, too, possesses intrinsic charm, the grass-clad slopes

[1] *Romania*, xxvii (1898), p. 537.
[2] E. K. Chambers, *Arthur of Britain* (London, 1927), pp. 125, 280 f.

of the Tor rising in the midst of miles of flat meadows
and tipped by the tower of St. Michael's. And when the
apple-trees are in bloom and, as sometimes happens, the
spring floods cover the meadows, the Isle of Avalon resumes
something of its ancient aspect. One is moved to repeat the
memorable closing lines of Arthur's farewell to Bedivere:

> 'I am going a long way . . .
> To the island valley of Avilion;
> Where falls not hail, or rain, or any snow,
> Nor ever wind blows loudly; but it lies
> Deep-meadowed, happy, fair with orchard lawns
> And bowery hollows crowned with summer sea,
> Where I will heal me of my grievous wound.'

XVI

The End of the Quest

WHAT, then, after this critical examination of the literature of the Grail in the Middle Ages, are the conclusions which can most reasonably be drawn about this prodigious and mysterious phenomenon? Where did it originate? What significance did the story bear in its earliest form or forms? How was it propagated and transmitted? What was the secret of its extraordinary appeal to the imagination? Why was there such an astonishing inconsistency and variety in its forms? What part did Glastonbury Abbey play in shaping and fostering the tradition? What other possible influences played upon it? Is there to be discovered in the Grail literature any central and significant messages for posterity? To these and other problems I would offer the following attempt at a solution.

1. The Grail legends form a branch of the enormously popular Arthurian cycle, and may therefore be interpreted most plausibly and realistically in accordance with what scholars have learned about the origin and development of that cycle, though doubtless special factors, mystical, ritualistic, and doctrinal, which hardly affected the other Arthurian romances, should be taken into account.

2. The starting-point of the Grail tradition was Ireland. The Irish derivation of several principal elements in the Tristan romance and of the Beheading Test or Game in *Gawain and the Green Knight* is now widely accepted by those familiar with the evidence, and there is a strong case for a similar origin for the various abductions of Guenevere and other recurrent Arthurian motifs. There is, therefore, an antecedent probability that similarities between the Grail

stories and the Irish sagas, though obscured by the time-interval and the transference from one cultural milieu to another, are not merely illusory or accidental.

3. The Irish sagas which present the most significant resemblance in outline or in conspicuous features to the versions of the visit to the Grail castle are classed as *echtrai*, and tell of the visits of mortals to the island homes or the palaces of the immortals, where they are regaled sumptuously with drink and food, and witness marvels. In the *echtrai* one finds counterparts of the inviting host, the damsel bearing a golden vessel, the disappearance of the host, the Waste Land which needs to be disenchanted, and chess-boards of precious metal. In other Irish sagas one discovers self-moving drinking horns, a damsel of hideous aspect who is metamorphosed into a radiant beauty, a blood-feud brought on by the slaying of the hero's father; and one modern Irish folk-tale seems to have preserved the unique counterpart of the question test.

4. Irish literature and oral tradition, as the best authorities agree, had a profound influence on the Welsh, and when the sagas mentioned passed over to Wales they blended with similar native traditions. In Welsh literature, moreover, one can detect the originals of the Maimed King and the Dwarf King in Brân and Beli, the nexus between the king's health and the fertility and prosperity of his kingdom, an island Elysium whose denizens are exempt from old age, and a group of magic talismans which offer a striking correspondence to the talismans of the Grail castle in *Perlesvaus*. Of these, the drinking-horn of Brân and the platter of Rhydderch are of supreme importance, the latter being the counterpart of the Grail.

5. Wales furnished also the names of a few persons most conspicuous in the Grail legends. Brân became Bron, Beli became Pelles and, through manuscript corruption, Pellehan, while there is some complex evidence to show that Pryderi became Perceval and that the epithet Gwallt-advwyn, meaning 'Bright-Hair', became first Galvagin and eventually Gawain.

6. In both the Irish and Welsh material it is not hard to find survivals of pagan mythology. The Grail castle was

originally a Celtic Elysium, where old age and disease were unknown and every desire was satisfied, provided the mortal visitor was worthy. The horn and the platter were originally the vessels of the gods, inexhaustible sources of drink and food. The prototype of the Grail Bearer and the Loathly Damsel was the divine personification of Ireland, Ériu; and the prototype of Lancelot du Lac was the sun and storm god, Lug Lonnbemnech. The Welsh Brân son of Llŷr, in his primitive aspect was probably a marine deity, while Beli ruled over a subterranean realm of noble dwarfs. When paganism was gradually suppressed in the Celtic countries, the process of euhemerization began. Gods became kings, their palaces tended to be localized, for example, near Tara or at Dinas Brân; their precious talismans were sometimes transferred to historic princes or heroes, for example, Arthur.

7. The transmission of this teeming mass of Celtic legend to the non-Celtic world was accomplished almost entirely by the cousins of the Welsh, the bilingual Bretons. A class of professional story-tellers and singers ranged the European continent and Great Britain, finding patrons wherever French was understood and creating a prodigious vogue for these novel and romantic tales, particularly in the courts of kings and counts and the halls of barons and knights. Though scorned and denounced at first by the clergy, these *conteurs* finally won their opponents over, to the extent that by the end of the twelfth century several romances can be attributed to clerical authorship, and by 1230 the great Vulgate cycle had been composed, at least in large part, in the cloister.

8. In the process of translating and adapting to French audiences and readers the somewhat wild and fantastic stories of Celtic heathendom, mistakes and misconceptions occurred inevitably. We have strong reason to believe that one mis-interpretation, frequently repeated, had momentous conse-quences for the development of the Grail legend. The words *cors beneïz* or *benoiz*, meaning 'blessed horn', and referring to the food- and drink-providing horn of Brân, must have occurred frequently in association with the words *sains graaus*,

referring to the holy dish of the same Brân, with its similar miraculous properties. Now the word *cors* in the nominative case could have several meanings besides 'horn', and the French were not any too familiar with holy drinking horns. On the other hand, they were constantly hearing and talking about the wonders wrought by the holy bodies of saints and particularly by the Corpus Christi, the body of Christ in the form of the consecrated Host. Since the word *cors* meant 'body', is it any wonder that under these circumstances the words *cors benoiz* or *beneïz* were regularly interpreted as the Blessed Body of Christ, the mass-wafer, which was credited with sustaining saintly persons, or as the historic body of the Crucified which Joseph of Arimathea took down from the cross and laid in the sepulchre?

9. Such errors would be all the more natural because of the persistent coupling of the *cors benoiz* with the *sains graaus*, the holy dish. But they would pose some riddles. They would force the perpetrators of the mistakes to speculate on the origin of the dish, the identity of its mysterious custodian, and its relationship to the *cors benoiz*, either in the sacramental or the historic sense. What theory but that propounded in the previous chapters accounts for the strange tale which Chrétien tells of the Host in the Grail, for Joseph of Arimathea's custodianship of this same Grail, employed by Christ at the Last Supper, and for the identification of Joseph of Arimathea with the Fisher King? What other theory would account so neatly for the name of the Grail castle, variously given as Corbenic, Cambenoyt, and Corlenot, as the supposition that it represented a corruption of the objective case *cor benoit*, 'blessed horn'? What other theory would account for the explanation of Corbenic as meaning 'most sacred vessel', which, though originally applying to the magic horn, was naturally taken to refer to the holy Grail?

10. The misconceptions and the more or less felicitous explanations which they provoked were almost inevitable in an era when all Christendom was obsessed by the cult of relics, particularly those of the Passion, was absorbed in the

problem of the Real Presence in the sacramental bread, and
was in a mood to believe in any vision or any miracle which
confirmed that doctrine. These same preoccupations and this
same receptivity assured a warm welcome for the legends of
the Grail as they became progressively Christianized, at first
by the *conteurs* and later by clerical men of letters. And we
may presume that because the same conditions prevailed
throughout Western Christendom and were not confined to
any one country or people, it was natural for Frenchmen to
respond, undeterred by national prejudices, to the fascination
of the legends about the wonder-working vessel that had
appeared in Arthur's time in the land of Logres. One can
understand why French poets and romancers in prose,
succumbing to that fascination, exercised their ingenuity and
their talents in the elaboration of this edifying material.

11. If the development of the Grail legends was accomplished under the conditions and with the motives set forth
above, and if mistranslation and misinterpretation were such
potent factors, then one must absolve the earliest at least of
the romancers who shaped the material, such as Chrétien de
Troyes and the author of the '*grant livre*', of conscious lying or
pious fabrication. They could claim, rightly, that the stories
came down from remote antiquity and deserved as much
credence as the marvels which marked the career of Alexander
the Great or the lives of the saints. The author of the '*grant
livre*' could have offered a reasonable argument why the Grail
must have been the dish of the Last Supper, and why its first
possessor must have been Joseph of Arimathea. The author
of *Sone de Nansai* could have defended by logic his identification of Joseph of Arimathea with the Fisher King on the
ground that both had been custodians of the *cors benoiz*, and,
since the Fisher King had also in his keeping the holy dish,
the *saint graal*, Joseph must have been its first keeper. Sincerity,
therefore, was quite consistent with what appears to us to be
brazen deception. The author of the *Queste del Saint Graal*,
if one may venture to analyse the workings of his mind,
probably believed that historical facts lay behind the narrative

he set down, but he would probably have admitted that some of the incidents were, like the parables of the New Testament, not strictly factual but were to be taken simply as illustrations of the eternal verities. The authors of the *Estoire del Saint Graal* and *Perlesvaus* are harder to psychoanalyse. Neither displays more than superficial religiosity, and both, though claiming celestial inspiration, incorporated in their works material that even their contemporaries would have considered hardly worthy of such a source. Both, we know, dealt very freely with their traditional material and indulged in much pure fabrication, at the same time that they pretended to have the highest sanction for their veracity. Perhaps the author of *Perlesvaus* was, as I have suggested, a mild case of schizophrenia, and so cannot be held to strict standards. As for the *Estoire*, its author, if sane, must have been aware that the Lord Jesus Christ had nothing to do with the story he himself told, and must be classed with Geoffrey of Monmouth and Baron Munchausen as the conscious purveyor of fiction under the guise of solemn truth. He, like Geoffrey, enjoyed a great success, for thanks to him the legend of Joseph of Arimathea was accepted, with modifications, not only by the monks of Glastonbury, but also by the official spokesmen of the English Church at the great Church councils.

12. What, finally, did the Grail legends mean? What truths were they intended to convey? Surely not the esoteric doctrines of heretical cults. Surely they were not invented or developed as propaganda for Glastonbury and against the papacy. In their earliest stages, when still following the patterns of Irish and Welsh myths and hero-tales, they dimly reflected the ideas and superstitions of a lingering paganism. Indeed, the Arthurian romances have been aptly described as the bright afterglow of Celtic heathendom. In the later stages, as we have seen, misconceptions of one kind or another played a powerful role, and the tales about the mysterious vessel were reshaped and expanded to illustrate the dominant ideas about the sacramental wafer as the veritable flesh and blood of God. Only the *Queste del Saint Graal* and *Parzival*,

however, can be said to offer food for the soul. The former is an allegory in which the Grail signifies the love of God, and the quest of the Grail the seeking after God through complete and joyous self-abnegation in the fellowship of the like-minded. The latter is the story of a less ascetic progress from ignorance and self-absorption and anger to understanding, humility, and compassion. These are the only medieval versions of the Grail legend, including, of course, Malory's abridgement of the *Queste*, which may be said to have still, and especially for those of the Christian faith, a real and lasting spiritual significance.

APPENDIX I

Bibliography of Critical Works
and of Major Texts of the Grail Legend

Surveys of earlier scholarship devoted to the elucidation of the problems of the Grail, together with synopses of some of the medieval texts, may be found in Alfred Nutt, *Studies on the History of the Holy Grail* (London, 1888), pp. 8–126; J. D. Bruce, *Evolution of Arthurian Romance from the Beginnings down to the Year 1300* (Baltimore, Göttingen, 1923), i. 219–362, 374–94, 419–25; ii. 1–19, 85–90, 104–35, 145–71, 308–12, 345–69. More recent views are represented in *Romans du Graal aux XIIe et XIIIe Siècles* (Paris, 1956).

1. Chrétien de Troyes, *Conte del Graal* or *Perceval*. Edited by Hilka as *Der Percevalroman (Li Contes del Graal)* (Halle, 1932); by W. Roach as *Le Roman de Perceval ou Le Conte du Graal*, 2nd ed. (Geneva, Paris, 1959). For recent special studies see R. S. Loomis, *Arthurian Tradition and Chrétien de Troyes* (New York, 1949), pp. 7–11, 335–471; J. Frappier, *Perceval ou le Conte du Graal*, Cours de Sorbonne (Paris, 1953); Frappier, *Chrétien de Troyes, L'Homme et l'Œuvre* (Paris, 1957), pp. 170–209; W. A. Nitze, 'Perceval and the Holy Grail, An Essay on the Romance of Chrétien de Troyes', *University of California Publications in Modern Philology*, xxviii (1949), No. 5.

2. Four Continuations of the same. The various versions of the First Continuation have been edited by W. Roach as vols. i, ii, iii of *Continuations of the Old French 'Perceval'* (Philadelphia, 1949, 1950, 1952). The other Continuations may be found in C. Potvin, *Perceval le Gallois* (Mons, 1866–71), vols. iii–vi. The best discussion of these is H. Wrede, *Fortsetzer des Gralromans Christians von Troyes* (Göttingen, 1952). See also A. W. Thompson in *Arthurian Literature in the Middle Ages*, ed. Loomis, pp. 206–17.

3. The best editions of *Parzival* are those of E. Martin (Halle, 1900–3) and of K. Bartsch, 4th ed., revised by M. Marti (1927–9). For commentaries in English see O. Springer in *Arthurian Literature in the Middle Ages*, ed. Loomis, pp. 218–50, and M. F. Richey, *Studies of Wolfram von Eschenbach* (Edinburgh, 1957). The most significant parts have been translated by Richey in *The Story of Parzival and the Graal* (Oxford, 1935), and the whole by H. M. Mustard and C. E. Passage (New York, 1961).

4. The texts of *Peredur* have been edited by J. Rhŷs and G. Evans, *Text of the Mabinogion and Other Welsh Tales from the Red Book of Hergest* (Oxford, 1887), and by J. G. Evans, *The White Book Mabinogion* (Pwllheli, 1907). The best translations are those of J. Loth, *Les Mabinogion*, 2nd ed. (Paris, 1913), ii. 47–120, and of Gwyn Jones and Thomas Jones, *The Mabinogion*, Everyman's Lib., pp. 183–227. I. L. Foster reviews the scholarship on the subject in *Arthurian Literature in the Middle Ages*, ed. Loomis, pp. 199–205.

5. The *Didot Perceval* was edited by W. Roach (Philadelphia, 1941). Discussed by P. Le Gentil in *Arthurian Literature*, ed. Loomis, pp. 257–62.

6. *Perlesvaus* was edited by W. A. Nitze and others as *Le Haut Livre du Graal, Perlesvaus* (Chicago, 1932–7), with full introduction and notes. An inaccurate translation by Sebastian Evans was published in Everyman's Library as *The High History of the Holy Grail*.

7. The Grail episodes in the Prose *Lancelot* may be found in H. O. Sommer, *Vulgate Version of the Arthurian Romances* (Washington, D.C., 1911–12), iv, v. For comments on the Prose *Lancelot* see Bruce, *Evolution of Arthurian Romance*, i. 397–418, and J. Frappier in *Arthurian Literature*, ed. Loomis, pp. 296–302.

8. The *Queste del Saint Graal* has been edited by Sommer, op. cit. vi. 3–199, and by A. Pauphilet (Paris). For commentary see Pauphilet, *Études sur la 'Queste del Saint Graal'* (Paris, 1921), and J. Frappier in *Arthurian Literature in the Middle Ages*, ed. Loomis, pp. 302–7. Translated by W. W. Comfort, *Quest of the Holy Grail* (London, 1926). Malory's version has been edited from Caxton's text by H. O. Sommer (London 1889), ii, and from the manuscript by E. Vinaver, *Works of Sir Thomas Malory* (Oxford, 1947), ii. 791–833, 853–1037. A new edition of the latter will shortly appear. See also *Essays on Malory*, ed. J. A. W. Bennett (Oxford, 1963).

9. *Joseph d'Arimathie* edited by W. A. Nitze as *Roman de l'Estoire dou Graal* (Paris, 1927). For commentary see P. Le Gentil in *Arthurian Literature in the Middle Ages*, ed. Loomis, pp. 251–6. Translated by M. Schlauch, *Medieval Narrative* (New York, 1928), pp. 179–95.

10. The *Estoire del Saint Graal*, edited by Sommer in *Vulgate Version*, i. For commentary see Frappier in *Arthurian Literature in the Middle Ages*, ed. Loomis, pp. 313–15, and Bruce, *Evolution*, i. 374–94.

11. *Sone de Nansai*, edited by M. Goldschmidt (Tübingen, 1899). A brief summary may be found in Bruce, *Evolution*, i. 350–3.

APPENDIX II

Illustrations

1. The miniature appears in MS. Bib. Nat., fr. 12577, which contains the long redaction of the First Continuation of the *Conte del Graal*. This redaction introduces a scene in which Chrétien's story of the visit to the Grail castle has been combined with features of Gawain's visit. Hence we have the Grail Bearer of the former text and the bier with a sword on it from the latter. See above, p. 68, and for the text *Continuations of the Old French 'Perceval'*, ed. W. Roach, ii (Philadelphia, 1950), vss. 3712–3833. The miniaturist did not read the text but only the rubric, which runs: 'Ci devise comment gauvain estoit a la table le roy pescheeur et aportoit on par devant la lance qui saingne et apres une pucele qui aportoit le saint Graal. Et apres vienent hommes qui portoient une biere e une espee desus.' In the text the squire bearing the lance is followed by a maiden with a *tailleor*, two squires with candelabra, and the Grail Bearer; the sword on the bier is broken; the lord of the castle is seated on a couch, and there is no crowned lady with him. Note the difference between text and illustration. For an account of the manuscript and reproductions of other miniatures from it see R. S. and L. H. Loomis, *Arthurian Legends in Medieval Art* (New York, 1938), p. 101, figs. 263–6. The miniaturist, not understanding the word *graal*, depicts the object as a ciborium.

2. The miniature appears in MS. Bib. Nat., fr. 344, which contains the *Estoire del Saint Graal* and the *Merlin*. The text reads: 'Lors fist Josefe aporter par devant lui le saint vaissel. Lors dist a alain je vous reves fait il de cest don dont jhesu cris [*sic*] meismes revesti son [*l.* mon] pere. Et quant vous trespasserez de cest siecle vous en poures revestir qui que vous voudrez. et il reçoit le vaissel moult liez et moult joians de ce don quil li a otroié.' Sommer's text may be found in *Vulgate Version of the Arthurian Romances*, i (Washington, 1909), p. 286, ll. 12–17. The miniaturist evidently had read the text and knew the equation made by the author between *graal* and *escuele*. Accordingly, he depicts a dish or bowl in the hands of Josephes. The date of the manuscript seems to lie in the first quarter of the fourteenth century.

3. The illustration comes from a stained-glass window at Langport church, near Glastonbury. As noted on p. 261, St. Joseph of Arimathea is depicted with two cruets, instead of the Grail, in accordance with the official Glastonbury *vita*. For a description of the Langport window see C. Woodforde, *Stained Glass in Somerset, 1250–1830* (London, 1946), pp. 33–35, 187 f. The date seems to be late in the fifteenth century.

APPENDIX III

The Elucidation

Perhaps the most confused and perplexing piece of Grail literature is a short prologue (484 verses) supplied by the Mons manuscript of Chrétien de Troyes's *Conte del Graal* and entitled 'Elucidation' by some wag who printed a prose summary of it in 1530. It leaves the reader more bewildered than before, because it is either irrelevant to Chrétien's poem or inconsistent with it. The author opens with the statement that the secret of the Grail may not be revealed unless Maistre Blihis is a liar—palpably a reference to the Welsh *conteur* Bleddri (Bleheris), but by no means a reliable one. There is a description (vss. 248–314) of a visit to the Grail castle, which shows verbal borrowings from the account in the First Continuation translated above, pp. 67–71, and which describes the Grail as serving the company without human agency; but it is not Gawain but Perceval who is the hero. Then we are told that the court of the Fisher King was found not once but seven times, and that seven 'gardes' will be devoted to them. There follows a rapid sketch of the contents of these 'gardes' which bears almost no correspondence either to Chrétien or his continuator. Either this part of the *Elucidation* was interpolated, a prologue to some lost text, or the poet himself was recalling in a drunken reverie various *contes* which he had heard or read. In fact, that is the impression left by the last part of this introduction to the *Conte del Graal*.

The more sober—and the most interesting—part seems to reflect with remarkable vividness a tradition of which there are various vestiges in Arthurian romance. (See Loomis, *Arthurian Tradition*, pp. 246–8.) The Waste Land motif is easily discernible, but the cause is not the sterilizing wound of the Fisher King but the outrage done to the maidens of the wells. These maidens had been accustomed to serve the wayfarer with whatever food or drink he desired. But when they were raped by King Amangon and his knights, and their golden cups were stolen from them, they no longer issued from the wells, the meads and flowers dried up, and the waters diminished. It is not too rash to suspect that we have here the survival of the pagan belief in the *nymphae* of the springs, prevalent in Britain and the Continent—a belief which attributed a drought to some offence done to the water-deities. What seems to be the same superstition survived into the nineteenth century in the folk-lore of Ogmore in Glamorganshire. Ogres used to carry off girls and imprison them in springs, and so long as certain wicked men lived by robbery and murder and neglected the fields the Shee Well near

Ogmore Mills remained dry and there were no fish in the stream. But when the ruffians promised to reform, the water flowed again and the people rejoiced. See Marie Trevelyan, *Folk-lore and Folk-stories of Wales* (London, 1909), pp. 19 f.

The *Elucidation* has been edited by A. Hilka in Christian von Troyes, *Percevalroman* (Halle 1932), pp. 417–29, and, with a good introduction, by Albert W. Thompson (New York, 1931). For comments see also Thompson in *Arthurian Literature*, ed. Loomis, pp. 207–9; H. Wrede, *Die Fortsetzungen des Gralromans Chrestiens von Troyes* (Göttingen, 1952), pp. 138–45; Loomis, *Arthurian Tradition*, pp. 171–4.

INDEX

MYTHOS: The Princeton/Bollingen Series in World Mythology

J. J. Bachofen / MYTH, RELIGION, AND MOTHER RIGHT

George Boas, trans. / THE HIEROGLYPHICS OF HORAPOLLO

Anthony Bonner, ed. / DOCTOR ILLUMINATUS: A RAMON LLULL READER

Jan Bremmer / THE EARLY GREEK CONCEPT OF THE SOUL

Joseph Campbell / THE HERO WITH A THOUSAND FACES

Henry Corbin / AVICENNA AND THE VISIONARY RECITAL

F. M. Cornford / FROM RELIGION TO PHILOSOPHY

Mircea Eliade / IMAGES AND SYMBOLS

Mircea Eliade / THE MYTH OF THE ETERNAL RETURN

Mircea Eliade / SHAMANISM: ARCHAIC TECHNIQUES OF ECSTASY

Mircea Eliade / YOGA: IMMORTALITY AND FREEDOM

Garth Fowden / THE EGYPTIAN HERMES

Erwin R. Goodenough (Jacob Neusner, ed.) / JEWISH SYMBOLS IN THE GRECO-ROMAN PERIOD

W.K.C. Guthrie / ORPHEUS AND GREEK RELIGION

Jane Ellen Harrison / PROLEGOMENA TO THE STUDY OF GREEK RELIGION

Joseph Henderson & Maud Oakes / THE WISDOM OF THE SERPENT

Erik Iversen / THE MYTH OF EGYPT AND ITS HIEROGLYPHS IN EUROPEAN TRADITION

C. G. Jung & Carl Kerényi / ESSAYS ON A SCIENCE OF MYTHOLOGY

Carl Kerényi / ELEUSIS: ARCHETYPAL IMAGE OF MOTHER AND DAUGHTER

Stella Kramrisch / THE PRESENCE OF ŚIVA

Roger S. Loomis / THE GRAIL: FROM CELTIC MYTH TO CHRISTIAN SYMBOL

Bronislaw Malinowski (Ivan Strenski, ed.) / MALINOWSKI AND THE WORK OF MYTH

Erich Neumann / AMOR AND PSYCHE

Erich Neumann / THE GREAT MOTHER

Maud Oakes with Joseph Campbell / WHERE THE TWO CAME TO THEIR FATHER